THE

ANCIENT ORDER

OF THINGS

T0149607

THE
ANCIENT ORDER
OF THINGS

ESSAYS ON THE MORMON TEMPLE

EDITED BY

Christian Larsen

SIGNATURE BOOKS | 2019 | SALT LAKE CITY

For Jacob

© 2019 Signature Books Publishing LLC. Signature
Books is a registered trademark. All rights reserved.
Printed in the USA. www.signaturebooks.com

The opinions expressed in this book are not necessarily
those of the publisher.

Design by Jason Francis.

FIRST EDITION | 2019

LIBRARY OF CONGRESS CATALOGING-IN-PUBLICATION DATA

Names: Larsen, Christian, 1988– editor.

Title: The ancient order of things : essays on the Mormon temple / edited
                 by Christian Larsen.

Description: First edition. | Salt Lake City : Signature Books, 2019. | Summary:
                 "From the first meetings of the Anointed Quorum in Nauvoo, Illinois,
                 to the dedication of the LDS Salt Lake temple, to modern-day Kirtland,
                 Ohio, The Ancient Order of Things: Essays on Mormon Temples
                 explores the historical, cultural, and sacred significance of the latter-day
                 temple"—Provided by publisher.

Identifiers: LCCN 2019037242 (print) | LCCN 2019037243 (ebook) |
                 ISBN 9781560852797 (paperback) | ISBN 9781560853732 (ebook)

Subjects: LCSH: Church of Jesus Christ of Latter-day Saints—Doctrines. |
                 Mormon temples. | Mormon Church—Doctrines.

Classification: LCC BX8643.T4 A53 2019 (print) | LCC BX8643.T4
                 (ebook) | DDC 246/.95893—dc23

                 LC record available at https://lccn.loc.gov/2019037242
                 LC ebook record available at https://lccn.loc.gov/2019037243

CONTENTS

EDITOR'S INTRODUCTION

Beginning shortly after the organization of the Church of Jesus Christ of Latter-day Saints in 1830, the temple has been central to both the longed-for and lived experience of believers. Indeed, church founder Joseph Smith emphasized the centrality of the temple to his followers when he taught that "the main object [of gathering together the people of God in any age] was to build unto the Lord [a] house whereby he could reveal unto his people the ordinances of his house and glories of his kingdom and teach the [people] the ways of salvation."[1]

The enormous theological and cultural weight placed on the temple has made it a symbol of faith and a locus of power in Mormonism. A frequently cited biblical passage speaks of a temple in exactly these terms and has been interpreted by many Latter-day Saints to refer to a temple of their own:

> And it shall come to pass in the last days, that the mountain of the Lord's house shall be established in the top of the mountains, and shall be exalted above the hills; and all nations shall flow unto it.
>
> And many people shall go and say, Come ye, and let us go up to the mountain of the Lord, to the house of the God of Jacob; and he will teach us of his ways, and we will walk in his paths: for out of Zion shall go forth the law, and the word of the Lord from Jerusalem. (Isa. 2:2–3.)

The temple as a locus of power has had implications not only for church leadership, but for the rank-and-file member as well. While it has acted as a rigorous sieve, regulating orthodoxy according to the pronouncements of church leadership, the temple has also served as one of the most dynamic sites of personal agency for the individual believer.

For example, in the temple Latter-day Saints who are separated from beloved family by great chasms of time and space are able to reconnect in ways that, for them, are real and meaningful. A few Latter-day Saints

---

1. Andrew F. Ehat and Lyndon W. Cook, eds., *The Words of Joseph Smith: The Contemporary Accounts of the Nauvoo Discourses of the Prophet Joseph Smith* (Provo, Utah: BYU Religious Studies Center, 1980), 212.

of African descent (as Tonya Reiter discusses in this volume) found in the temple a way to participate in priesthood ordinances by being baptized (though not *baptizing*) for the dead before women and men of African heritage were admitted to the priesthood and to the temple ceremonies. Women (who are still not ordained to the LDS priesthood) may officiate in the temple in some priesthood ordinances for other women, actions that in all other contexts are reserved only for men. These are examples of how individual members leverage the power of the temple to exercise their own agency in ways they would not otherwise be able to do outside of the temple.

When Joseph Smith spoke by revelation, presaging a yet-to-be-constructed temple, he promised an "endowment of power from on high" (LDS D&C 38:32). When viewed through this lens, Smith's prophesy is fulfilled in a very real way (though perhaps not in the way Smith intended) in the lives and faith of Latter-day Saints worldwide.

However, in Mormonism the temple has never been about the individual believer only. While sacred rites are carried out in LDS temples by, for, and in behalf of individuals, and the temple is uniquely empowering for individual believers, it is foundationally about much more than that. Indeed, the temple is the culmination of Smith's project to restore the most ancient order of things.

It was another American restorationist, Alexander Campbell, who called for a "restoration of the ancient order of things" in a series of articles published in the *Christian Baptist*.[2] He sought a return to what he determined was ancient Christian practice. But Smith sought, rather, to reach backward—and forward—by many more millennia. Brigham Young, Smith's successor as LDS Church president, articulated Smith's vision saying, "the human family ... must be joined together, so that there would be a perfect chain from Father Adam to his latest posterity."[3]

---

2. W. Dennis Helsabeck Jr., "Names of the Movement," in Douglas Allen Foster et al., eds., *The Encyclopedia of the Stone-Campbell Movement* (Grand Rapids, Michigan: William B. Eerdmans, 2004), 551.

3. Richard S. Van Wagoner, comp., *The Complete Discourses of Brigham Young,* 5 vols. (Salt Lake City: The Smith–Pettit Foundation, 2009), 1:188.

This grand and encompassing vision of temple work persists to this day. In the words of one modern-day LDS scholar:

[The temple] signifies the eternal human saga by which men and women progressively constitute fuller and richer relationships to divine parents, in the pilgrimage from incarnate spirits, through adoption into Christ's family, assuming greater levels of commitment and higher standards of holiness, entering into binding covenants that reify and extend human and divine connectedness, until cleansed and sanctified by the sacrificial offering of Christ's own flesh, they enter into the divine presence, part of an eternal sociality with those they love.[4]

Unfortunately, the temple has also sometimes fallen short of this vision and has alienated and disempowered faithful believers. Elements such as ritual nudity (which John-Charles Duffy addresses in this volume), certain ritualistic gestures, the exclusion of Latter-day Saints of African descent from receiving the endowment and sealing ceremonies, and the barring of LGBTQ members from full participation have taken their toll on more than a few of the faithful.

This reality has necessitated adjustments to both the temple ceremonies and the temple itself over the years. In fact, in early 2019 significant adjustments were made to the language of several LDS temple rites to improve gender equity. These include realigning the focus of a woman's covenant on God rather than on her husband, expanding the role and dialogue of Eve in the Creation drama, and equalizing the language and promises a bride and groom make to each other during the temple sealing ceremony.[5] These changes have been met with an enthusiasm that underscores the significance the temple holds in the lives of Latter-day Saints, and this enthusiasm suggests that the power of the temple is not waning. If past remains prologue, believers can certainly expect future changes that will preserve the significance and power of the temple in their lives just as these most recent adjustments have done.

This volume seeks to capture the power of the Mormon temple from a historical perspective, both in the context of its time and in

---

4. Terryl L. Givens, *Feeding the Flock* (New York: Oxford University Press, 2017), 314.

5. Jana Riess, "Major Changes to Mormon Temple Ceremony, Especially for Women," *Religion News Service*, Jan. 8, 2019, accessed Mar. 4, 2019, at www.religionnews.com/2019/01/03/major-changes-to-mormon-temple-ceremony-especially-for-women.

the lives of those who worshipped there. The authors explore aspects of the temple and its history that span time and tradition. While this volume makes no attempt to be all-inclusive, it does seek to gather together unique facets of temple scholarship in one place. This volume also makes no pretension to cover comprehensively some topics that deserve more extensive exploration, including the role of women and the inclusion of LGBTQ Saints in temple rites. Because dialogue on these and other issues is ongoing, it will be left to future scholars to give them the attention that they deserve.

In addition to those already mentioned, the essays gathered here address the history of the Mormon temple beginning with the first prayer meetings of the Quorum of the Anointed in Nauvoo, Illinois (Devery S. Anderson), through the interim following the western exodus (Richard E. Bennett), to the dedication of the Salt Lake temple in 1893 (Brian H. Stuy). Others address the implications of the temple rites themselves, including sacramentalism's "conquest of death" (Ryan G. Tobler) and the place of the temple ceremonies in LDS canon (Kathleen Flake). They also reach beyond the scope of the LDS tradition to embrace the history of the Mormon temple more broadly in Lyman Wight's Texas community (Melvin C. Johnson), the dispute over control of the Independence, Missouri, temple lot (R. Jean Addams), and the history of the Kirtland temple in the decades after the departure of the Saints from Ohio (Christin Craft Mackay and Lachlan MacKay). Each author explores her or his topic while remaining mindful of the sensitive nature of the temple for believers. Both scholars and observers—whatever their beliefs—will find, I believe, much of interest in this collection.

I offer my thanks to the authors who contributed their scholarship to this volume. I also express my grateful acknowledgments to the staff of Signature Books, especially to Gary James Bergera, who helped to bring this volume to completion.

Wednesday, [May] 4 [1842].—I [Joseph Smith] spent the day in the upper part of the [Red Brick] Store [in Nauvoo, Illinois], i.e.,: in my private office (so called, because in that room I keep my sacred writings, translated ancient records, and received revelations) and in my general business office, or lodge room (i.e. where the masonic fraternity met occasionally, for want of a better place) in council with General James Adams of Springfield [Illinois], Patriarch Hyrum Smith, Bishops Newel K. Whitney and George Miller, [William Marks, Wm Law] and Presidents Brigham Young, Heber C. Kimball and Willard Richards, instructing them in the principles of order of the priesthood, attending to washings, anointings, endowments and the communication of Keys pertaining to the Aaronic Priesthood, and so on to the highest order of Melchisedek Priesthood, setting forth the order pertaining to the Ancient of Days, and all those plans and principles by which any one is enabled to secure the fullness of those blessings which have been prepared for the Church of the First born, and come up and abide in the presence of the Eloheim in the eternal worlds. In this Council was instituted the ancient order of things for the first time in these last days. And the communications I made to this Council were of things spiritual, and to be received only by the Spiritual minded: and there was nothing made known to these men, but what will be made known to all the saints of the last days, so soon as they are prepared to receive, and a proper place is prepared to communicate them, even to the weakest of the Saints; therefore let the Saints be diligent in building the [Nauvoo] Temple, and all houses which they have been, or shall hereafter be commanded of God to build; and wait their time with patience in all meekness, faith perseverance unto the end, knowing assuredly that all these things referred to, in this council, are always governed by the principle of revelation.

Thursday, 5.—General Adams started for Springfield, and the remainder of the Council of yesterday, continued their meeting at the same place, and myself and brother Hyrum received in turn from the other[s], the same that I had communicated to them the day previous.

—*History of Joseph Smith and the Church of Jesus Christ of Latter-day Saints: A Source- and Text-Critical Edition, Volume 5: 1842–1843,* ed. Dan Vogel (Salt Lake City: Smith–Pettit Foundation, 2015), 3–4.

ONE

THE ANOINTED QUORUM, 1842–45

DEVERY S. ANDERSON

On May 4, 1842, Joseph Smith and nine men assembled in the upstairs room of his red brick store in Nauvoo, Illinois, and, with older brother Hyrum, administered to the other eight certain rites that would later be reserved for the new Nauvoo temple, slowly rising in gleaming limestone on the bluff above them. The men were James Adams, Heber C. Kimball, William Law, William Marks, George Miller, Willard Richards, Newell K. Whitney, and Brigham Young. The next day the men, except Adams, who had returned to Springfield, administered the same rituals—special washings, anointings, and instructions—to Joseph and Hyrum.

LDS historian Glen M. Leonard describes these rituals as presenting

> a pattern or figurative model for life. The teachings began with a recital of the creation of the earth and its preparation to host life. The story carried the familiar ring of the Genesis account, echoed as well in Joseph Smith's revealed book of Moses and book of Abraham. The disobedience and expulsion of Adam and Eve from the Garden of Eden set the stage for an explanation of Christ's atonement for that original transgression and for the sins of the entire human family. Also included was a recital of mankind's tendency to stray from the truth through apostasy and the need for apostolic authority to administer authoritative ordinances and teach true gospel principles. Participants were reminded that in addition to the Savior's redemptive gift they must be obedient to God's commandments to obtain a celestial glory. Within the context of these gospel instructions, the initiates made covenants of personal virtue and benevolence and of commitment to the church. They agreed to devote their talents and means to spread the gospel, to strengthen the church, and to prepare the earth for the return of Jesus Christ.[1]

---

1. Glen M. Leonard, *Nauvoo: A Place of Peace, A People of Promise* (Salt Lake City: Deseret Book Co., 2002), 258–59. The LDS endowment today, according to the *Encyclopedia of Mormonism*, has "four main aspects": first, "a ceremonial washing and anointing, after which

The apex of the ceremonies, which are also termed the endowment, seems to have been to teach and practice the true order of prayer, which permitted initiates to pray with the confidence that their petitions would be answered.

By participating in these rituals, this group of men (and later women) set themselves apart from the rest of the church and formed the beginnings of what later would be called the Quorum of the Anointed, Anointed Quorum, and Holy Order, an elite body of church members possessing special spiritual power and status.[2] Joseph Smith would introduce only one more temple ordinance before his death. This was the second anointing (also "fullness of the priesthood"), which he conferred beginning in 1843.[3] This essay explores the individuals who

---

the temple patron dons the sacred clothing of the temple [both undergarment and robes]"; second, "a recital of the most prominent events of the Creation, a figurative depiction of the advent of Adam and Eve and of every man and every woman, the entry of Adam and Eve into the Garden of Eden, the consequent expulsion from the garden, their condition in the world, and their receiving of the Plan of Salvation leading to the return to the presence of God"; third, making personal covenants to "observe the law of strict virtue and chastity, to be charitable, benevolent, tolerant and pure; to devote both talent and material means to the spread of truth and the uplifting of the [human] race; to maintain devotion to the cause of truth; and to seek in every way to contribute to the great preparation that the earth may be made ready to receive ... Jesus Christ"; and fourth, a "sense of divine presence," meaning that temple ordinances "are seen as a means for receiving inspiration and instruction through the Holy Spirit, and for preparing to return to the presence of God." Alma P. Burton, "Endowment," in *Encyclopedia of Mormonism,* ed. Daniel H. Ludlow, 4 vols. (New York: Macmillan Publishing Co., 1992), 2:455. Prior to 1990, the covenants aspect included the administration of various so-called Masonic-informed "penalties" to emphasize the importance of keeping the covenants.

2. The terms "Anointed Quorum" and "Quorum of the Anointed" are not found in any of the known surviving contemporary relevant documentary sources, but the group was often referred to as simply the "quorum." Endowment initiates and church historians subsequently employed the terms to refer to those church members who received the endowment ceremonies and met together as a group during Joseph Smith's lifetime. Thus, I find them useful in discussing the early participants in what become the LDS temple endowment.

3. The function and purpose of the Quorum of the Anointed must be understood in the broader context of Joseph Smith's developing understanding of temple theology and ordinances. Although such a history lies outside the scope of this essay, it includes "power from on high" associated with ordination to the Melchizedek priesthood in Kirtland, Ohio (1831), the construction and dedication of the Kirtland House of the Lord (1833–36), the establishment of the School of the Prophets (1832–33), the ordinance of washing feet (1833), the development of the concept of sealing, washings and anointings (1836), baptism for the dead (1840), the Nauvoo temple (begun 1840), marriage for eternity and plural marriage (1841), the establishment of a Masonic lodge in Nauvoo (1841), and the endowment ritual (begun May 1842).

made up the Quorum of the Anointed, the evolution of that quorum over time, particularly before Joseph Smith's death, and its purpose. From references to this group of people scattered throughout the diaries and reminiscences of participants, it is possible to reconstruct its meeting schedule, typical procedure, and goals. Although sometimes viewed as having a political purpose, this quorum instead served almost exclusively a spiritual function, uniting participants in prayer and bringing them consolation as they faced increasing tensions in Nauvoo after the deaths of Joseph and Hyrum.[4]

The ten men (including Joseph and Hyrum Smith) who were the first to experience what Latter-day Saints today understand to be the LDS temple endowment were all members of Nauvoo's Masonic lodge. Three had been Masons for more than two decades. Hyrum Smith had apparently joined sometime before 1821; Heber C. Kimball became a member in 1823; and George Miller had been a Mason since 1819. James Adams had joined a lodge in Illinois after the Saints had entered the state in 1839.[5] Joseph and the other men had become Masons only during the preceding two months. Joseph's explanation of similarities between elements of Masonic and Mormon rituals, according to Kimball, was that "masonry was taken from [Mormon] priesthood but has become degenerated."[6] Nineteenth-century accounts of certain aspects of the two ceremonies show that they contain more than a few identical, or nearly

---

4. For a history of the meetings of the quorum from its beginnings until the opening of the Nauvoo temple, see Devery S. Anderson and Gary James Bergera, eds., *Joseph Smith's Quorum of the Anointed, 1842–1845: A Documentary History* (Salt Lake City: Signature Books, 2005).

5. Andrew F. Ehat, "Joseph Smith's Introduction of Temple Ordinances and the 1844 Mormon Succession Question," (master's thesis, Brigham Young University, 1982), 42–43.

6. Heber C. Kimball to Parley and Mary Ann Pratt, June 17, 1842, Church History Library, Church of Jesus Christ of Latter-day Saints, Salt Lake City, Utah (hereafter CHL). Michael Homer suggests that it may not have been coincidental that the original quorum of the anointed was composed of ten men: "A Royal Arch Chapter, also known as the Holy Order of the Royal Arch, consists of at least nine Master Masons, and was the next logical step in Freemasonry for those who had advanced to the third degree." Homer, "'Similarity of Priesthood in Masonry': The Relationship Between Freemasonry and Mormonism," *Dialogue: A Journal of Mormon Thought* 27, no. 3 (Fall 1994): 34. See also Homer, *Joseph's Temples: The Dynamic Relationship Between Freemasonry and Mormonism* (Salt Lake City: University of Utah Press, 2014), 245–49.

identical, words and gestures.[7] For those believing in the restoration of all things, such similarities pointed to a belief in the ancient origins of Freemasonry.[8] Historian D. Michael Quinn observes that, despite the parallels, "the Mormon endowment or Holy Order had the specific purpose of preparing the initiate for 'an ascent into heaven,' whereas Freemasonry did not."[9] Another factor, whose impact on the endowment was just as (if not more) important, was Joseph's translation of the Book of Abraham, especially the vignette called Facsimile 2, which lists items "that cannot be revealed unto the world; but is to be had in the Holy Temple of God." Explaining the role of the Egyptian papyri that Joseph used in producing the book, Latter-day Saint writer Hugh Nibley asserted that "early fathers of the Church" noted similarities "between Christianity and other, notably Egyptian, beliefs and practices." Nibley termed these early rituals an "Egyptian endowment," and Latter-day Saints today believe that Joseph Smith's study of Egyptian and biblical texts inspired him to restore a purer, truer form of temple rites.[10]

By 1840, Masonry had developed from a network of Renaissance craft guilds into a fraternity emphasizing personal study, self-improvement, and service. One of Masonry's benefits from a Mormon standpoint was the pledge of protection and loyalty that members swore to each other. Joseph supported the idea of a Nauvoo lodge for the prestige it would bring to the city and church. Initial requests to the Grand Lodge in June 1841 for a Nauvoo dispensation were denied, yet four months later

---

7. David John Buerger, *The Mysteries of Godliness: A History of Mormon Temple Worship* (San Francisco: Smith Research Associates, 1994), 53–55.

8. The erroneous view that Masonry originated during the construction of King Solomon's temple has been abandoned by modern scholars, and most Mormons today do not believe that the efficacy of the endowment depends on the ancient origins of Masonry. LDS scholar Armand L. Mauss explains "that the Masonic ceremony itself changed and evolved even in recent centuries does not necessarily invalidate Joseph Smith's claim that he was restoring, by revelation, an even more ancient temple ceremony to which the Masonic one bore certain resemblances. On the other hand, neither does that claim constitute a declaration of the total independence of the Mormon temple ceremony from any external cultural influences, including Masonry." Mauss, "Culture, Charisma, and Change: Reflections on Mormon Temple Worship," *Dialogue: A Journal of Mormon Thought* 20, no. 4 (Winter 1987): 79–80.

9. D. Michael Quinn, *The Mormon Hierarchy: Origins of Power* (Salt Lake City: Signature Books/Smith Research Associates, 1994), 115.

10. Hugh Nibley, *The Message of the Joseph Smith Papyri: An Egyptian Endowment* (Salt Lake City: Deseret Book Co., 1976), xii–xiii. See also Leonard, *Nauvoo*, 212.

Abraham Jonas of the Columbus Lodge approved the Saints' application. In December 1841, eighteen Masons met to organize a Nauvoo lodge in Hyrum Smith's home. Jonas officially installed the lodge and its officers on March 15, 1842. Joseph Smith and Sidney Rigdon, his counselor in the First Presidency, were both initiated on this occasion, which took place in the red brick store's upstairs room. More than 500 Mormon men joined or were advanced within the first five months, causing Nauvoo Masons to outnumber all other Masons in Illinois combined.[11]

In addition to their Masonic membership, these first ten men were among the highest ranking and most trusted leaders of the church. Joseph was church president, Hyrum assistant president; William Law was a member of Joseph's First Presidency; Brigham Young, Heber C. Kimball, and Willard Richards were members of the Quorum of Twelve Apostles; William Marks was Nauvoo Stake president; Newell K. Whitney was a presiding bishop; and James Adams and George Miller held positions of local leadership.

The Anointed Quorum met on at least two subsequent occasions (perhaps as many as four) before the end of 1842. Vinson Knight apparently became the next man to be initiated that year, although this is not certain.[12] Those who left accounts of these meetings record that they received instruction, discussed items of business and current interest, and engaged in group prayer. For example, on June 26 and 28, 1842, meetings focused on "the situation of the pine country & Lumbering business" where men were logging Wisconsin timber for the Nauvoo temple. On each occasion, quorum members "united in solemn prayer," asking, for example, for aid in dealing with legal matters facing the church and for protection of a quorum member who was to leave the next day to bring his family to Nauvoo.[13]

---

11. Homer, *Joseph's Temples*, 158.

12. John C. Bennett, *A History of the Saints; or, An Exposé of Joe Smith and Mormonism* (Boston: Leland & Whiting, 1842), 247–48. Bennett cites a letter from George W. Robinson dated August 8, 1842, which claims that Vinson Knight had been endowed. Because Knight had died a week earlier on July 31, 1842, his initiation, if Bennett is correct, must have occurred between May 6 and the end of July. Because he was bishop of Nauvoo's Lower Ward and an early polygamist, he is included in the list of members in this essay.

13. Anderson and Bergera, *Joseph Smith's Quorum of the Anointed*, 10–16; Andrew H. Hedges, Alex D. Smith, and Richard Lloyd Anderson, eds., *The Joseph Smith Papers: Journals, Volume 2: December 1841–April 1843* (Salt Lake City: Church Historian's Press, 2011), 68–71.

Following meetings in July (and possibly September), the Anointed Quorum did not meet again until May 1843. The gap between meetings most probably resulted from the John C. Bennett crisis that placed most of the church's business on hold. Bennett, who had moved to Nauvoo in September 1840, quickly rose to prominence in the new community. Within five months he was mayor of Nauvoo, chancellor of the University of Nauvoo, and major general of the Nauvoo Legion. Two months later he was sustained as an acting counselor to Joseph Smith. Church leaders soon learned, however, that Bennett had been secretly practicing his own version of plural marriage (Joseph had begun teaching his doctrine of plural wives to other church leaders, including some of the Twelve Apostles, in mid- to late-1841). Bennett's practice—which occurred as Joseph was attempting to introduce plural, or celestial, marriage—did not involve a marriage ceremony, and Joseph disavowed any connection to Bennett's activities. Bennett, who was never a member of the Anointed Quorum, withdrew from the church shortly after the quorum's organization in May 1842.

During the fall of 1842, an embittered Bennett published a book-length exposé of Joseph Smith. Although many of Bennett's sensational claims were based on hearsay, others reflected first-hand knowledge, and the situation posed a dilemma for Joseph, who wanted to keep knowledge of both plural marriage and the Anointed Quorum private. Public discussion over Bennett's charges of "spiritual wifery" forced Joseph to denounce Bennett's allegations publicly while privately continuing to teach and practice plural marriage.[14]

The situation intensified when Hyrum Smith, William Law, and William Marks, all members of the Anointed Quorum who were unaware of Joseph's plural marriages, tried to rid the church of such

---

14. For Bennett's role in Nauvoo as a polygamy insider, see George D. Smith, *Nauvoo Polygamy "... But We Called It Celestial Marriage,"* (Salt Lake City: Signature Books, 2008), 82, 222, 263, 269, 285. See also Brian C. Hales, *Joseph Smith's Polygamy, Volume 1: History* (Salt Lake City: Greg Kofford Books, 2013), 547–74, for an alternate view of Bennett. Other important studies of the practice in Nauvoo are Todd M. Compton, *In Sacred Loneliness: The Plural Wives of Joseph Smith* (Salt Lake City: Signature Books, 1997); Richard S. Van Wagoner, *Mormon Polygamy: A History* (Salt Lake City: Signature Books, 1986); and Kathryn M. Daynes, *More Wives Than One: Transformation of the Mormon Marriage System, 1840–1910* (Urbana: University of Illinois Press, 2002).

teachings. Joseph's private secretary, William Clayton, recorded on May 23, 1843: "Conversed with H[eber] C. K[imball] concerning a plot that is being laid to entrap the brethren of the secret priesthood by Brother H[yrum] and others."[15] According to Brigham Young's later reminiscence, apparently within a day or two, Hyrum approached him: "I have a question to ask you," Hyrum began. "You and the twelve know some things that I do not know. I can understand this by the motions, and talk, and doings of Joseph, and I know there is something or other, which I do not understand, that is revealed to the Twelve. Is this so?" Young responded: "I do not know any thing about what you know, but I know what I know." Hyrum continued: "I have mistrusted for a long time that Joseph has received a revelation that a man should have more than one wife, and he has hinted as much to me, but I would not bear it. ... I am convinced that there is something that has not been told me." Young then reportedly responded:

> [B]rother Hyrum, I will tell you about this thing which you do not know if you will sware with an uplifted hand, before God, that you will never say another word against Joseph and his doings, and the doctrines he is preaching to the people. He replied, "I will do it with all my heart;" and he stood upon his feet, saying, "I want to know the truth, and to be saved." And he made a covenant there, never again to bring forward one argument or use any influence against Joseph's doings. Joseph had many wives sealed to him. I told Hyrum the whole story, and he bowed to it and wept like a child, and said, "God be praised." He went to Joseph and told him what he had learned, and renewed his covenant with Joseph, and they went heart and hand together while they lived, and they were together when they died, and they are together now defending Israel.[16]

Hyrum's conversion to plural marriage and the renewed intimacy of the two brothers may have prompted the meeting of the Anointed Quorum on May 26, 1843, the first after at least eight months. The interval between William Clayton's diary entry, Hyrum's conversation with Young, and the quorum's meeting was only three days. Clayton recorded

---

15. George D. Smith, ed., *An Intimate Chronicle: The Journals of William Clayton* (Salt Lake City: Signature Books/Smith Research Associates, 1991), 105.

16. Brigham Young, quoted in Ehat, "Joseph Smith's Introduction of Temple Ordinances," 57–59.

in his diary on May 26 that "Hyrum received the doctrine of priesthood," generally understood to mean that he accepted plural marriage.[17]

LDS researcher Andrew Ehat suggests that the discussion of Hyrum's conversion to plural marriage may not have occurred in this meeting of the Anointed Quorum because William Law, who never accepted plural marriage, was present: "According to his testimony, William Law never knew from Joseph Smith that plural marriage was a practice of the Church until D&C 132 was recorded. This was seven weeks *after* the 26 May meeting."[18] Joseph may have broached the topic indirectly, theoretically, or not at all. D. Michael Quinn, another historian of the Anointed Quorum, believes that Hyrum's conversion prompted Joseph at the May 26 meeting to re-endow—that is, to repeat the washings, anointed, and teachings for—everyone who had been endowed the previous year. William Marks and George Miller were the only members of the Anointed Quorum absent from this meeting. Whether or not Joseph instructed quorum members in plural marriage at this time, Hyrum's acceptance revitalized the quorum and Joseph's plans for it. One result, according to Quinn, was that Joseph decided two months later to designate Hyrum his successor and church president. After the May 26 meeting, according to Quinn, "Events in the Quorum of Anointed and other groups associated with the secret practices of Nauvoo were often more crucial than events occurring within open, public forums."[19]

On this occasion, the quorum also renewed the practice of group prayer circles—or the true order of prayer—a ritual which became increasingly important in quorum meetings and remains an important part of LDS temple worship. These ritual prayers imparted to members the "endowment of power" they believed they possessed.[20] Contemporary diary entries mentioning, for example, "prayer meeting at J[oseph Smith]'s old house"[21] usually refer to meetings of the Anointed Quorum.

On May 28, 1843, two days after this crucial meeting, Joseph

---

17. Anderson and Bergera, *Joseph Smith's Quorum of the Anointed*, 17–19; Smith, *Intimate Chronicle*, 106.

18. Ehat, "Joseph Smith's Introduction of Temple Ordinances," 62, emphasis original.

19. Quinn, *Origins of Power*, 54–55.

20. D. Michael Quinn, "Latter-day Saint Prayer Circles," *BYU Studies* 19, no. 1 (Fall 1978): 79–105.

21. Willard Richards, diary, Nov. 12, 1843, CHL.

introduced another ceremony to the Anointed Quorum: marriage seal-ings for eternity.[22] On that day, Joseph and James Adams were sealed to their civil spouses, Emma Hale Smith and Harriet Denton Adams. This was an important moment for the Smiths, as Emma Smith, like Hyrum, had originally opposed her husband's teachings on plural marriage (and would again), yet had apparently reconciled herself suffi-ciently to the doctrine and practice, for "in the background of Joseph's introduction of the temple ordinances was the principle of plural mar-riage."[23] The next day, Hyrum, Brigham Young, and Willard Richards were all sealed to their civil wives.[24]

Four months later, on September 28, the first women were initiated into the quorum, beginning with Emma, who received her endowment on or just before that date. The previous year, Joseph had organized the women's Relief Society and, using Masonic terminology, had instructed the women in his vision of their organization. "Let this Presidency serve as a constitution," he said, proposing two weeks later "that the So-ciety go into a close examination of every candidate ... that the Society should grow up by degrees." He added that God would "make of this Society a kingdom of priests as in Enoch's day."[25]

At the Anointed Quorum's meeting on September 28, 1843, Joseph

22. Anderson and Bergera, *Joseph Smith's Quorum of the Anointed*, 19–21. Joseph had actually begun marriage sealings for eternity in April 1841 when, according to reminiscent accounts, he married his first documented plural wife, Louisa Beaman.

23. Ehat, "Joseph Smith's Introduction of Temple Ordinances," 74–75. Ehat adds: "Jo-seph had persuaded Emma to accept plural marriage in part by assuring her she could choose his wives. Shortly before her 28 May sealing, she designated Emily and Eliza Partridge and Sarah and Maria Lawrence and witnessed their weddings to her husband. She did not know that Joseph had already married at least sixteen women, including the Partridge sisters, two months earlier. By July 1843 when Joseph dictated the revelation sanctioning polygamy (D&C 132), Emma had changed her mind. Hyrum Smith read it her, after which he reported to Joseph: 'I have never received a more severe talking to in my life. Emma is very bitter and full of resentment and anger.'" Quoted in Linda King Newell and Valeen Tippetts Avery, *Mormon Enigma: Emma Hale Smith* (Garden City, New York: Doubleday, 1984), 142–52.

24. Anderson and Bergera, *Joseph Smith's Quorum of the Anointed*, 21–22; Andrew H. Hedges, Alex D. Smith, and Brent M. Rogers, eds., *The Joseph Smith Papers: Journals, Volume 3: May 1843–June 1844* (Salt Lake City: Church Historian's Press, 2015), 25–26. Hyrum Smith and Adams were not polygamists at this point; Young and Richards were. Smith, *Nauvoo Polygamy*, 615–16, 635–37.

25. Nauvoo Female Relief Society Minute Book, Mar. 17 and 30, 1842, in Jill Mulvay Derr et al., eds., *The First Fifty Years of Relief Society: Key Documents in Latter-day Saint Women's History* (Salt Lake City: Church Historian's Press, 2016), 31, 42–43. These words

"was by common consent and unanimous voice chosen President of the quorum and anointed and ord[ained] to the highest and holiest order of the priesthood (and companion [i.e., Emma])."[26] This ordinance, called the second anointing, ostensibly fulfilled the promise of the first anointing (which occurred during the early stages of the endowment).[27] According to Glen M. Leonard, this "crowning ordinance" was "a promise of kingly powers and of endless lives. It was the confirmation of promises that worthy men could become kings and priests and that women could become queens and priestesses in the eternal worlds."[28] "For any person to have the fullness of that priesthood," Brigham Young explained, "he must be a king and priest. A person may have a portion of that priesthood, the same as governors or judges of England have power from the king to transact business; but that does not make them kings of England. A person may be anointed king and priest long before he receives his kingdom."[29] Those who receive their second anointings, according to twentieth-century LDS apostle Bruce R. McConkie, "means that the Lord seals their exaltation upon them while they are yet in this life. ... [T]heir exaltation is assured."[30] During the ordinance, explains LDS historian Lyndon W. Cook, a husband is "ordained a priest and anointed a king unto God," while wives are "anointed priestesses and queens unto their husband."[31] "These ordinances," Ehat adds,

> depending on the person's ecclesiastical position, made the recipient a "king and priest," "in," "in and over," or (as only in Joseph Smith's case) "over" the Church. Moreover, the recipient had sealed upon him the power to bind and loose on earth as Joseph explained in his definition of the

were also common Masonic terms and prompted Bennett to accuse Joseph of establishing a lodge of female Masonry. Quinn, "Latter-day Saint Prayer Circles," 85–86.

26. Anderson and Bergera, *Joseph Smith's Quorum of the Anointed*, 25; Hedges, Smith, and Rogers, *Journals, Volume 3*, 104.

27. David John Buerger, "'The Fulness of the Priesthood': The Second Anointing in Latter-day Saint Theology and Practice," *Dialogue: A Journal of Mormon Thought* 16, no. 1 (Spring 1983): 10–44.

28. Leonard, *Nauvoo*, 260–61.

29. Joseph Smith Jr. et al., *History of the Church of Jesus Christ of Latter-day Saints*, ed. B. H. Roberts, 7 vols. (Salt Lake City: Deseret News Press, 1902–12, 1932, 5:527.

30. Bruce R. McConkie, *Mormon Doctrine*, 2nd ed. (Salt Lake City: Bookcraft, 1966), 109–10.

31. Lyndon W. Cook, *Joseph C. Kingsbury: A Biography* (Provo, Utah: Grandin Book, 1985), 94.

fulness of the priesthood. Another blessing, growing out of the promise of the sealing power was the specific blessing that whatever thing was desired it would not be withheld when sought for in diligent prayer.[32]

"There is no exaltation in the kingdom of God," Joseph Fielding Smith, writing as official LDS Church Historian and apostle, "without the fulness of priesthood."[33] Members who received the second anointing understood that their reward lay not in this, but in the next, life.

Throughout the remainder of 1843, the Anointed Quorum continued to expand, with eternal sealings and second anointings following initiation as members. Such ordinances consumed a significant portion of the time, but the quorum also addressed important issues confronting the church. For example, on November 15, 1843, after Alpheus and Lois Cutler received their second anointing, "I [Joseph Smith] spoke of a petition to Congress, my letter to [James Arlington] Bennett, and intention to write a proclamation to the kings of the earth." On December 3, with "all present except Hyrum and his wife," W. W. Phelps read Joseph's appeal to the Green Mountain Boys of Vermont to require Missouri to redress its wrongs against the Saints. Joseph's written appeal "was dedicated by prayer after *all* had spoken upon it."[34] As Quinn points out, these meetings during November and December 1843 were the first time in church history that men and women together discussed theocratic issues. Other such meetings would follow.[35]

However, the Anointed Quorum was not an administrative or legislative body. Its authority stemmed from the members' anointings and endowments, both of which were strictly spiritual in nature. They discussed the appeal to the Green Mountain Boys, then made it a matter of prayer. The quorum did vote on matters that affected the group, however. For example, when William Law rejected plural marriage and stopped attending quorum meetings, the group voted to expel him in early 1844. Bathsheba Bigler Smith, a member of the quorum and wife

---

32. Ehat, "Joseph Smith's Introduction of Temple Ordinances," 95–96.

33. In Bruce R. McConkie, comp., *Doctrines of Salvation: Sermons and Writings of Joseph Fielding Smith* (Salt Lake City: Bookcraft, 1956), 3:132.

34. Anderson and Bergera, *Joseph Smith's Quorum of the Anointed*, 35–36; Hedges, Smith, and Rogers, *Journals, Volume 3*, 138; emphasis added.

35. Quinn, *Origins of Power*, 116.

of George A. Smith, who attended this meeting, said that "each one present vot[ed] yes or no in his [or her] turn."[36] Quinn summarizes, "All available evidence shows that the Holy Order's only administrative function pertained to ... the endowment ordinances from 1843 to 1845," and stresses that "even when male members of the Anointed Quorum conducted administrative business, they sometimes made a distinct separation between meeting in their church capacity to discuss administrative matters and meeting as the quorum of Anointed to have a prayer circle about the matters discussed."[37]

By the end of 1843, the quorum numbered at least thirty-eight individuals and had met at least thirty-two times, mostly to endow new members, advance others in the ordinances, and engage in group prayer. Eighteen women had been initiated into the quorum and been endowed. Fifteen members had received the second anointing, while as many as seventeen couples had been sealed for eternity.

As the quorum grew, it is important to note the family relationships between Joseph and other quorum members (see Table 1). Although the quorum included a number of Joseph's biological kin and relatives by marriage, relationships established by his and other plural unions also broadened the familial connections. Eventually, some thirty-nine initiates (44 percent of all quorum members) shared a family connection to Joseph, thus strengthening existing bonds of loyalty and increasing the trust Joseph hoped to foster and maintain within the group.

The year 1844 proved to be a difficult, yet prosperous twelve months for the quorum. Members were added by vote. In late January, for example, William Clayton recorded: "Brother [Reynolds] Cahoon came to my house to say that a vote had been taken on my being admitted into the quorum and I was accepted."[38] It is unknown if recommendations for admission came solely from Joseph or also from other quorum members. However, each member had a say in the matter and admissions

---

36. Bathsheba W. Smith, Testimony, Mar. 16, 1892, in *Complainant's Abstract of Pleading and Evidence, In the Circuit Court of the United States, Western District of Missouri, Western Division at Kansas City. The Reorganized Church of Jesus Christ of Latter Day Saints, Complainants vs. The Church of Christ at Independence, Missouri* (Lamoni, Iowa: Herald Publishing House, 1893), 360.

37. Quinn, "Latter-day Saint Prayer Circles," 90–91.

38. Smith, *Intimate Chronicle*, 125.

TABLE 1. Family Connections to Joseph Smith of Quorum Members, 1842–45

Member	Connection to Joseph Smith
Lucy Mack Smith	mother
Hyrum Smith	brother
Mary Fielding (wife of Hyrum Smith)	sister-in-law
Mercy Fielding Thompson (sister of Mary Fielding Smith and Hyrum Smith's plural wife)	sister-in-law by marriage
Joseph Fielding (Mary and Mercy's brother)	brother-in-law by marriage
Hannah G. Fielding (wife of Joseph Fielding)	sister-in-law by marriage
Samuel H. Smith	brother
William Smith	brother
John Smith (brother of Joseph Smith Sr.)	uncle
Clarissa Lyman Smith (wife of John Smith)	aunt by marriage
George A. Smith (son of John and Clarissa Smith)	first cousin
Bathsheba Bigler Smith (wife of George A. Smith)	cousin-in-law by marriage
Emma Hale Smith	first wife
Louisa Beaman/Beman	plural wife
Mary Adeline Beaman/Beman Noble (sister of Louisa Beaman)	sister-in-law
Joseph Bates Noble (husband of Mary Beaman)	brother-in-law by marriage
Olive Grey Frost	plural wife
Mary Ann Frost Pratt (sister of Olive Frost)	sister-in-law
Parley Pratt (husband of Mary Ann Frost)	brother-in-law by marriage
Marinda Nancy Johnson Hyde	plural wife
Orson Hyde (husband of Marinda Nancy Johnson)	co-husband
Helen Mar Kimball	plural wife
Heber C. Kimball (father of Helen Mar Kimball)	father-in-law

TABLE I. *continued*

Member	Connection to Joseph Smith
Vilate Murray Kimball (mother of Helen Mar Kimball)	mother-in-law
Fanny Murray Young	plural wife
Vilate Murray Kimball (stepmother of Fanny Young)	stepmother-in-law
Heber C. Kimball (stepfather of Fanny Young)	stepfather-in-law
Rhoda Richards	plural wife
Levi Richards (brother of Rhoda Richards)	brother-in-law
Willard Richards (brother of Rhoda Richards)	brother-in-law
Jennetta Richards Richards (wife of Willard Richards)	sister-in-law by marriage
Sarah Ann Whitney	plural wife
Joseph C. Kingsbury (civil husband of Sarah Ann Whitney; and son-in-law; wife, Caroline Whitney [deceased])	co-husband
Newel K. Whitney (father of Sarah Ann Whitney)	father-in-law
Elizabeth Ann Whitney (mother of Sarah Ann Whitney)	mother-in-law
Agnes M. Coolbrith	plural wife
Elizabeth Davis Durfee	plural wife
Zina D. H. Jacobs	plural wife
Mary E. Rollins Lightner	plural wife
Sylvia Porter Sessions	plural wife
Eliza Roxcy Snow	plural wife

received unanimous votes. In her reminiscence of the decision to drop William Law, Bathsheba Smith also recalled: "One member hesitated to vote, which called forth earnest remarks from the Prophet Joseph. He showed clearly that it would be doing a serious wrong to retain him longer. After his explanation the vote was unanimous."[39]

---

39. Smith, Testimony, 360.

Although the quorum met primarily for prayer and ordinance work, meetings also included instruction on scripture and doctrine. For example, on January 28, 1844, in addition to the usual prayer circle, Joseph spoke on the coming of Elijah as recorded in Malachi 4. The following week, he expounded on the scriptural teaching of the 144,000 in the book of Revelation. At an earlier meeting that month, John Taylor had addressed the quorum and "made some appropriate remarks unto edification."[40] The quorum met more than twenty times in January and February 1844, averaging at least two and often three times a week.

After William Law's expulsion from the Anointed Quorum, he became further estranged from Joseph and was excommunicated three months later on April 18, 1844, along with his wife, Jane, and brother, Wilson. Three days later, William Law helped to found the Reformed Mormon Church and for the next two months worked to brand Joseph a "fallen" prophet. Meetings of the Anointed Quorum became less frequent as church leaders dealt with these latest challenges: only four times in March, once in April, and six times from May until Joseph's and Hyrum's deaths in late June. Meetings also dealt less with spiritual matters and more with the crisis with dissidents and reformers. For example, William Clayton recorded on April 28: "We united [in prayer] for President Joseph the Church, the presidency contests the Lawsuits. The apostates, the sick &c. &c." Still, Clayton added, "We had a good time."[41] The friendship, trust, and unity experienced within the quorum was, no doubt, a welcome respite from the turmoil in the community at large.

On June 7, 1844, Law and others published the first (and only) issue of the *Nauvoo Expositor*, which detailed Joseph's plural marriage teachings and advocated repeal of Nauvoo's city charter. Joseph, as mayor of Nauvoo, and the city council, declared the *Expositor* a nuisance and ordered its total destruction. Joseph was charged with inciting a riot and other potentially treasonous activities. While awaiting trial in Carthage Jail, he and Hyrum were killed by a group of men on June 27.

---

40. Anderson and Bergera, *Joseph Smith's Quorum of the Anointed*, 60–62; Wilford Woodruff, *Wilford Woodruff's Journal, 1833–1898*, typescript, ed. Scott G. Kenny, 9 vols. (Midvale, Utah: Signature Books, 1983–85), 2:344, 348, 346.

41. Smith, *Intimate Chronicle*, 131.

The deaths placed in a special category those who had already joined the Anointed Quorum compared to those initiated during the next year and a half, before the completion of the Nauvoo temple. What role did plural marriage play in quorum membership? Although there was a high correlation, not all in the Anointed Quorum were polygamists. (See Table 2.) Of the thirty-seven men and twenty-nine women (sixty-six total) initiated during Joseph's lifetime, sixteen men and twenty women (54.5 percent of members) were polygamists either before or after initiation. These sixteen men represented 43 percent of male initiates (24 percent of members); the twenty women represented 69 percent of female initiates (30 percent of members). Thus, while practicing plural marriage was not required for admission into the quorum, acceptance of the teaching was.[42]

Regarding the second anointing, while receipt of this "higher" ordinance required the first anointing, admission into the Anointed Quorum did not guarantee receipt of the second anointing during Joseph's lifetime. Of the men and women initiated into the quorum while Joseph was alive, nineteen men and seventeen women (56 percent of all initiates) received their second anointing prior to Joseph's death. (See Table 3.) These nineteen men represented 51 percent of male members (29 percent of all members), the seventeen women 59 percent of female members (26 percent of all members). Of the nineteen husbands who received the second anointing during Joseph's lifetime, eleven (58 percent) were polygamists, eight (42 percent) monogamists. As can best be determined, no plural wife ever received the higher ordinance until after Joseph's death, leading D. Michael Quinn to conclude that, during this period, "polygamy was only an appendage" to receipt of the second anointing."[43] Had Joseph lived, requirements for initiation into the quorum and the ordinances themselves may have evolved further, especially considering the changes that had taken place while he was alive.

During the succession crisis that followed Joseph's death, some of the drama played out in the Anointed Quorum. As Quinn points out, in the weeks following, "the primary format for discussing [presidential]

---

42. See the list of Nauvoo polygamists in Smith, *Nauvoo Polygamy*, 574–656
43. Quinn, "Latter-day Saint Prayer Circles," 88.

TABLE 2. Plural Marriage among Quorum Members
during Joseph Smith's Lifetime

I. Husbands and Plural Wives Initiated	
Husbands	*Wives*
James Adams	Harriet Denton Adams, Roxena Repshire*
Reynolds Cahoon	Thirza Stiles Cahoon, Lucina Roberts*
William Clayton	Ruth Moon Clayton, Margaret Moon
Orson Hyde	Marinda Nancy Johnson Hyde, Martha Rebecca Browett,* Mary Ann Price*
Heber C. Kimball	Vilate Murray Kimball, Sarah Peak Noon*
Vinson Knight	Martha McBride Knight,* Philinda Clark Eldredge Myrick*
Isaac Morley	Lucy Gunn Morley, Hannah Blakeslee Finch Merriam*
Parley Pratt	Mary Ann Frost Pratt, Elizabeth Brotherton*
Willard Richards	Jenetta Richards Richards, Sarah Longstroth*
Hyrum Smith	Mary Fielding Smith, Mercy R. Fielding Thompson, Catherine Phillips*
John Smith	Clarissa Lyman Smith, Mary Aikens,* Julia Ellis Hills*
Joseph Smith	Emma Hale Smith, Agnes M. Coolbrith, Elizabeth Davis Durfee, Marinda Nancy Johnson Hyde, Fanny Young Murray, Louisa Be[a]man,* Prescindia L. H. Buell,* Sarah Kinsley Cleveland,* Hannah Ells,* Olive Grey Frost,* Desdemona Fullmer,* Elvira Annie Cowles Holmes,* Zina D. H. Jacobs,* Almera Woodward Johnson,* Helen Mar Kimball,* Martha McBride Knight,* Maria Lawrence,* Sarah Lawrence,* Mary E. Rollins Lightner,* Melissa Lott,* Sarah Scott Mulholland,* Emily Dow Partridge,* Eliza Maria Partridge,* Rhoda Richards,* Ruth Vose Sayers,* Patty Bartlett Sessions,* Sylvia Porter Sessions,* Delcena Johnson Sherman,* Eliza Roxcy Snow,* Lucy Walker,* Sarah Ann Whitney,* Nancy Maria[h] Winchester,* Flora Ann Woodworth*

TABLE 2. *continued*

Husbands	Wives
William Smith	Caroline Amanda Grant Smith,* Mary Ann Covington Sheffield,* Mary Jones*
John Taylor	Leonora Cannon Taylor, Elizabeth Kaighan,* Jane Ballantyne*
Lyman Wight	Harriet Benton,* Jane Margaret Ballantyne*

* Not a member of the Anointed Quorum during Joseph Smith's lifetime.

II. Husbands Practicing Plural Marriage
Who Were Not Initiated during Joseph Smith's Lifetime

George F. Adams	John E. Page
Ezra T. Benson	Ebenezer Richardson
Howard Egan	William Sagers
William Felshaw	Erastus Snow
William D. Huntington	Theodore Turley
Joseph A. Kelting	Edwin D. Woolley
Joseph Bates Noble	Lorenzo Dow Young

succession was at meetings of the Quorum of Anointed. Three-fourths of the apostles and other leaders were weeks away from Nauvoo. Unlike all other quorums, the Quorum of Anointed had no requirement that a majority be present to conduct business."[44] However, quorum members were divided on appointing a trustee for the church; some wanted to act immediately, others wanted to await the apostles' return.[45] The second group prevailed. The quorum met six times between June 27 and August 8: on June 30, and July 4, 7, 12, 14, and 24.

Following the arrival in Nauvoo of most apostles, Sidney Rigdon, Joseph's first counselor, presented the case for his appointment as "guardian" of the church at a public meeting on August 8.[46] However, most church members favored the leadership of the Quorum of the Twelve, with Brigham Young as its president. At Rigdon's excommunication

44. Quinn, *Origins of Power*, 149.
45. Quinn, 150
46. Quinn, 164.

TABLE 3. The Second Anointing and Plural Marriage among Quorum Members during Joseph Smith's Lifetime

Husbands	Wives	Marital Status at the Time
Reynolds Cahoon	Thirza Stiles Cahoon	Polygamist
Alpheus Cutler	Lois Lathrop Cutler	Monogamist
Orson Hyde	[Anointed without wife]	Polygamist
Heber C. Kimball	Vilate Murray Kimball	Polygamist
Cornelius Lott	Permelia Darrow Lott	Monogamist
William Marks	Rosannah Robinson Marks	Monogamist
Isaac Morley	Lucy Gunn Morley	Polygamist
William W. Phelps	Sally Waterman Phelps	Monogamist
Orson Pratt	[Anointed without wife]	Monogamist
Parley P. Pratt	[Anointed without wife]	Polygamist
Willard Richards	Jennetta Richards Richards	Polygamist
Georg A. Smith	Bathsheba Bigler Smith	Monogamist
Hyrum Smith	Mary Fielding Smith	Polygamist
John Smith	Clarissa Lyman Smith	Polygamist
Joseph Smith	Emma Hale Smith	Polygamist
[Husband deceased]	Lucy Mack Smith	Monogamist
John Taylor	Leonora Cannon Taylor	Polygamist
Newel K. Whitney	Elizabeth Ann Smith Whitney	Monogamist
Wilford Woodruff	Phoebe Carter Woodruff	Monogamist
Brigham Young	Mary Ann Angell Young	Polygamist

the next month, Apostle Orson Hyde denounced Rigdon's claims and observed that the dilemma could have been resolved elsewhere: "There is a quorum organized where revelations can be tested." Although Hyde did not identify the Anointed Quorum by name, he seems to have been thinking of its prayer circles.[47] The day after Rigdon's failed bid, Young assembled the Anointed Quorum, and its members voted to stop admitting new initiates "till times would admit."[48]

47. Quinn, 171.
48. Anderson and Bergera, *Joseph Smith's Quorum of the Anointed*, 82–84; Willard Richards, diary, Aug. 9, 1844.

The meetings of the Anointed Quorum were also curtailed; three in September, two in October, none in November, and one in December. At December's meeting, quorum members voted to admit three women, though the women actually joined the quorum later. During the first three-quarters of 1845, Brigham Young convened and presided over 146 meetings of the quorum, often five and ten times a month. During the final quarter, from October 2 to December 11, the quorum met daily. They also added more than twenty members. In the process, according to Quinn, Young helped to "make polygamy an institution instead of furtive practice" by increasing the percentage of plural wives within the quorum from 7.6 percent during Joseph's lifetime to 57.1 percent.[49] Young also resumed the administration of second anointings in 1845.

In addition to admitting members, the quorum regularly held prayer circles. They prayed for deliverance from their enemies, for example, asking that Thomas Sharp, editor of the hostile *Warsaw Signal*, "be visited with judgements." They also implored divine retribution on troublemakers inside the church, such as William Smith (Joseph's younger brother), who believed the Smith family should lead the church and "is endeavoring to ride the Twelve down."[50] At a time when the Saints were struggling to complete their temple and simultaneously having to deal with internal and external strife, many of the quorum's meetings lasted late into the evening. On May 18, 1845, for example, the quorum was in session until 2:00 a.m.; on May 22, the meeting ended at midnight; on May 29, quorum members did not return home until 1:30 a.m. It is obvious from the sources that the spiritual power they collectively invoked while engaged in prayer motivated them to unite together until they could open the temple, endow as many of the Saints as possible, and finally evacuate Nauvoo.

The Anointed Quorum met for the first time in the Nauvoo temple on December 7, 1845. Three days later, they launched the monumental process of endowing the general adult membership of the church. Although the temple was unfinished, the attic level was completed,

---

49. Quinn, *Origins of Power*, 176.
50. Smith, *Intimate Chronicle*, 167.

allowing endowments to be performed for over 5,000 men and women until February 6, 1846.

While the Nauvoo era of Mormon history is remembered, in part, for developments associated with the temple, the Anointed Quorum set the stage for those teachings. It was the Anointed Quorum that met together for three and a half years, participating in sacred rites and receiving instruction from Joseph Smith, Brigham Young, and other church officials. Any study of Nauvoo must treat the Anointed Quorum as a facet of Joseph's contribution to temple-related theology. The quorum should be recognized for its comforting and invigorating spiritual power, acting as a separate group from those governing the church administratively.

TWO

"NOT TO BE RITEN"
THE MORMON TEMPLE RITE AS ORAL CANON

KATHLEEN FLAKE

By letter of June 1842, one of Joseph Smith's closest associates in the formative days of the Church of Jesus Christ of Latter-day Saints ("LDS Church" or "the LDS") writes to another of the newly received temple ceremony: "I wish you was here so as to feel and hear for your Self. we have recieved some pressious things through the Prophet … that would cause your soul to rejoice I can not give them to you on paper fore they are not to be riten."[1]

In the ensuing 170-plus years, the LDS Church has not wavered from its earliest insistence that its temple rite is "not to be riten," but only to be experienced by the faithful who "feel and hear for" themselves by participating in the ritual. If accused of conducting secret rites, the church will protest that its temple ceremony is sacred, not secret: "Because the temple ceremony is sacred to us, we don't speak about it except in the most general terms. …"[2] To Latter-day Saints, each of their more than 160 operating temples (as of 2019) is the "house of the Lord" necessarily set apart from the world. Believing the indictment of Israel—"they have put no difference between the holy and profane, neither have they showed difference between the unclean and the clean" (Ezek. 22:26)—the LDS have placed their core canon[3] within the temple and strictly limited access to it and its ritual

---

1. Heber C. Kimball to Parley P. Pratt, June 17, 1842, Church History Library, Church of Jesus Christ of Latter-day Saints, Salt Lake City, Utah (hereafter CHL).

2. "Mormons Drop Rites Opposed by Women," *New York Times*, May 3, 1990, 1.

3. The tendency to conflate the meanings of canon and scripture has created some confusion and, hence, it may be necessary at the outset to stipulate that the term "canon" here denotes a rule or norm, not the privileging of certain writings as authoritative. That this rule or canon is orally maintained by the community makes it no less a source of law. As has

content. Not all within the church are admitted,[4] and, for those who are, even general discussion about the ritual outside of the temple proper is discouraged by LDS scriptural and ecclesiastical guidelines regarding the temple's sacredness: "That which cometh from above is sacred, and must be spoken with care, and by constraint of the Spirit" (D&C 63:64). Clearly, the content of the LDS temple rite is both sacred and secret: sacred to the initiated in that it is "set apart" by the way it is treated vis-à-vis their other knowledge and secreted from the uninitiated in that they are not to know it at all. Refusing to make a text of the rite publicly available and insisting that its specific content not be revealed exact a considerable price from the church. Not only does it engender suspicion in the general population from which the church desires acceptance, it creates tension within the church itself, resulting in loss of temple privileges by and even excommunication of some members.[5] Consequently, the practice invites the question: what interests are served at such costs? I suggest that the answer to this question lies not in theological discourse on the sacred and the profane, but in theories of ritual and oral tradition.

The LDS temple ritual is not, by virtue of its being embodied in ritual, a form of human activity existing separate from belief or existing for the purpose of acting out belief recorded in LDS scriptural

---

been noted of Judaism, "Even if the oral law does not defile the hands [as does the holiness of the sacred text], it may provide a more explicit and pragmatically significant register of the demands of a holy life in Judaism than one can find simply reading the written law" (Gerald T. Sheppard, "Cannon," *Encyclopedia of Religion* [New York: Macmillan Publishing Company, 1987]).

4. Participation in the temple ritual is available only to mature members of the church in good standing. This determination is made annually through a two-tier interview process conducted by the ecclesiastical leaders at the LDS equivalent of the parish and diocesan levels. "Questions are asked to ascertain one's faith in God ... and inquiry is made regarding the person's testimony of the restored gospel and loyalty to the teachings and leaders of the church. Worthiness requirements include being honest, keeping the commandments, such as chastity—sexual continence before marriage and fidelity within marriage—obeying the laws of tithing and the Word of Wisdom, fulfilling family responsibilities and avoiding affiliation with dissident groups" (Robert Tucker, "Temple Recommend," *Encyclopedia of Mormonism*, ed. Daniel H. Ludlow, 4 vols. [New York: Macmillan Publishing Co., 1992], 4:1446).

5. "Mormons Summon Those who Spoke to Media of Temple Rites," *Los Angeles Times*, June 2, 1990, 12. "Most Mormon Church members quoted last month in news stories about revisions in the church's confidential ceremony have been summoned for interviews by church officials, it was learned this week."

canon.[6] Thus, the particular emphasis of my analysis it not on the relative authoritativeness or particular content of the temple rite vis-à-vis LDS scripture,[7] but on the form of the temple canon: ritualized and orally maintained, not textualized. I will first discuss ways in which the temple rite operates as canon within the church. Then I will describe in what ways the church's maintenance of this canon constitutes a strategic use of the conventions of an oral tradition by a modern, literate society.[8] Third, I will suggest that the effect of oral traditioning, in conjunction with ritual practice, is to preserve the legitimacy of the canon and the solidarity of community it orders and reorders. Preliminarily, however, it is necessary to establish that the LDS temple ritual is a form of canonical belief, an authoritative locus of transcendent meaning and law both expressed and negotiated in the embodied activity of its performance.

THE LDS TEMPLE RITE AS CANON

The LDS temple rite constitutes canon in both senses of the word: its original meaning as the rule or standard by which all else is measured and later as the rule or law by which persons are governed ecclesiastically. Indeed, what has been said of ancient temple-building cultures could be said of Latter-day Saint society: "The origin of law and of legal traditions must be sought in a ritual setting. More importantly, *law is introduced and mediated ritually*, in a temple setting. Failure to

---

6. For an analysis of the conceptual distinctions between thought and activity and their effect in limiting the outcomes of analysis of ritual, see Catherine Bell, "Discourse and Dichotomies: The Structure of Ritual Theory," *Religion* 17 (1987): 95–118. Note also Mary Collins's related observation that "the human body's very centrality to the ritual action may be the prime reason that rites are judged by academics to be insignificant sources of transcendent meaning" ("Critical Ritual Studies: Examining an Intersection of Theology and Culture," in *Worship: Renewal to Practice* [Washington, DC: Pastoral, 1987]).

7. LDS written canon is comprised of four equally authoritative volumes of scripture: the Bible (typically the King James Version), the Book of Mormon, Doctrine and Covenants, and the Pearl of Great Price, which includes the Book of Abraham and the Book of Moses. Though believed to present in narrative form the cosmology and soteriology dramatized in the temple rite, these books neither contain the text of nor serve as the locus of authority for the rite as performed in the temple.

8. For the sake of brevity, when the context keeps the meaning clear, I will refer to this strategic use of the conventions of an oral tradition simply as "oral traditioning."

understand the full implications of this fact has led occidental scholarship into the trap of animosity toward the temple."[9]

The LDS Church's theology and practice of temple worship are among its more obvious deviations[10] from traditional Christianity and, as such, deserve a fuller treatment than permitted by the scope of this paper. For present purposes, it must suffice to note that Mircea Eliade's conclusion regarding temples generally is specifically true of LDS temples. Patterned on celestial prototypes, temples symbolically represent the "transformation of chaos into cosmos … by giving it forms and norms."[11] Or, as described by Mormonism's most prolific writer on this subject: "What makes a temple different from other buildings is not its sacredness, but its form and function … a temple, good or bad, is a scale-model of the universe."[12] The faithful who enter this "scale-model" are instructed in the laws which govern the cosmos and commit themselves by covenant to obey them. As stated in the most detailed of the few authorized descriptions of the rite:

> Participants in white temple clothing assemble in [the temple's] ordinance rooms to receive … instruction and participate in the unfolding drama of the Plan of Salvation [including narratives of the Creation and the Garden]. They are taught … the laws and ordinances required for reconciliation through the Atonement of Christ; and a return to the presence of God. … [S]olemn covenants are made pertaining to truthfulness, purity, righteous service, and devotion. In this way, the temple is the locus of consecration to the teaching of the law and the prophets and the ways of God and his Son.[13]

Thus, while the LDS temple is the preeminent expression of LDS cosmology, its purpose is not a static, descriptive one. It is also prescriptive

---

9. John M. Lundquist, "Temple, Covenant, and Law in the Ancient Near East and in the Old Testament," in *Temples of the Ancient World*, ed. Donald W. Parry (Salt Lake City: Deseret Book Co., 1994), 279; emphasis original.

10. As stated by one LDS commentator, "The temple and its ceremonies remain as one of the very few aspects of Mormonism still able to evoke suspicion about how 'normal' Mormons really are" (Armand L. Mauss, "Culture, Charisma, and Change: Reflections on Mormon Temple Worship," *Dialogue: A Journal of Mormon Thought* 20, no. 4 [Winter 1987]: 77).

11. Mircea Eliade, *Cosmos and History: The Myth of the Eternal Return* (New York: Harper, 1959), 12, 16.

12. Hugh Nibley, "What Is a Temple?" in *Mormonism and Early Christianity* (Salt Lake City: Deseret Book Co., 1987), 357.

13. Allen Claire Rozsa, "Temple Ordinances," *Encyclopedia of Mormonism*, 4:1444.

of the manner in which life is to be lived and the standards by which good and evil are discerned. While the law obtained in the LDS temple consists, as indicated above, of such common values as "truthfulness, purity, righteous service, and devotion," these communal values are "enthroned within that community through a temple covenant ceremony. It is in this sense that law cannot be said to exist outside of an ordered, cosmic community. ... The elaborate ritual, architectural, and building traditions that lie behind temple construction and dedication are what allow the authoritative, validating transformation of a set of customary laws into a code."[14]

The temple is the cosmically authoritative source without parallel in the LDS Church of the laws which bind the LDS faith community, incorporating by reference LDS scriptural canon,[15] but standing independent of it as a source of God's word.

Stanley Tambiah's observations about cosmological rituals are directly applicable to the LDS temple rite: it establishes those "orienting principles and conceptions that are held to be sacrosanct, are constantly used as yardsticks, and are considered worthy of perpetuating relatively unchanged."[16] Not surprisingly, then, one finds the north star, the ancient and unfailing instrument of orientation, represented on the Salt Lake temple's western wall. The most symbolically expressive in its architecture of any of the church's temples, the Salt Lake temple (dedicated 1893) is to Latter-day Saint the fulfillment of Isaiah's prophesy that "In the last days, ... the mountain of the Lord's house shall be established in the top of the mountains. ... And many people shall go and say, Come ye, and let us go up to the mountain of the Lord ... and he will teach us of his ways, and we will walk in his paths: for out of Zion shall go forth the law" (Isa. 2:2–3).

The church's nineteenth-century temple-builders wrote a hymn still sung by their progeny: "For God remembers still his promise made of

---

14. Lundquist, "Temple, Covenant, and Law, 282.

15. Note analogous usage of text described by Catherine Bell, "Ritualization of Texts and Textualization of Ritual in the Codification of Taoist Liturgy," *History of Religions* 27 (1988): 366–92.

16. S. J. Tambiah, "A Performative Approach to Ritual," *Proceedings of the British Academy* 65 (1979): 121.

old that He on Zion's hill truth's standard would unfold! ... We'll now go up and serve the Lord; obey his laws and learn his word."[17] Latter-day Saints "go up" to the primordial hill to be taught the law which orders them within the cosmos. As surely as God ordered the world out of chaos, the Saints come to be ordered in their community. They receive the "rule" by which they should "walk," in Pauline terms (Philip. 3:16), and are taught, in modern theological terms, "the law in force in the Church, which governs its activity as a society."[18]

In summary, the LDS temple ceremony can be said to constitute the most complete expression of the church's canon: both as "reed" and as *regula*. The authority of the LDS temple canon is established *inter alia* by the cosmological dimensions of its ritualization within a "scale model of the universe." It is offered as the unique law by which time and space are to be transcended, and, thus, it is believed to be timeless, even unchanged from the beginning of time. In the words of one LDS writer, it is "relevant to the eternities. The modern world is as unstable as a decaying isotype, but the temple has always been the same. The ordinances are those taught by an angel to Adam."[19]

Yet it is axiomatic that even rituals which seek to embody the timelessness of sacred cosmic ordering must adapt to the dynamics of time or become irrelevant to or incapable of "heal[ing] or amend[ing] personal or social disorder"[20] experienced by those who live in time. Paradoxically, the socially transformative power of such ritual schemes lies, in part, in their timeliness: in their capacity to fit into evolving patterns of human choice and action occurring outside of the ritual enactment and to reorder them according to the cosmic pattern provided within the enactment. The ritual which does not respond to time is not timeless but meaningless and, hence, ineffectual. Herein lies the particular challenge to the LDS Church in the maintenance of both

---

17. *Hymns of the Church of Jesus Christ of Latter-day Saints* (Salt Lake City: Church of Jesus Christ of Latter-day Saints, 1985), 5.

18. "Canon Law" in *Dictionary of Theology*, eds. Karl Rahner and Hebert Vorgrimler (New York: Crossroad, 1985, 2nd ed.).

19. Hugh Nibley, *Temple and Cosmos: Beyond This Ignorant Present* (Salt Lake City: Deseret Book Co., 1992), 34.

20. Victor Turner, *Dramas, Fields, and Metaphors* (Ithaca, New York: Cornell University Press, 1974), 149.

the authority and vitality of its ritualized canon. On the one hand, it must be accepted by the faithful as fixed, a timeless standard by which they order their lives. On the other hand, it must shift to accommodate life as experienced by successive generations, if it is to have any relevancy and, hence, power to order their lives. How can these prescribed standards for traversing the lower, middle, and higher worlds within the cosmos shift on their *axis mundi* in time without disorienting the faithful and their identity as a community based on shared, timeless belief? This paper suggests that an answer lies in the church's peculiar methods of administering its temple rite, namely, its strategic use of the conventions of oral tradition to shield its core canon from the divisive effects of discursive thought and public debate.

THE ORAL TRADITIONING OF THE CANON

Notwithstanding its canonical status, from the beginning[21] the LDS temple rite was "not to be riten" or to be written about, as indicated in the correspondence cited earlier. First performed in 1842 under the direction of Joseph Smith, the church's founder and prophet, the ritual was not reduced to writing until beginning in 1877 by Brigham Young, his successor. In the intervening thirty-five years, the canon was maintained only as given in ritual performance by those who received it directly from Joseph Smith.[22] In the absence of official explanation, the reasons for creating a written version of the rite can only be surmised from history. No doubt the aging first generation of church leadership desired to fix the content of the rite as they were about to pass it on to the next generation. In addition, convert baptisms from foreign cultures were pouring into the Salt Lake Valley, bringing with them their own "webs of significance"[23] to apply to this highly symbolic ritual. Finally, the Saints had just completed the first temple to operate outside of the immediate geographic influence of

---

21. For a discussion of the origins and development of the LDS temple ritual, see David John Buerger, *Mysteries of Godliness: A History of Mormon Temple Worship* (San Francisco: Smith Research Associates, 1994, 2002).

22. Buerger.

23. Clifford Geertz, "Thick Description: Toward an Interpretive Theory of Culture," in *The Interpretation of Cultures* (New York: HarperCollins, 1973), 5.

the president of the church.[24] Any of these factors could have motivated leadership to create a text. Regardless, the inclination to fix
the canon is so logical in a literate society as not to need explanation.
What this paper addresses is the reverse phenomenon: an apparently
illogical unavailability of an authorized text of and the absence of any
definitive exegesis on the specific content of the LDS temple rite.

No text is read during the temple rite. It is performed from memory
both by those who lead the rite and those who participate in it. Indeed,
it is not generally acknowledged that a script of the ritual exists. Such
authorized written accounts of the ceremony as exist are rare and made
available only to those lay women and men (called "temple workers") who
are set apart to administer the temple ordinances.[25] Even here, however,
only that portion of the text relevant to the temple worker's liturgical
role is available within a room of the temple reserved for such purposes,
and, almost without exception, it may not be taken outside the temple.
Hence, such text as exists is made available in part and for the sole purpose of committing it to memory for performance within the temple. A
worker may officiate in the rites once the memorized text has been repeated verbatim to his or her mentor. Since neither an authorized text of
the LDS temple rite nor any descriptive exegesis of it is licitly available to
either nonmembers or members of the church, full authorized knowledge
of the two-hour rite and its specific meaning are obtainable only by oral
representation within the temple during the rite's performance.

Nevertheless, beginning in 1842 and continuing to the present,
there have been numerous unauthorized versions of the temple ceremony published in a variety of media by those who no longer affiliate
with the church or who believe that Mormonism poses a cultic threat to
traditional Christian faith. Viewed as products of "apostates who seek to
injure or destroy the Church ... usually distorted,"[26] these texts are ig-
nored by the church. The faithful are strongly discouraged from reading
or speaking of the rite, and, with extraordinarily few exceptions, they

24. In 1877, the LDS dedicated a temple in St. George, Utah, approximately 300 miles from
church headquarters in Salt Lake City. The textualization of the rite was done on its premises.

25. Robert L. Simpson, "Temples: Administration of Temples," *Encyclopedia of Mormonism,* 4:1456–58.

26. Boyd K. Packer, *The Holy Temple* (Salt Lake City: Bookcraft, 1980), 30.

do not. Their general attitude in this regard is illustrated in a letter to the editor of an Arizona newspaper: "Discussing the temple ceremonies openly is as insensitive as burning the Torah, stomping on the Eucharist and desecrating a mosque. Just because you disagree with a religious practice does not mean it is justified to hold it up to ridicule."[27] Here we see expressed those attributes of the LDS temple already discussed, namely, its role as source of religious law, divine presence, and sacred space. Worthy of special note, however, is the author's equating publicity of the rite with its profanation. While less dramatic in tone, official church statements share the sentiment that the temple ritual is not to be revealed to the uninitiated or spoken of, except in most general terms, outside of the temple itself.[28] Thus, the few books published by the LDS Church on this subject[29] are typically devoted to analyses of the role of temple ordinances in the church's soteriology or to oblique analogizing of LDS temple practices to those of ancient civilizations.[30]

In sum, the LDS treat their temple canon in a manner most analogous to an oral tradition, and, in practical effect, it operates as such among the faithful. Though an authorized text exists, it is not generally known to exist and is not employed during the rite. Neither the text nor its performance is commented on in writing, and both are subject to discussion only in the most oblique terms. Finally, no authorized text is available to the participants except under discrete circumstances and, even then, not in its entirety and for only the amount of time required to memorize it. Thus, while the ritual may not be obtained licitly in writing by the uninitiated, neither can it be obtained in writing by the initiated. The price of access to the rite and its specific contents is the same for all: participation in the ritualized social body which is created by the ritual and creative of the ritual as it is handed down personally, even orally, from generation to generation.

I suggest that there are at least two reasons for the church's employing

---

27. *Arizona Republic*, May 5, 1993, A16.

28. Packer, *The Holy Temple*, 26.

29. E.g., Parry, *Temples of the Ancient World*.

30. The *Encyclopedia of Mormonism* (1992) published by Macmillan with cooperation from church authorities contains, under several subject headings, the most thorough description by the church of the temple ceremony and ordinances, but nevertheless refrains from providing a text of ceremony or description of the gestures associated with its performance.

the conventions of an oral tradition within its modern, literate community. First, doing so protects the canon's perceived legitimacy as a source of immutable truth, notwithstanding the rite's periodic modification. Second, it maximizes ritual's capacity to negotiate the meaning of the canon without fragmenting the community ordered by the canon. Each of these hypotheses is discussed below.

THE EFFECT OF ORAL TRADITION IN THE CANON

The surest way to fix a notion—to obtain maximum uniformity of expression and dictate meaning—is to record it and read it. In writing, consciousness is deemed "liberate[d] from the tyranny of the present."[31] Unfortunately for cosmologies, however, consciousness then becomes subject to the tyranny of the past because writing also "favors awareness of inconsistency."[32] As discussed at length in Goody and Watt's seminal essay on the effects of literacy,[33] it is the nature of language to make distinctions and it is the consequence of writing to preserve these distinctions, compounding a history of conceptual boundaries and barriers which fragment a society's confidence in the existence of definable truth. As observed by Stanley Tambiah, it is not the idea that is fixed by writing, but rather the articulation and critique of the idea's temporal context—"the epistemological and ontological understandings of the particular age."[34] Paul Ricoeur adds, "What we write, what we inscribe, is the *noema* of the speaking. It is the meaning of the speech event, not the event as event."[35]

Rituals are, however, not only meaning, but also event—even religion's "generative and regenerative processes."[36] Generative rituals are ill suited to being fixed and are undermined by the self-consciousness or historical-consciousness of writing down or writing about. This

---

31. Oswald Spengler, quoted in Jack Goody and Ian Watt, "The Consequences of Literacy," in *Literacy in Traditional Societies*, ed. Jack R. Goody (Cambridge: Cambridge University Press, 1968), 53.

32. Goody and Watt, 49.

33. Goody and Watt.

34. Tambiah, "A Performative Approach to Ritual," 165.

35. Paul Ricoeur, "The Model of the Text: Meaningful Action Considered as a Text," *Social Research* 38 (Autumn 1971): 532.

36. Victor Turner, *From Ritual to Theater: The Human Seriousness of Play* (New York: Performing Arts Journal, 1982), 86.

dynamic underlies what Ronald Grimes labels academia's "fears [of] explaining ritual away"[37] and is caused by the fact that literate societies "cannot discard, absorb, or transmute the past. ... [T]heir members are faced with permanently recorded versions of the past and its beliefs; and because the past is thus set apart from the present, historical inquiry becomes possible. This in turn encourages scepticism; and scepticism, not only about the legendary past, but about received ideas about the universe as a whole. From here the next step is to see how to build up and to test alternative explanations."[38]

Ritual cosmologies, of course, seek the reverse effect: the unquestioning sense of a "received ... universe as a whole." They resist writing's invitation to find in private thought, not communal experience, the means of discerning truth.

The communal experience of the LDS temple ritual, not private thought, is the privileged source of LDS truth. The rite is, therefore, carefully protected from "historical inquiry" and even an awareness of its having a history independent of its mythos of having been given to Adam by an angel. By scrupulously maintaining the ritual as an oral tradition—not making its text available or otherwise discussing it publicly for others to record authoritatively its specific contents—the church enables the temple ceremony to "function ... as a series of interlocking face-to-face conversations in which the very conditions of transmission operate to favour consistency between past and present, and to make criticism—the articulation of inconsistency—less likely to occur; and if it does, the inconsistency makes a less permanent impact, and is more easily adjusted or forgotten."[39]

In the LDS community, these homoeostatic functions of oral traditioning—its facilitation of forgetting and transmuting inconsistency—operate at an overt and public level. Those parts of the temple canon which are deemed to be no longer relevant or necessary are discarded or transformed "without a whisper of announcement."[40] News of change and

---

37. Ronald L. Grimes, *Beginnings in Ritual Studies* (Lanham, Maryland: University of America Press, 1982), 32.

38. Goody and Watt, "The Consequences of Literacy," 67–68.

39. Goody and Watt, 48.

40. "Veil of Secrecy Hides Changes in Mormon Rituals," *The Independent*, May 5, 1990, 11.

its explanation comes from the newspaper, not church administration: "While [a spokesperson for the church] described the church's basic beliefs and obligations as 'timeless and binding,' she said 'the ceremony itself needs to meet the needs of the people.' The revised ritual is 'more in keeping with the sensitivities we have as a society,' she added."[41]

Notwithstanding such acknowledgments to the community outside of the church, no official comment is made to the church community itself. No doctrinal foundation for, much less commentary on the "sensitivities" which inspired, the changes is supplied. No theologizing on the implications of the changes is offered or invited. Indeed, the changes themselves are not even identified except as they are directly experienced by the participants in the course of performing the ritual. And, with each performance, the conventional forms of the ritual—formality, stereotypy, condensation, and redundancy[42]—restore the sense of the ritual's timelessness and immutability. Personal knowledge and experience of change is neither remarked upon nor long remembered, and the sense of collective, shared experience in one eternal round of ordered life is retained. Thus, notwithstanding changes to the rite since its inception and increasing publicity about modern adaptations,[43] the perception of the faithful remains that the temple rite and its canon are today as they were first revealed by Joseph Smith. For example, one LDS historian has referred to "the formidable task of describing and explaining what happened on 4 May 1842, the day our ... [temple rite] was first administered as given in our temples today."[44]

---

41. *New York Times*, May 3, 1990, 2.

42. Tambiah, "A Performative Approach to Ritual," 123.

43. Even after the creation of the beginnings of a text in 1877, it appears that actual performance of the rite continued to vary considerably until 1927 when efforts were made to write down a "single unified ceremony for all temples" (Thomas G. Alexander, *Mormonism in Transition: A History of the Latter-day Saints, 1890–1930* [Urbana: University of Illinois Press, 1986], 302). While the exact nature and number of changes to the ritual and the canon it constituted cannot be known, absent official texts, one study concludes that "the history of the [LDS temple rite] ... shows specific content and procedural alterations were made in 1845, 1877, 1883, 1893, 1919–1927, the early 1960s, and 1968–1972" (David John Buerger, "The Development of the Mormon Temple Endowment Ceremony," *Dialogue: A Journal of Mormon Thought* 20, no. 4 [Winter 1987]: 67). Additional changes occurred in 1990, 2005, and 2008 (*New York Times*, May 3, 1990, 1; http://www.ldsendowment.org/timeline.html).

44. Andrew F. Ehat, "'Who Shall Ascend into the Hill of the Lord?' Sesquicentennial Reflections of a Sacred Day: 4 May 1842," in Parry, *Temples of the Ancient World*, 49.

Approaching this phenomenon with the assumptions of a textual literature and ritually illiterate society, it is possible to conclude that LDS use of oral conventions to adapt and forget is, at best, secrecy in service of willful ignorance or, at worst, deceit in service of social control. To do so, however, ignores that "the issue of truthfulness as a matter of conforming to what exactly happened at some point in the past [is] probably not the issue that [is] most important for an oral community."[45] If asked, the vast majority of temple-going Latter-day Saints—and certainly the academics referenced in this paper—will acknowledge that the temple rite has changed over time, even recently. They will, however, in the same breath protest the relevancy of change to their present experience of the transcendent through the medium of temple ritual. Thus the LDS historian who assumes the "formidable task of describing" the original enactment of the rite ultimately resorts to discussing instead the meaning of the temple to the faithful. He says, "In temples, we have a staged representation of the step-by-step ascent into the presence of the Eternal while we are yet alive."[46] This is, of course, ultimately what religion aspires to provide and, paraphrasing Catherine Bell, the "most important issue for [the Latter-day Saints acting here as] an oral community."

After all, as Victor Turner said, religion is "not a cognitive system, a set of dogmas, alone, it is meaningful experience and experienced meaning."[47] This is what Latter-day Saints seek in their temples and attempt, by means of oral traditioning, to shelter from discursive thought and public debate. A primary benefit of doing so is illustrated in James Smart's expression of ambivalence with regard to the success of biblical criticism:

> One cannot help welcoming the excavation of every fresh feature of the human story, but at the same time one must recognize the distortion that is taking place with the limination of the participation and action of the living God from the story. That elimination of a living God from the biblical history can so easily be also the elimination of a living God from our own present history. That, in fact, was the disastrous influence upon the

---

45. Catherine Bell, "The Authority of Ritual Experts," *Studia Liturgica* 23 (1993): 106.
46. Ehat, "'Who Shall Ascend into the Hill of the Lord?'" 49.
47. Turner, *From Ritual to Theater*, 86.

faith of Christians of a historicist biblical science that in clearing away the mythological language of the biblical witnesses reduced their living God, whose powerful presence they knew, to a religious concept or ideal.[48]

Orally traditioning the LDS canon is a means of attempting to prevent in a modern, literate community the "elimination of a living God from [its] own present history" by remaining aloof from "the excavation of every fresh feature of the human story." The church's refusal to textualize its ritualized canon and submit it to the literacy of even the faithful sets the rite apart, secrets it from discursive thought and attendant public debate. In this way, orally traditioning the rite maximizes the "muteness," in Bell's terms, inherent in the ritualization of this canon: "Ritualization is embedded within the dynamics of the body defined within a symbolically structured environment. An important corollary to this is the fact that ritualization is a particularly 'mute' form of activity. It is designed to do what it does without bringing what it is doing across the threshold of discourse or systematic thinking."[49]

Hence, the conventions of both ritual and of oral tradition contribute materially to the maintenance of the canonicity of the LDS temple rite. They prevent fragmentation of understanding and belief: what Goody describes as, the "scepticism" which follows from "criticism—the articulation of inconsistency."[50] They also protect religious experience of the divine from what Stewart identifies as criticism's conceptual reductionism.[51] In sum, both orally traditioning and ritually embodying the canon cooperate to immunize from a sense of history the canon's authoritativeness and perceived legitimacy, sustaining it as a timeless and immutable source for ordering successive generations of the faithful.

There is, however, a second effect of oral traditioning of the temple canon, and it is primary to the integrity of the LDS community, not just

---

48. James D. Smart, *The Past, Present, and Future of Biblical Theology* (Philadelphia: Westminster, 1979), 123–24.

49. Catherine Bell, *Ritual Theory, Ritual Practice* (New York: Oxford University Press, 1992), 93.

50. See, for example, the skepticism expressed in a critique, by those affiliated with the church, challenging the historicity of LDS scriptural canon, in Brent Lee Metcalfe, ed., *New Approaches to the Book of Mormon: Explorations in Critical Methodology* (Salt Lake City: Signature Books, 1993). Goody and Watt, "The Consequences of Literacy," 48.

51. Smart, *The Past, Present, and Future of Biblical Theology*, 124.

its doctrine. The strategic use of oral homeostasis and ritual muteness which sustains the sense of ordered wholeness in their canon is ultimately protective of the LDS sense of who they are and how they relate as a community. The temple canon enables the faithful's meaningful experience not only with a "living God," but also with each other.

THE EFFECT OF ORAL TRADITION ON THE COMMUNITY

It is a given that, whatever else rituals may be, they are social undertakings both expressing and creating relationships. For example, though it is the "passage" aspect of the "rites of passage" that seems to capture most attention on the subject, the passage exists for the ultimate purpose of putting the initiate in right relationship to the ritual community. Victor Turner is well known for characterizing the relationship created in complex rituals as "communitas" or "society as an unstructured or rudimentarily structured and relatively undifferentiated *comitatus*, community, or even a communion of equal individuals who submit together to the general authority of the ritual elders."[52]

The sense of community generated by the ritualized canon of the LDS Church is enhanced by the way in which oral traditioning of the temple rite structures the relationships within the ritual community itself. None is set apart to interpret the rite: all are under the same requirement to maintain it as an oral tradition. During the ritual, all present are enacting the ritual and all are eligible to officiate in those parts which require it. The rite is devoid of reference to ecclesiastical position and title. The ritual is always transmitted within the temple proper by a person who knows the ritual to another who does not. The one mentors the other by *inter alia* teaching questions and giving answers. It is an immediate exchange between ritually identified persons, not persons and textualized ideas. What Goody said of the Socratic method could also be said of the LDS temple rite. It is a "social process, in which initiates pass on their knowledge directly to the young; a process indeed, in which only a long personal relationship can transcend the inherent incapacity of mere words to convey

---

52. Turner, *The Ritual Process*, 82.

ultimate truths—the forms or ideas which alone can give unity and coherence to human knowledge."[53]

The solidarity of the LDS community—its sense of ordered wholeness on a social, not only a conceptual level—is enhanced by the oral traditioning of its temple rite. As observed by Goody, "on the whole there is less individualization of personal experience in oral cultures, which tend, in Durkheim's phrase, to be characterized by 'mechanical solidarity'—by ties between persons, rather than between individuals in a variety of roles."[54] In this manner, the strategic use of oral conventions within the modern, literate LDS Church is basic not only to its cosmos-building, but also to its Zion-building intentions. After all, "out of Zion shall go forth the law" (Isa. 2:3), and, to the Latter-day Saints, Zion is defined by the nature of its community: "And the Lord called his people ZION, because they were of one heart and one mind, and dwelt in righteousness; and there were no poor among them" (Moses 7:18). The function of the temple canon is to create such a community "by giving it forms and norms."[55]

In their zeal to build Zion, the Saints have always manifest separatist tendencies; not the least of which was their westward trek beyond the borders of the United States to the Great Salt Lake Basin. There the Saints hoped to "put behind them the misunderstanding, dissensions, persecution, and temptation of contemporary American society and to build a new and better civilization in the Zion of their mountain stronghold."[56] Today, the mountains have long since ceased to be a stronghold. The rise of the global village, as well as the Saints' own proselytizing intentions and temporal prosperity, makes it impossible for them to find their communal identity in economic, political, or geographic separatism, as they did in the past. It is the final hypothesis of this paper that the church's oral traditioning of the temple canon is today no less creative of their identity than these other, more obvious strategies once were. More subtle than LDS economic utopianism and social engineering, both

---

53. Goody and Watt, "The Consequences of Literacy," 50.
54. Goody and Watt, 62.
55. Eliade, *Cosmos and History*, 10.
56. Leonard J. Arrington and Davis Bitton, *The Mormon Experience: A History of the Latter-day Saints* (Urbana: University of Illinois Press, 1992), 110.

the ritualization and oral traditioning of the church's core canon make of the LDS temple a unique source of self-identification and cohesion in a rapidly growing and increasingly diverse population. The church appears to be increasingly turning to it as the *sine qua non* of membership identification. Note, for example, inaugural statements made by church president Howard W. Hunter which denominate the temple "the great symbol of our membership."[57] The LDS temple solidifies, through the conventions of ritual and oral traditioning, the LDS faith community. It defines the community's internal cohesiveness and the external boundaries in terms of cosmically defined, historically impervious canon assumed by covenant. No longer able or desiring to isolate themselves in the Rocky Mountain West or to particularize themselves by separate commercial or marital economies, the Saints can be expected to rely increasingly upon the temple for their sense of separateness which is also their sense of cosmic wholeness and solidarity as a community.

Such solidarity does not, however, mean that the community is immune to change. Neither is it wise to conclude that the church's strategies for creating doctrinal and communal solidarity merely stave off change. Rather, as will now be discussed, the oral and ritual strategies which engender the faithful's sense of conceptual and communal unity are paradoxically the same conventions which facilitate change in the rite. They adapt the community to its temporal reality without requiring it to abandon its sense of relational and ideological wholeness. Only one example can be given here.

CHANGING THE CANON, CHANGING THE COMMUNITY

If complex ritual "ossifies" when it does not "speak to the minds and hearts of succeeding generations facing change and upheaval,"[58] it is

---

57. *Ensign*, Oct. 1994, 5. This emphasis coincides with the church's increasing commitment of resources to building temples. In the first half of the twentieth century, the LDS Church built four temples; in the last half, another sixty. And in the present century thus far (2019), especially after the implementation of a smaller, standardized design for temples, almost another 140 have been built, are under construction, and/or been announced. This number is expected to continue to increase. While indicative of membership growth, the financial commitment represented here also reveals the importance of temple worship in LDS religious life and identity.

58. Tambiah, "A Performative Approach to Ritual," 165.

not surprising that in the early 1990s "[t]he Mormon Church has changed some of its most sacred rituals, eliminating parts ... viewed as offensive to women."[59] Gender roles are at the heart of the LDS temple rite and no aspect of life in this generation of the church has been as subject to "change and upheaval" as gender identity. Hence, the church's adaptation of its canon illustrates *inter alia* that ritualizing and orally traditioning the LDS canon facilitates not only the ordering, but also the peaceful reordering of the LDS community.

Few notions are as critical to LDS self-definition as that of the relationship between men and women, most often expressed in their theologizing upon the family. Consequently, as one might expect, the LDS *communitas* ordered by the temple ritual is "rudimentarily structured"[60] by the specific "value-laden distinction"[61] of gender. When entering the temple, all participants remove their street clothing, including jewelry and any other insignia of socio-economic status, and "wear white temple robes symbolizing purity and the equality of all persons before God the Father and his Son Jesus Christ."[62] No titles are employed other than "brother" or "sister." Temple worship is conducted in groups called "sessions," which begin as often as every twenty minutes with multiple, identical sessions held daily. Consequently, the group gathered in one session is indistinguishable from those in another, except by the time of day the participants arrive. In fact, the only distinctions made in the temple rite are those based on gender. Some of these distinctions are practical, as in the separation of dressing rooms within the temple. Others have to do with the marking of ritual space (e.g., seating in the temple sessions is by gender, not by familial relationship or personal status); ritual identity (e.g., differences in temple clothing); and ritual action (e.g., the majority[63] of the ordinances

---

59. *New York Times*, May 3, 1990, 2.

60. Turner, *Ritual Process*, 82.

61. "Acting ritually is first and foremost a matter of nuanced contrasts and the evocation of strategic, value-laden distinctions" (Bell, *Ritual Theory, Ritual Practice*, 90).

62. Alma P. Burton, "Endowment," *Encyclopedia of Mormonism*, 2:454–56.

63. The only temple ordinance not administered by women is the marital sealing rite. Only men who have received a separate ordination to certain priesthood authority, which is limited to the administration of the sealing ordinances in the temple, may officiate in an LDS temple marriage sealings. Men who have been ordained only to perform the variety of

are administered by women to women and by men to men). In this manner, the LDS temple ritual suspends all distinctions except the one which it seeks to ritualize, namely, gender. Such value-laden gender distinctions, like those of all other churches, are a source of contention within the LDS Church.

When these struggles are conducted in the discursive mode, they appear to be primary motivation for ecclesiastical discipline, including excommunication.[64] Ecclesiastical authority has classified feminist critique as a particular threat to the church. In an unpublished speech given to the LDS All Church Coordinating Council on May 18, 1993, one of the most senior members of the church hierarchy cautioned its middle management against "dangers [that have] ... made major invasions into the membership of the Church ... the feminist movement and the ever present challenge from the so-called scholars or intellectuals."[65] Understood in light of the theory discussed in this paper, this is not an unexpected response by church authority. To speak of changes made in belief and practice, to debate them publicly, to write them down and create a history of disparate definitions of, for instance, LDS priesthood and its operations with respect to women can, indeed, engender skepticism. Because discursive and literate forms directly challenge belief, the LDS Church will not, and, we could say in light of these theories, cannot, employ these means to experiment with and to respond to modern sensibilities without jeopardizing its sense of a shared universe as a whole, immune to human history. Though the church must evolve or become irrelevant, it will likely do so through that method which "is designed to do what it does without bringing what it is doing across the threshold of discourse or systematic thinking."[66] It will rely on the conventions of ritual to adapt its core canon.

---

functions associated with the administration of the church and those ordinances not unique to the temple, such as baptism and confirmation, may not officiate in temple sealings.

64. "Six Intellectuals Disciplined for Apostasy," *Sunstone*, Nov. 1993, 68, with respect to the excommunications of D. Michael Quinn and Maxine D. Hanks, writer and editor respectively of "Mormon Women Have Had the Priesthood Since 1843," in *Women and Authority: Re-emerging Mormon Feminism* (Salt Lake City: Signature Books, 1992).

65. Boyd K. Packer, Speech given May 18, 1993, photocopy in my possession; reported in "Elder Packer Names Gays/Lesbians, Feminists, and 'So-called Scholars' Three Main Dangers," *Sunstone*, Nov. 1993, 74.

66. Catherine Bell, *Ritual Theory, Ritual Practice*, 93.

Catherine Bell provides a theoretical basis for this conclusion when she reasons that ritual is "the mute interplay of complex strategies within a field structured by engagements of power."[67] Because participants are free to act and understand differently, they make choices, determining the extent of their acceptance of the ritual order. This makes ritual not only a structured, but a structuring, environment: "The person who has prayed to his or her god, appropriating the social schemes of the hegemonic order in terms of an individual redemption, may be stronger because these acts are the very definitions of power, personhood, and the capacity to act."[68]

Thus, for example, the woman who in the LDS temple prays to her god—bodily officiates in administering rites of purifying and sanctifying significance; takes upon herself the signs and tokens of immortality; and receives her husband by covenant and gives herself to him by the same covenant—is, according to Bell, not performing meaning, but obtaining a practical knowledge, even "a mastery that experiences itself as relatively empowered, not as conditioned or molded."[69] Of course, bringing with them as they do contemporary sensibilities, this generation of LDS ritualizers is affected by receiving or observing a woman's cultic activity within the temple. Neither she nor they are required to believe or disbelieve an ideology, but only to consent to a version of the dominant values which they negotiate as they embody the ritual and choose among symbolic multivalence. The negotiation is "mute" because it operates "below the level of discourse" which permits her and them to "misrecognize both the source of the schemes and the changes these schemes undergo in the temporal process of projection and embodiment."[70] It has even been argued that cosmological rituals, in particular, are designed to invite such changes.[71]

In addition, the strategic oral traditioning of the LDS rite maximizes ritual's "mute interplay" and openness to new contents by enabling the

---

67. Bell, 204.
68. Bell, 118.
69. Bell, 221.
70. Bell, 206–27.
71. Tambiah, "A Performative Approach to Ritual," 136, has concluded that "complex rites, and long recitations, usually have some sequences more open than others, more open in terms of structure and more open to new contents."

entire community to "misrecognize" change for stasis and to peace-
fully reorder itself. The homoeostatic conventions of forgetting and
transmuting operate so as to "not lead to deliberate rejection and rein-
terpretation of social dogma ... [but] to semi-automatic readjustment
of belief."[72] Discursive thought, either written or spoken, which aspires
to clarify ambiguity by identifying distinctions, requires "deliberate rejection" of the old belief, the conscious choosing among historically
sensitive alternatives. Not all in the community will make the same
choice, and some may base a given choice on reasons incidental to
a meaningful experience with a "living God." Moreover, having once
deliberated, others will continue to choose to make distinctions that
separate not only their ideas, but also themselves one from another.
In short, because they do not allow a community to make "semi-automatic readjustment" to change, written words and their critique do
not have the power to heal what they have breached—to transmute
without comment what is transmitted and misrecognize while negoti-
ating new belief and new community. Orally traditioned ritual enables
communities to live with ambiguity and to misrecognize change for
stasis, even to believe that "the modern world is as unstable as a decaying isotope, but the temple has always been the same."[73]

It is in this paradoxical capacity to mutate what it establishes as
immutable that the particular social genius of the LDS temple rite is
revealed: "It is the work of ritual action to join into a whole, again and
again, what is in fragile relationship and always in danger of disintegra-
tion, namely, the future, the present, and the past of a people."[74] While
ritual produces power relationships, they are in a constant flux of negotiation which constitutes "mute interplay," rather than "mechanical
solidarity."[75] Or as summarily stated by a female participant in the LDS
temple rite: "Like any other ritual, you make it your own."[76] The opportunity it provides to make meaning one's "own," or, in other words,
to negotiate the meanings of gender in the rite, makes the temple the

---

72. Goody and Watt, "The Consequences of Literacy," 48.
73. Nibley, *Temple and Cosmos*, 34.
74. Collins, "Critical Ritual Studies," 95.
75. Bell, *Ritual Theory, Ritual Practice,* 204.
76. Bell.

most likely forum for "mutely" working out the relation between men and women that is so fundamental to LDS doctrine and community. As in the past, the LDS Church can be expected in the present also to reorder itself by means of its ritualized and orally traditioned temple canon. This will enable the church community to adjust old belief in light of new belief without having to experience ideological contradiction and the communal conflict it engenders. Though, no doubt, too slow a process for some, it will nonetheless preserve for most the sense of ordered wholeness provided by the LDS core canon: the law that creates and is created by their temple-building community.

CONCLUSION

Many questions remain to be considered, including several related to ritual authority as it is exercised in the modification of the temple's ritualized canon. For example, one might well ask what is the influence of discursive thought and debate from certain quarters of the church upon the hierarchically mandated changes to the canon? Other questions remain regarding the restrictions placed upon access to the temple within the faith community—such as, do the limitations on access to the temple rite within the faith community itself dilute its agency as an instrumentality of change? Do they create a community within a community of the LDS Church? Of course, there remain the more historical questions related to the temple rite's evolution in the nineteenth and twentieth centuries and its theological dimension. Has the rite been responsive to both the needs of the people and the demands of the LDS gospel? In short, is it an authentic expression of the faith of the worshiping community?

This article, however, must remain limited to one issue, simply stated by a member of the LDS community: "In an age of so much communications [sic], there may be some value in having something you only think about and share in a special place."[77] I have suggested that for Latter-day Saints that value consists in the peaceful reordering of LDS community around its core canon as it necessarily evolves from generation to generation. The oral traditioning and ritualization of the

---

77. *New York Times*, May 3, 1990, 1.

LDS temple canon enables a "mute" evolution of belief and working out of social conflict, such as that related to gender. It is the figurative and literal "muteness" of the LDS oral and ritual tradition that has the potential to preserve the religious community it is also changing. In sum, the classic gifts of ritual—order, community, and transformation[78]—are strategically augmented by oral tradition to provide in the LDS temple canon "a way of coming to rest in the heart of cosmic change and order."[79]

---

78. Tom Driver, *The Magic of Ritual: Our Need for Liberating Rites that Transform Our Lives and Our Communities* (San Francisco: HarperCollins, 1991), passim.

79. Grimes, *Beginnings in Ritual Studies*, 43.

THREE

"SAVIORS ON MOUNT ZION"
MORMON SACRAMENTALISM, MORTALITY, AND BAPTISM FOR THE DEAD

RYAN G. TOBLER

When Seymour Brunson died, they gave him a soldier's funeral. Thousands of Mormons in the Illinois town of Nauvoo, growing fast on the Mississippi River, turned out on August 10, 1840, trailing Brunson's corpse in a procession that stretched out a mile long. They came to mourn a patriot and protector: Brunson had fought as a boy of fourteen in the War of 1812. Later, he joined the Mormon Church and served as a captain in the Mormons' own militia, guarding against the depredations of Missouri mobs. When the Saints relocated to Illinois, Brunson acted as a bodyguard to the Mormon Prophet Joseph Smith and as a member of the city's ecclesiastical high council.

Ironically, however, it was illness that caused Brunson's death. After purchasing and surveying the area in 1839, the Mormons in Nauvoo were still just settling in. "Commerce," as the city had previously been called, provided a "resting place" for the Saints after the Missouri conflicts, a sense of rest that was captured in its new Hebrew name, "Nauvoo."[1] But it was also a sickly place. The marshy riverfront constantly bred malaria and other diseases, and scores of inhabitants fell ill.[2] The summer of 1840 had been especially deadly; Mormon families throughout the city had suffered casualties, and news from the town often came as a catalogue of loss. "There has been rizing of fifty Deaths," wrote one alarmed mother, hoping that a new influx

---

1. Glen M. Leonard, *Nauvoo: A Place of Peace, A People of Promise* (Salt Lake City: Deseret Book Co., 2002), 57–59.

2. Robert Bruce Flanders, *Nauvoo: Kingdom on the Mississippi* (Urbana: University of Illinois Press, 1965), 50–54.

of settlers would "help build up the place," and make it less morbid.[3] Journals and diaries reflect the ordeals of fevers, sweats, and chills, attributed to everything from "swamp fever" and cholera to "the ague." Citizens looked on helplessly as family members were confined to their sickbeds, sometimes vomiting, sometimes shaking violently. As part of an era of mortality, Mormons asked that God shield them and their loved ones from the indiscriminate threat of illness. "Look upon us O Lord in this time of need," prayed one, "and help us … for thou alone art able to deliver from the grasp of death."[4]

Although still robust at age forty, Seymour Brunson went out one evening to drive away some stray cattle and caught cold, which led to something more serious, and then to his untimely death. When Brunson finally succumbed, lying in a sickbed in Joseph Smith's home, he was put to rest with full military honors. Indeed, at the moment of his passing, some said that the spirits of his comrades, fallen Mormon soldiers, came to "waft him home."[5] To the Saints, the death of a hardy soul like Brunson was unsettling; it was one of those occasions, as Joseph Smith later put it, through which "we have again the warning voice sounded in our midst which shows the uncertainty of human life."[6]

Considering the experiences of early Latter-day Saints, like those in Nauvoo, scholars have long debated the appeal and potency of Mormonism, wondering why it resonated so deeply with many early Americans, and why the concepts at its core have been (and are) so attractive and enduring. Many explanations have been proffered for Mormonism's essential power in the nineteenth century, including the solutions it provided for contemporary "sectarian divisions, republican contradictions, nascent capitalism, social dislocation, and a quest for authority."[7] Most recently, scholarship has added critical insights about

---

3. Vilate Kimball to Heber C. Kimball, Sep. 6, 1840, MS 3276, Church History Library, Church of Jesus Christ of Latter-day Saints, Salt Lake City, Utah, hereafter CHL.

4. John Smith, Journal, Sep. 16, 1840, MS 1326, CHL.

5. Heber C. Kimball to John Taylor, Nov. 9, 1840, CHL. See also Andrew F. Ehat and Lyndon W. Cook, eds., *The Words of Joseph Smith: The Contemporary Accounts of the Nauvoo Discourses of the Prophet Joseph Smith* (Provo, Utah: BYU Religious Studies Center, 1980; rpt., Orem, Utah: Grandin Book, 1991), 49.

6. Ehat and Cook, *Words of Joseph Smith*, 106.

7. Richard Lyman Bushman, "Joseph Smith and the Creation of the Sacred," in *Joseph*

how Mormonism's central principles offered early adherents powerful spiritual and cultural resources to confront the menace of human death. Indeed, apprehension and fear of mortality represent one of the most relentless problems of human life, a problem that early Mormons often found close at hand. As scholars have recently shown, however, rather than being terrorized by mortality, Mormons in the mid-nineteenth century fought back, mounting an aggressive "conquest of death" that challenged the oppressive power of mortality. The religious doctrines and rituals they came to embrace ensured that neither salvation nor relationships were endangered when death came.[8]

Studying the unique performance of saving rituals or "sacraments" among early Mormons highlights yet another dimension of Mormonism's appeal. As the faith matured in the late 1830s and early 1840s, saving ordinances came to assume an increasing and unusual importance. These rituals offered Mormons a way of living their faith different from that common in American Protestantism; confronted with premature and unexpected death, for instance, Mormon "baptism for the dead" gave adherents not only solace and hope, but ability and saving power. Through this new religious sacrament, ordinary people were deputized as agents of salvation, empowered by their physical bodies to help mitigate death's effects upon their fellow beings. Indeed, the rich theological innovations of the Nauvoo period taught Mormons that they were not only akin to God, and joint heirs with Jesus Christ, but also joint laborers with him. In partnership with the divine Savior, Mormon people were not only embryonic gods, but also vital aides, or "saviors," in the work of human redemption.

BAPTISM FOR THE DEAD

Joseph Smith spent much of his time in early Nauvoo visiting and laying hands on those, like Brunson, who were ill and ailing. His house, at

---

Smith Jr.: Reappraisals after Two Centuries, eds. Reid L. Neilson and Terryl L. Givens (New York: Oxford University Press, 2009), 94.

8. The fullest expression of this line of thought about the significance of human death to the development of early Mormonism is Samuel Morris Brown, *On Heaven as It Is on Earth: Joseph Smith and the Early Mormon Conquest of Death* (New York: Oxford University Press, 2012).

times, overflowed with the sick.[9] Disease in 1839 was so prevalent that
Smith had to reassure the Saints that it was not a sign of God's displea-
sure but came upon all people naturally "by reason of the weakness of
the flesh."[10] His journal charted the outbreak and recession of sickness
in the community, and he was often called on to speak at the funerals of
those who passed on.[11] And indeed, funerals in Nauvoo became the occasion for many of the Prophet's most radical and profound teachings.
With their dead before them, Mormons were subdued and thoughtful,
receptive to whatever consolation their prophet could offer. And ap-
propriately, in Nauvoo Smith became an orator adopting the habit of
speaking frequently to large assemblies of people, often in the open air.
The precepts about God, human life, and saving sacraments that Smith
gave at these liminal moments first rattled the windows, then blew off
the door of Christian orthodoxy.

Initially, the eulogy that Smith gave for Brunson in 1840 seemed
like a standard Christian homily. Turning to a common text, Smith
took up Paul's first epistle to the Corinthians and preached the tran-
scendence of the Christian resurrection.[12] He affirmed Paul's testimony
that the redemptive power of Jesus Christ would ultimately conquer
the great and last enemy of death. But then he went further. Observing
the widow Jane Neyman among his listeners, Smith changed course,
weaving her tragic story into the discourse. He told the audience about

---

9. "It was a very sickly time and Joseph had given up his home in Commerce to the
sick, and had a tent pitched in his dooryard and was living in that himself. The large number
of Saints who had been driven out of Missouri, were flocking into Commerce; but had not
homes to go into, and were living in wagons, in tents, and on the ground." Wilford Woodruff, *Leaves from My Journal* (Salt Lake City: Juvenile Instructor Office, 1882), 62.

10. Dean C. Jessee, Mark Ashurst-McGee, and Richard L. Jensen, eds., *The Joseph
Smith Papers: Journals, Volume 1: 1832–1839* (Salt Lake City: Church Historian's Press,
2008), 352–53.

11. Jessee, Ashurst-McGee, and Jensen, 348–53.

12. No direct account of Smith's discourse after Brunson's death exists; the contours of
the event are reconstructed from recollections and correspondence. Neyman left an account
recorded in the Church Historian's office in Salt Lake City in 1854 in company with Vienna
Jacques. It is catalogued with the Joseph Smith History Documents, ca. 1839–60, CR 100
396, CHL. Simon Baker, who likewise attended the sermon, also gave a later account that
was incorporated into the Journal History of the Church of Jesus Christ of Latter-day Saints
(a chronological scrapbook of typed entries and newspaper clippings, 1830–present), Aug.
15, 1840, CR 100 137, CHL. See also Lewis Brunson, "Short Sketch of Seymour Brunson,
Sr.," *Nauvoo Journal* 4 (1992): 3–4.

her son—who had also died, but had sadly not been baptized—and drew their attention to a fearful dilemma. If Christian baptism and discipleship were necessary for salvation, as they believed, then what about those who had not received them? Seymour Brunson seemed safely confirmed in the faith. But what about this young boy, who had died even more prematurely? And what of his bereft mother? The redemption of Christ was indeed great and consoling, but how could it assuage the grief of this good woman? Were there no "glad tidings" in the Christian gospel for her?

With a radically innovative reading of scripture, Smith assured the audience that, indeed, the solace of Christianity extended even to this apparently dire circumstance. In fact, evidence of this could be found, he taught, in the very same Pauline epistle. Pointing them to the fifteenth chapter and its cryptic twenty-ninth verse, he read: "Else what shall they do which are baptized for the dead, if the dead rise not at all? why are they then baptized for the dead?"

It was an obscure and puzzling passage, one with which America's most learned pastors and ministers routinely tussled. As they struggled to square the verse with their own senses of orthodoxy, Christian exegetes gave a wide spectrum of interpretations.[13] Despite the literalism of the period, most concurred that a direct reading—one that somehow sanctioned some sort of ritual for the deceased—was inadmissibly bizarre. Indeed, some commentators sternly condemned this explanation, insisting that had such a thing ever existed "it was a superstition ... wholly unauthorized by the word of God."[14] Others assured their readers that such speculation could be easily put to rest: one could, in other words, "very properly [set] aside ... all attempts to explain the

---

13. Christian newspapers and exegetical journals in Bible-breathing America published a steady stream of analyses of this verse and the idea of "baptism for the dead" throughout the nineteenth century. See, for instance, "Baptism for the Dead," *Gospel Herald* (New York), Jan. 28, 1823; "Baptism for the Dead," *Christian Intelligencer and Eastern Chronicle* (Portland, ME), June 26, 1829, 102; "Baptism for the Dead," *Episcopal Watchman* (Hartford, CT), Jan. 9, 1830; "Baptism for the Dead," *Christian Observer* (Louisville, KY), Dec. 12, 1845, 197; S[amuel] W. Whitney, "Baptism for the Dead," *Christian Review* (Boston), Apr. 1852, 296–302; and Arthur Wilde Little, "Baptism for the Dead—Its Bearing upon the Resurrection," *American Church Review* (New York), Oct. 1884, 162–75.

14. "Baptism for the Dead," *Christian Observer*, Dec. 12, 1845.

passage by inventing customs which did not then exist." Most agreed that the right approach was to "examine the passage with the most critical minuteness"—an approach that led to many nuanced discussions of audience, context, and metaphor.[15] Still, some of the most eminent interpreters conceded that the passage was unyielding and that not even the most vigorous or ingenious readings seemed to satisfy.[16]

By contrast, the explanation that Joseph Smith gave was far less ambivalent. Rather than endeavoring to contextualize Paul's statement or turning to metaphors, Smith exhibited early Mormonism's "marvelous literalism," heralding the idea of baptizing for the dead as an authentic Christian doctrine.[17] Paul's glancing comment, according to Smith, was an allusion to an ancient rite of posthumous baptism—baptism of a living person in behalf of a dead one—that was once known and practiced among primitive Christians.[18] God was now revealing this

---

15. "Baptism for the Dead," *New York Evangelist*, Dec. 8, 1864.

16. In his popular biblical commentary, the English theologian Adam Clarke described 1 Corinthians 15:29 as "certainly the most difficult [passage] in the New Testament; for, notwithstanding the greatest and wisest men have laboured to explain it, there are to this day nearly as many different interpretations of it as there are interpreters." Clarke, *The New Testament of Our Lord and Saviour ... With a Commentary and Critical Notes* (New York, 1826), 6:272. Samuel Thomas Bloomfield's influential commentary *Greek Testament with English Notes* (Philadelphia, 1837), 2:166, agreed that "if we were to judge of the difficulty of the passage from the variety of interpretations ... we should say that this is the most obscure and least understood verse in the N.T."

17. "Marvelous literalism" and "creative literalism" have been used to describe early Mormons' unique biblical exegesis, which often involved the discovery of profuse meaning in seemingly obscure passages. Baptism for the dead represents a prime example. Brown, *In Heaven as It Is on Earth*, 11n11.

18. For scholarship on the religious practices of ancient Christiasn related to the dead, including posthumous baptism, see Jeffrey A. Trumbower, *Rescue for the Dead: The Posthumous Salvation of Non-Christians in Early Christianity* (New York: Oxford University Press, 2001). For extensive analysis of salvation for the dead theology in historical Christianity and Mormonism, from a Mormon perspective, see Hugh W. Nibley, "Baptism for the Dead in Ancient Times," in *Mormonism and Early Christianity* (Salt Lake City: Deseret Book Co., 1987), 100–67. See also the following series of articles in *The Journal of the Book of Mormon and Other Restoration Scripture*: Roger D. Cook, David L. Paulsen, and Kendel J. Christensen, "The Harrowing of Hell: Salvation for the Dead in Early Christianity," 19, no. 1 (2010); 56–77; David L. Paulsen and Brock M. Mason, "Baptism for the Dead in Early Christianity," 19, no. 2 (2011); 22–49; David L. Paulsen, Kendel J. Christensen, and Martin Pulido, "Redeeming the Dead: Tender Mercies, Turning of Hearts, and Restoration of Authority," 20, no. 1 (2011): 28–51; and David L. Paulsen et al., "Redemption of the Dead: Continuing Revelation after Joseph Smith," 20, no. 2 (2011): 52–69.

doctrine, long lost and forgotten, once again, and "people could now act for their friends who had departed this life." The practice showed God's forethought and his provisions for the unredeemed dead. This was, according to Smith, an "independent" revelation he had received himself, but it was visible in the Bible as well.[19]

The mourners were startled, yet exhilarated. It was, one observer concluded, a "very beautiful discourse."[20] Another found it "astonishing to him to think he had read the Bible all his life and he had never looked at it in that light before."[21] It meant that, in the face of death, there was hope not only for those, like Brunson, who fought a good fight as Christian soldiers, but also for those many who had never known or entered into the Mormon fold. By means of this new principle, widow Neyman could experience the joy of Christian redemption, and her son could be saved.

Vilate Kimball had written to her missionary husband, Heber, about the sobriety of the Brunson oration—another dark day in a season of fatality. "And yet," she said, "the day was joyful because of the light and glory that Joseph set forth. I can truly say my soul was lifted up."[22] For many, "baptism for the dead" was, as Smith later characterized it, a "glorious truth ... well calculated to enlarge the understanding, and to sustain the soul under troubles, difficulties, and distresses."[23]

It was also a teaching and a rite whose implications, implementation, and development would thoroughly transform the Mormon faith. Born near the outset of a surging Mormon sacramentalism, baptism for the dead became one of an accruing number of salvific rites and "ordinances" within the faith. As a new variation on a familiar theme, proxy baptism catalyzed the development of proxy ordinances and the idea of vicarious salvation in Mormonism, opening the way for further theological development. In conjunction with

19. On "independent" revelation, see Joseph Smith to the Council of the Twelve, Dec. 15, 1840, ID 588, The Joseph Smith Papers, http://josephsmithpapers.org (accessed Mar. 15, 2013); and Vilate Kimball to Heber C. Kimball, Oct. 11, 1840, MS 18732, CHL.

20. Journal History, Aug. 15, 1840.

21. William M. Allred, "Recollections of the Prophet Joseph Smith," *Juvenile Instructor*, Aug. 1, 1892, 4782.

22. Vilate Kimball to Heber C. Kimball, Sep. 6, 1840, MS 2737.

23. Ehat and Cook, *Words of Joseph Smith*, 77–78.

other ascendant doctrines, it altered the trajectory of Mormonism throughout the nineteenth century. Ultimately the impulse to save and redeem the dead would become a central impulse in modern Mormon belief and practice.

PRECEDENTS

Although Joseph Smith first publicly taught the doctrine of baptism for the dead in 1840, precedents for the idea had long been percolating in his mind. Like many of Mormonism's signal doctrines, the concept was the gradual product of Smith's unfolding insights and cumulative experience. He was only seventeen when his brother Alvin, seven and a half years his senior, suddenly sickened and died in the fall of 1823. Alvin was a pillar in the Smith family, a favorite of his mother, and a model of family devotion.[24] Tall and sober, he was virtuous by all accounts; but like others in his family, he had avoided churches and a formal religious affiliation. When he died unbaptized, a Presbyterian minister reportedly made the consequences of this status all too clear: because Alvin had not been a Christian, he probably could not be saved. Instead, as one of the Smiths remembered, the minister "intimated very strongly that he had gone to hell."[25] It was an insinuation that the Smith family found both offensive and terrifying.

The crisis of Alvin's death drove home the urgency of questions about salvation and introduced Joseph to the gravity of human loss.[26] What actually did happen to friends and family upon death? What assurances could there be of salvation, of "going to heaven," for those who had no "proper" faith? It was a personal form of the question that had unsettled Christian thinkers for centuries. How would God deal with those who were, for one reason or another, unenlightened and

---

24. On Alvin Smith, see Richard Lyman Bushman, *Joseph Smith: Rough Stone Rolling* (New York: Alfred A. Knopf, 2005), 42.

25. Dan Vogel, *Early Mormon Documents*, 5 vols. (Salt Lake City: Signature Books, 1996–2003), 1:512–13.

26. Joseph Smith's bereavement experience has been interpreted as highly significant for the development of Mormonism. Douglas J. Davies argues that Alvin's death "was of crucial significance as a motivating force in the thinking of the Prophet" and "has been seriously underestimated in accounts of Mormonism." Davies, *The Mormon Culture of Salvation: Force, Grace, and Glory* (Aldershot, England: Ashgate, 2000), 86–90.

unconverted to Christianity? Surely it was unreasonable and unfair of God to punish ignorance. The dogma of previous centuries would have said that even asking such questions of a sovereign God was irreverent, but sentiments were changing. More and more in America, man was sovereign, God answered to reason, and even Providence must be just.[27] The dilemma of the ignorant and unredeemed dead was a problem that was becoming more critical, drawing God's basic beneficence into question.

Questions about the fairness of God and the exclusivity of salvation had been a longstanding source of angst in the Smith family. Like an increasing number of Americans, both Joseph's father, Joseph Smith Sr., and his grandfather, Asael Smith, became deeply uncomfortable with the severity of Reformed theology, with its dogmas of total depravity and limited atonement. Finding these teachings unbearably and unreasonably harsh, they sympathized with Universalism, a popular humanistic sentiment that prevailed in parts of America during the late eighteenth century.[28] In the Universalist message, these progenitors found a mercy of extensive scope. God had created his people for salvation, said the Universalists, not to be damned. Ultimately there would be a "universal restoration" of all people to God's presence, wherein sinners—and all humankind were sinners—would be saved. Universalist arguments brought relief, but criticism as well; more conservative Christians said it encouraged licentiousness and destroyed God's law. This contest between schemes of salvation was a conflict Joseph Smith would inherit as he came of age in the early nineteenth century.[29] Part of his prophetic career, beyond being a visionary, a purveyor of scripture, and a religious organizer, would be to deliver an alternative scheme—a

---

27. One account of this ideological transformation, which had social, political, and religious ramifications, is Nathan O. Hatch, *The Democratization of American Christianity* (New Haven: Yale University Press, 1989).

28. On American Universalism, see Ann Lee Bressler, *The Universalist Movement in America, 1770–1880* (New York: Oxford University Press, 2001).

29. Richard L. Bushman, *Joseph Smith and the Beginnings of Mormonism* (Urbana: University of Illinois Press, 1984), 26–29. See also Casey Paul Griffiths, "Universalism and the Revelations of Joseph Smith," in *The Doctrine and Covenants: Revelations in Context*, eds. Andrew H. Hedges, J. Spencer Fluhman, and Alonzo L. Gaskill (Provo, Utah: BYU Religious Studies Center, 2008), 168–87.

divine "plan of salvation" that sustained God's justice, delivered God's mercy, and made provisions for everyone.

For nearly a decade, from 1830 to 1839, as Smith experienced a steady outpouring of divine revelations, he accumulated insight into death, the dead, and God's mechanisms of salvation. Most of these revelations seemed to take Mormonism further away from orthodox Christian thinking and toward something like Universalism. One of the most dramatic breakthroughs occurred in 1832, when Joseph Smith and Sidney Rigdon experienced a splendorous encounter with heaven that Mormons reverently came to call "The Vision." Contrary to their expectations, the eternity that Smith and Rigdon experienced was not the stark binary of heaven and hell evoked in contemporary sermons, the Bible, and even in the Book of Mormon.[30] It was instead a place where few were truly damned and mercy seemed plentiful, even for the sinner.

By visionary observation, Smith and Rigdon came to understand that the hereafter was a stratified existence where virtue and obedience to God's laws in life were rewarded by a corresponding "degree of glory," a conception that completely redefined the Christian afterlife. When written down and circulated among the Saints, "The Vision" proved to be controversial: some Mormons welcomed the insight; others found it too permissive. "My traditions were such," Brigham Young remembered, "that when the Vision came first to me, it was so directly contrary and opposed to my former education, I said, wait a little; I did not reject it, but I could not understand it." His brother Joseph Young also conceded, "I could not believe it at first. Why the Lord was going to save everybody."[31] The vision and the startling implications that flowed from it left Mormons grappling with a dramatically different view of salvation.

Smith and Rigdon's experience gave insight not just to God's mercies

---

30. Bushman, *Joseph Smith: Rough Stone Rolling*, 200.

31. Brigham Young, Aug. 29, 1852, *Journal of Discourses*, 26 vols. (London: Latter-day Saints' Book Depot, 1854–86), 6:281. Joseph Young, "Discourse," *Deseret Weekly News*, Mar. 18, 1857, 11. On "The Vision," see Matthew McBride, "The Vision," Revelations in Context, LDS Church History, http://history.lds.org/article/doctrine-and-covenants-revelations-in-context-the-vision?lang=eng (accessed Mar. 28, 2013). I am indebted to this source for the citations above.

upon the sinner, but also to his forbearance toward "those who died without law" and who "received not the testimony of Jesus in the flesh, but afterward received it." These people, the "honorable men of the earth" would, echoing language in 1 Peter, have the gospel preached to them after death. According to the vision, they would inhabit the secondary "terrestrial world" in the afterlife.[32] Four years later, in 1836, Joseph Smith described another theophany which seemed even more generous. With God in the heavens, Smith was amazed to see not only Adam and Abraham—but Alvin Smith. Confused, Joseph said he wondered how this could be. Alvin had died "before the Lord [had] set his hand to gather Israel ... and had not been baptized for the remission of sins"—a condition considered necessary for full salvation. But Smith then said he heard the voice of God, clarifying: "All who have died with[out] a knowledge of this gospel, who would have received it, if they had been permitted to tarry, shall be heirs of the *celestial* kingdom of God—also all that shall die henceforth without a knowledge of it, who would have received it, with all their hearts, shall be heirs of that kingdom; For I, the Lord, will judge all men according to their works[,] according to the desire of their hearts."[33]

Seemingly mindful of how messy life on earth could be, the revelation confirmed sentiments previously held by Smith, that God would expect no more than humankind could give. He had written to his uncle in 1833 that "men will be held accountable for the things which they have and not for the things they have not," and this revelation seemed to bear that doctrine out.[34] Here was a god who looked on the heart and acknowledged extenuating circumstances.[35] A full, celestial salvation

---

32. Robin Scott Jensen, Robert J. Woodford, and Steven C. Harper, eds., *The Joseph Smith Papers: Revelations and Translations: Manuscript Revelation Books, Facsimile Edition* (Salt Lake City: Church Historian's Press, 2009), 415–33 (D&C 76:71–80; all D&C citations are from the LDS 1981 ed.). On early understandings of preaching to the dead, see Gregory A. Prince, *Power from on High: The Development of Mormon Priesthood* (Salt Lake City: Signature Books, 1995), 143.

33. Jessee, Ashurst-McGee, and Jensen, *Journals, Volume 1*, 167 (D&C 137:7–8); emphasis mine.

34. Lavina Fielding Anderson, ed., *Lucy's Book: A Critical Edition of Lucy Mack Smith's Family Memoir* (Salt Lake City: Signature Books, 2001), 588.

35. On evolving perceptions of salvation for the dead and proxy baptism, see Prince, *Power from on High*, 142–46.

was available to everyone with a good heart and righteous desires. God would hold nothing back from those who died unenlightened.

The issue, however, was still not settled. It was comforting to know that God was empathetic, even accommodating, but Mormonism still faced the ineluctable question that confronted Universalists and others. What were God's criteria for salvation? Were they different for the living and the dead? Was God ultimately a god of laws or a god of mercy? Smith's revelations seemed increasingly to suggest that God could somehow save those who had not had access to the means of salvation. And yet Mormons' commitment to the essentiality of baptism and the growing importance of rituals complicated the picture. How did God's salvation of the dead square with the biblical injunction, often repeated, that "except a man be born of water and of the spirit, he cannot enter into the kingdom of God" (John 3:5)?

By the summer of 1838, Smith was nearing a solution.[36] In an editorial Q&A in the *Elders' Journal*, a church-owned newspaper, he responded to a question about the fate of those who had died without embracing Mormonism. "If Mormonism be true," asked the inquiry, "what of all those who died without baptism?" The editorial offered a new, suggestive response. "All those who have not had an opportunity of hearing the Gospel, and being administered unto by an inspired man in the flesh," it said, "must have it hereafter, before they can be finally judged."[37] It was a reply that opened another dimension of possibilities, since it appeared to extend the scope of human action beyond the grave. If not only gospel instruction, but the "administration" of saving ordinances, were somehow available in the afterlife, the shape of God's designs for human salvation changed substantially.[38]

---

36. It is not clear precisely when, between July 1838 and August 1840, Smith settled on the practice of proxy baptism as a solution for the problem of redeeming the dead. Mormon convert William Appleby wrote that Smith told him he had received revelation on the subject "nine years or nearly after the Church was organized," possibly dating the doctrine to sometime during 1839. William I. Appleby, Autobiography and Journal, 75, MS 1401, CHL.

37. Joseph Smith, "In Obedience to Our Promise ...," *Elders' Journal*, July 1838, 43.

38. Alexander L. Baugh, "'For This Ordinance Belongeth to My House': The Practice of Baptism for the Dead outside the Nauvoo Temple," *Mormon Historical Studies* 3, no. 1 (Spring 2002): 47.

NAUVOO THEOLOGY

Baptism for the dead appeared in Nauvoo amid a surge of profound developments in Mormon theology, all of which affected and catalyzed each other. Indeed, the short period between settlement in 1839 and Smith's death in mid-1844 is perhaps the most theologically dynamic period of Mormon history, bringing rich reformulations and expansions that thoroughly transgressed the boundaries of American Christianity. In Nauvoo, Smith revealed and taught a cascade of innovative and arresting doctrines. "It is my meditation all the day," he said in 1843, "to know how I shall make the Saints of God comprehend the visions that roll like an overflowing surge before my mind."[39] His extraordinary teachings broke like waves over his followers, at once elating and bewildering. As early as 1840, one Mormon woman related, "President Smith has been bringing many strange doctrines this season." They were, as she said, no child's milk, but "strong meat."[40] Yet Smith wanted to move still faster; he bemoaned the fact that his people were not prepared to receive all that he could and wished to tell them.

Priestly Power and Rituals

One great axis of Smith's revelations previous to Nauvoo had been religious authority—what he called "priesthood." From the organization of the church in 1830, Smith came to define authority in a way that differed significantly from contemporary Protestantism. According to Smith, "priesthood" was divine authority that came not by a calling of the Spirit, not through the enlightening medium of scripture—only by an authorized form of direct and manual ordination. He maintained that he himself had received this authority by ordination under the hands of angelic beings. Over the ensuing years, Smith's revelations gradually extended and clarified the functions of priesthood, organizing it into branches and spheres of action that governed the church and addressed the needs, both spiritual and temporal, of its people. In keeping with the biblical model of authority,

---

39. Ehat and Cook, *Words of Joseph Smith*, 196; punctuation standardized.
40. Phoebe Woodruff to Wilford Woodruff, Oct. 6, 1840, MS 19509, CHL.

Smith established in Ohio a Quorum of Twelve Apostles and other priesthood offices that were intended to reflect the authoritative order of the apostolic church.[41]

But Mormon priesthood authority was not only about the church's leadership and welfare; it was also "priestly" in the sense that it authorized essential religious rituals, such as baptism. Smith taught that holders of priesthood (and they alone) were empowered by God to perform saving rites effectively. Unlike Catholicism, ordination to this priesthood was not the perquisite of a religious order. All men of the church were eligible to hold priesthood authority, so long as their conduct was worthy. In many ways, this practice suited the leveling spirit of contemporary American Protestantism. Nowhere had there been such a "priesthood of all believers," as in the antebellum United States where unlikely but impassioned believers seized the reins of religious leadership.[42] But ordained Mormon men were not only exhorters, itinerant preachers, and empowered healers; they were also ordained "priests," authorized to officiate in God's sacred ordinances and rites.

The presence of this priestly authority made possible an unusual sacramentalism that began emerging in Mormonism in the late 1830s. Running counter to the general thrust of a Protestant evangelical context that still frowned on ritual, ceremony, and other elaborate forms of liturgy, Mormonism had through its first decade developed a surprisingly robust ritualistic impulse. Mormons had gone well beyond the few rituals common to many Protestants (baptism, the Lord's Supper), and had embraced many others (washing, healing, ordination, anointing). In Nauvoo, however, the emphasis on ritual accelerated, and Mormons developed a distinct, higher order of religious sacraments

---

41. On the historical development of Mormon priesthood authority, see Prince, *Power from on High,* and D. Michael Quinn, *The Mormon Hierarchy: Origins of Power* (Salt Lake City: Signature Books/Smith Research Associates, 1994). On the nature of priesthood authority in Mormonism, see Robert L. Millett, "Joseph Smith, the Book of Mormon, and the Legal Administrator," and Steven C. Harper, "Angels in the Age of Railways," in Robert L. Millett, ed., *By What Authority: The Vital Questions of Religious Authority in Christianity* (Macon, Georgia: Mercer University Press, 2010), 108–23 and 124–43, respectively.

42. Hatch, *Democratization of American Christianity,* 44–46, 170–78.

unlike anything in the Protestant milieu.[43] These formal sacraments came to be closely associated with Mormons' building of temples; Smith's revelations indicated that sacred acts needed to be performed in sacred spaces, and he built temples for this purpose. By the end of the Nauvoo period, Mormon sacramentalism encompassed an ornate suite of temple rituals with rich dramaturgical and symbolic elements. Proxy baptism for the dead anticipated and catalyzed this emerging "sacramental" impulse.

At the same time that they introduced new forms and kinds of religious ritual, Smith's revelations also created a deeper logic for religious ritual itself. Drawing on biblical and Book of Mormon language, as well as on Protestant rhetoric of the "binding" and "sealing" capacities of God's power, Smith taught that rituals and acts performed by virtue of the divine priesthood were indispensable for salvation.[44] When performed properly, these acts had eternal significance. Hence, when exercised in harmony with the will of God, priesthood authority underwrote saving rituals both in heaven and on earth and actualized a condition needed for salvation. "It may seem to some," Smith acknowledged, a "very bold doctrine we speak of—a power that ... binds on earth and binds in heaven." But this definitive "sealing" power, he insisted, had "always been given" to authorized prophets throughout human history.[45] It was this power that drove the saving rituals, both for the living and the dead. "There is a way to release the spirit of the dead," Smith taught in 1841, "that is, by the power and authority of the Priesthood—by binding and loosing on earth."[46]

---

43. For treatment of the many important rituals encompassed by early Mormonism, see Brown, *In Heaven as It Is on Earth*, 157–61; and Jonathan A. Stapley and Kristine L. Wright, "The Forms and the Power: The Development of Mormon Ritual Healing to 1847," *Journal of Mormon History* 35, no. 2 (Summer 2009): 42–87. My argument is that Nauvoo largely introduced and centralized an emphasis on "sacraments" and "sacramentalism," terms which delineate ritual action understood to be formally and strictly necessary for salvation.

44. Brown, *In Heaven as It Is on Earth*, 146–51. Brown traces the Protestant precedents for "seals" and covenants.

45. Robin Scott Jensen, Richard E. Turley Jr., and Riley M. Lorimer, eds., *The Joseph Smith Papers: Revelations and Translations, Volume 2: Published Revelations* (Salt Lake City: Church Historian's Press, 2011), 683–84 (D&C 128:9).

46. Ehat and Cook, *Words of Joseph Smith*, 76–79.

Collective Salvation

Baptism for the dead also merged in concert with evolving Mormon ideas about religious community and collective salvation.[47] From 1830 to 1838, Smith's revelations and teachings had abounded with references to the scriptural concept of "Zion," the holy, archetypal community of the faithful that Mormons had attempted to create in Missouri, and which remained paradigmatic for the Nauvoo period that followed.[48] In Nauvoo, however, the mechanisms for social unity and collective salvation shifted. Emphasis on the broad bonds of community and society merged with new emphasis on kinship and family; solidarity increasingly rested on the concrete ties of marriage and blood. Rather than attempting to bind his people together through consecration of property and communal covenants, as he had endeavored to do in Missouri, Nauvoo saw Smith use the power of priesthood authority to unite them.[49]

Like many theological developments in early Mormonism, these new insights about priesthood and human relationships unfolded through the motif of a biblical prophecy. Rehearsed at the outset of Smith's prophetic career, when he was seventeen years old, and repeated thereafter, the ancient prophecy of Malachi foretold a time when Elijah the prophet would be sent to "turn the heart of the fathers to the children, and he heart of the children to their fathers, lest I [God] come and smite the earth with a curse" (Mal. 4:6). The prophecy was little understood until 1838, when Smith and Oliver Cowdery reported that Elijah appeared to them in the Kirtland, Ohio, temple, reiterated the prophecy and transferred important elements of authority to

---

47. Samuel M. Brown, "Early Mormon Adoption Theology and the Mechanics of Salvation," *Journal of Mormon History* 37, no. 3 (Summer 2011): 3–52, offers the fullest explanations of Smith's complex initiative to create an integrated, eternal human family through sealing rituals. The article also provides valuable insight to early Mormon soteriology, suggesting that Joseph Smith offered a "sacramental guarantee of salvation that was in its very essence communal" (5–6).

48. "The religious worldview behind the attempt to establish a Zion place and a Zion society ... offers the most useful window for understanding the Nauvoo period." Leonard, *Nauvoo*, 5.

49. Brown, *In Heaven As It Is on Earth*, 203–08; and Bushman, *Joseph Smith: Rough Stone Rolling*, 421–23, 440–46.

accomplish it.[50] These were the priesthood "keys," evidently, through which the prophecy could be fulfilled.

In Nauvoo, the sealing authority found its object, and Malachi's prophecy took on additional meaning. At the same time as he contemplated the necessity of baptism and salvation for the virtuous dead, Smith reflected on this newly granted power of priesthood authority, and the two considerations evidently merged. Smith realized that the sealing power would somehow have to be applied, to be executed "upon some subject or other." In order to be effective, in other words, priesthood power would need a medium in which it could work. "And what is that subject?" Smith asked rhetorically. His conclusion was: "It is the baptism for the dead."[51] The rite of proxy baptism could both provide the means of salvation to the unevangelized dead and invoke the sealing power, binding the Saints to their progenitors and together into the Kingdom of God.[52]

Embodiment and Surrogacy

In its development, baptism for the dead partook of Mormons' increasingly exceptional beliefs about matter and the human body.[53]

---

50. Jessee, Ashurst-McGee, and Jensen, *Journals, Volume 1*, 219–22 (D&C 110:13–16).

51. Jessee, Ashurst-McGee, and Jensen, 48 (D&C 128:18). Prior to this time, Latter-day Saints had different understandings of "sealing" which were more clearly Protestant: to be "sealed up" to God was to be assured a condition of salvation in the afterlife; one could also be "sealed" unto damnation. This conception of sealing was associated with the priesthood authority from the Church's organization in 1830, and in subsequent years "Mormon elders sealed congregations to eternal life." Early LDS patriarchs also "sealed" up those they blessed to salvation. Brown, *In Heaven as It Is on Earth*, 148–49.

52. For Smith's thinking about the priesthood keys and sealing the human family together, ca. 1839, see Ehat and Cook, *Words of Joseph Smith*, 8–11. The widespread Christian doctrine of adoption into the kingdom of God, which many Latter-day Saints identified with baptism, may have enabled Joseph Smith to understand baptism for the dead as a way to seal people together. Brown, "Early Mormon Adoption Theology," 15–19. Over time, as Smith came to teach that all of the emerging temple rituals, not just baptism for the dead, would be necessary to finalize the sealing together of the human family, he seems to have used the term "the baptism for the dead" to refer to the concept of proxy ordinances as a whole. Hence, Smith's later sermons on "the baptism for the dead," may have been synecdochic for all ordinances performed for the dead.

53. On embodiment, see Davies, *Mormon Culture of Salvation*, 122–23; Benjamin E. Park, "Salvation through a Tabernacle: Joseph Smith, Parley Pratt, and Early Mormon Theologies of Embodiment," *Dialogue: A Journal of Mormon Thought* 43, no. 2 (Summer 2010): 1–44; and Bushman, *Joseph Smith: Rough Stone Rolling*, 420–21.

For centuries, many Christians had lauded the spirit but loathed the flesh, which they saw as carnal and corruptive. For Mormons, however, that perception began to wane as new revelations emerged that seemed to give the human body new purpose and dignity. The fundamental unit of human identity, Smith revealed in 1832, was actually not the human spirit alone, but that spirit in conjunction with a corporeal body.[54] Flesh was, Mormons learned, a vital and permanent element of the self. Smith also taught, as early as 1841, that God and Jesus had glorified bodies of flesh and bones.[55] Human bodies were, therefore, actually a divine inheritance, a consequence of having been created in God's image. "The great principle of happiness," Smith pronounced, "consists in having a body."[56]

Revelations about the body also affected Mormons' understanding of religious ritual. If the body was an essential vehicle for the human spirit, then it became significant that religious rituals were performed in the flesh as bodily sacraments. "Deeds done in the body," particularly the saving rituals of the faith, were of great consequence; the body was an essential part of the ordinances that enabled salvation.[57] However, the significance of the body also created dilemmas. Persons who had died without the saving rites could not, of course, hope to receive them without their fleshly bodies; hence those in this circumstance faced a seemingly insurmountable barrier to redemption. "What kind of beings," Smith asked rhetorically, "can be saved although their bodies are mouldering in the dust?"[58] The disembodied dead clearly could not attend to rituals that required a fleshly tabernacle.

Smith's radical solution for this problem was a principle of ritual surrogacy.[59] In order to ensure fairness to all human beings, he taught,

54. Jensen, Woodford, and Harper, *Manuscript Revelation Books, Facsimile Edition*, 479–505 (D&C 88:15).

55. Ehat and Cook, *Words of Joseph Smith*, 60. A revelation on this subject was received in 1843 but not canonized until 1981 (D&C 130:22).

56. Ehat and Cook, *Words of Joseph Smith*, 60.

57. Ehat and Cook., 78. See 2 Cor. 5:10.

58. Ehat and Cook, *Words of Joseph Smith*, 360.

59. John L. Brooke, *The Refiner's Fire: The Making of Mormon Cosmology, 1644–1844* (New York: Cambridge University Press, 1994), 28, 44, 242–43, posits that the concept of baptism for the dead may have come to Mormonism through a radical German pietist group in Ephrata, Pennsylvania. Brooke notes that a form of baptism by proxy in behalf

God's divine economy allowed for living, embodied human beings to act in behalf of deceased persons in saving rituals. Thus those on the earth with bodies and access to priesthood power could participate in Mormonism's rituals, including baptism, "for and in behalf of" their dead kin. The dead may not have the capacity to be baptized, Smith acknowledged, but "why not deputize a friend on earth to do it for them"?[60] By "actively engaging in rites of salvation substitutionally," he said, Latter-day Saints "became instrumental in bringing multitudes of their kin into the kingdom of God." He was careful to clarify that the Saints themselves did not themselves hold saving power—that it "was the truth, not men that saved them."[61] But by acting in this way, Mormons would ensure that their deceased ancestors could satisfy the ritual requirements on earth and gain salvation.

Dynamic understandings of priesthood, sealing, and surrogacy converged in Nauvoo and met in the ritual of baptism for the dead, which in turn served as a catalyst for their further development. Baptism was, by far, the most familiar of religious rites, and as Smith and the Latter-day Saints began to appreciate the importance of sacraments, and their applications for the dead, it was the ubiquitous rite of baptism that served as a primary model. Other saving rituals would not be confirmed as such until later. It had been the principle of baptism that had prompted Mormon leaders' initial inquiries about the nature of religious authority. Now it was through the lens of baptism that Smith first sensed God's larger designs for the future of the human race.

A MORMON "REVIVAL"

By the end of the church's semiannual conference in October of 1840, just two months after it had been first articulated, the new doctrine of baptism for the dead had enthralled the Latter-day Saints. During

---

of the dead was introduced in a cloister there sometime in the mid-eighteenth century and suggests that it had some level of diffusion among local German immigrants. Despite Brooke's assertion, however, scholars have not found evidence suggesting a connection between Ephrata and Mormonism. See Davies, *Culture of Salvation*, 90; and Terryl L. Givens, *By the Hand of Mormon: The American Scripture that Launched a New World Religion* (New York: Oxford University Press, 2002), 170.

60. Phoebe Woodruff to Wilford Woodruff, Oct. 6, 1840.

61. Ehat and Cook, *Words of Joseph Smith*, 77.

the conference, which drew several thousand Mormons into Nauvoo, Smith and others had preached at length on the new doctrine, expounding the idea and its meanings to the assemblies. And the Saints had embraced the principle with enthusiasm: in the adjournments between meetings, many went to the riverbank and immediately began to perform the ritual. Reporting on the October conference to her missionary husband, Heber, Vilate Kimball said that "Brother Joseph has opened a new and glorious subject of late, which has caused quite a revival in the Church … that is, the baptism for the dead."[62]

During the months following its introduction, performances of proxy baptism became a form of communal worship in Nauvoo. Hundreds of ordinances were performed as Latter-day Saints congregated together at the broad Mississippi. On Sabbath days especially, they assembled on the riverbank, waded out into the current, and submerged one another in behalf of dead parents, grandparents, children, siblings, spouses, and other relations. Wading again to shore, they knelt, placing their hands upon one another's heads, ritually confirming each other in behalf of their dead relations as members of the church, precisely as was done for the living.

The collective energy that the Saints brought to baptism for the dead could be spectacular. Vilate Kimball wrote to Heber, "Since this order has been preached here, the waters have been continually troubled."[63] Phoebe Woodruff likewise wrote to her husband, Wilford, that "this doctrine is cordially received by the Church and they are going forward in multitudes." One Nauvoo friend, she said, was "clear carried away with it." Many returned again and again: "Some are going to be baptized as many as 16 times."[64] Years later Wilford Woodruff recollected: "How did we feel when we first heard the living could be baptised for the dead? We all went to work at it as fast as we had an opportunity, and were baptised for every body we could think of." He recalled wading into the river with Smith and other church leaders on a summer Sunday evening, "[Joseph] baptized a hundred. I baptized a hundred. The next man, a few rods

---

62. Vilate Kimball to Heber C. Kimball, Oct. 11, 1840.
63. Kimball to Kimball.
64. Phoebe Woodruff to Wilford Woodruff, Oct. 6, 1840.

from me, baptized another hundred. We were strung up and down the Mississippi, baptizing for our dead."[65]

Converts and visitors to Nauvoo found the scale of the activity startling. "It is surprising," one new Mormon recorded, "to see both men and women, on the Sabbath in particular, after worship retire to the River for Baptism. Four hundred and fifty (I was informed) had been baptised of an afternoon. Hundreds are Baptising for their dead, people are coming hundreds of miles to see the Prophet, and attending to this ordinance, in behalf of their departed relatives."[66] Outsiders who visited Nauvoo told tales of how assiduously Mormons went about the task. "They baptize here," related a visiting minister, Reverend M. Badger, incredulously, "not only for the living, but for the *dead*. ... I saw one old man who had been baptized 13 times for his deceased children, because they were not Mormon."[67] As records began to be kept following the ritual's introduction, these efforts added up. During 1841, for instance, the Saints performed at least 6,500 proxy ordinances. This and other remarkable figures have led to the conclusion that "baptism for the dead was a major religious activity" in Mormon Nauvoo.[68]

Mormons' collective eagerness to embrace baptism for the dead was presumably, like the energy of other contemporary American religious revivals, the product of deep anxiety and existential concern. During the period, introspective Methodists, Baptists, and others despaired at the depth of their own sin, yearned for rebirth, and gloried in the grace of God—feelings that galvanized their camps and assemblies. Confronted with sickness, death, and the sorrow of human separation, Mormons in Nauvoo turned to priesthood baptism as an opportunity to avail

---

65. Wilford Woodruff, "Remarks," *Deseret News*, May 27, 1857, 4; "Discourse Delivered by President Wilford Woodruff ... April 6, 1891," *Deseret Weekly*, Apr. 25, 1891, 554.

66. Appleby, Autobiography and Journal, 80.

67. M. Badger, "Joseph Smith at Home," *New York Observer and Chronicle*, Aug. 6, 1842, 128; emphasis original.

68. M. Guy Bishop, "What Has Become of Our Fathers?: Baptism for the Dead at Nauvoo," *Dialogue: A Journal of Mormon Thought* 23, no. 2 (Summer 1990): 88. Bishop offers helpful quantitative analysis. The original records of baptism for the dead in Nauvoo are located in CR 342 10, CHL. A published and annotated, but incomplete reproduction is Susan E. Black and Harvey B. Black, eds., *Annotated Records of Baptisms for the Dead, 1840–1845: Nauvoo, Hancock County, Illinois*, 7 vols. (Provo, Utah: BYU Center for Family History and Genealogy, 2002).

themselves and their loved ones of God's mercy. Together, the rite and the river brought Mormons a sense of "dramatic empowerment."[69]

Inevitably, proxy baptisms drew outside attention. The Mormons had expected the practice to be ridiculed; and when eastern visitors and newspapers learned that the Mormons were performing baptisms in behalf of national celebrities like George Washington, the satire began.[70] Reverend Badger chuckled that he had heard of eighty-year-old Mormon Stephen Jones, a Revolutionary War veteran, who was baptized "for George Washington and La-Fayette; then for Thomas Jefferson; and then applied in behalf of Andrew Jackson! but they told him the General was not yet dead, and so he waits awhile."[71] Another correspondent feigned relief that "after these fifty years [George Washington] is out of purgatory and on his way to the 'celestial' heaven!"[72] Other voices, less amused, denounced the ritual as alarming and blasphemous. "There is a danger," one critic insisted, "of pressing the importance of outward rites, which are of easy compliance to the neglect of those spiritual views which make religion a work of the heart." This lesson was, in what was ostensibly an allusion to Catholic ritualism, "the testimony furnished by the history of the Church in every age."[73]

---

69. Michael Pasquier, ed., *Gods of the Mississippi* (Bloomington: Indiana University Press, 2013), x.

70. "Surely the Gentiles will mock, but we will rejoice in it." Vilate Kimball to Heber C. Kimball, Oct. 11, 1840.

71. Badger, "Joe Smith at Home." Stephen Jones's proxy baptisms for George Washington, the Marquis de Lafayette, and Thomas Jefferson evidently took place on July 4, 1841, in conjunction with the holiday. A week later, in a dispatch that was widely reprinted, the antagonistic *Warsaw Signal* issued a sardonic report of the proceedings: "The doctrine of the Mormons appears to be, that those who are living must be baptized by one having authority from Joe Smith, or else go to hell; but those who are already dead may be brought out of torment by a friend or relation receiving the baptismal rites in their behalf. The nation may rejoice, therefore, that the illustrious patriots above named, are now taken from the possession of the Prince of Darkness, and admitted into the fellowship of the Saints!!!" "Baptism for the Dead," *Warsaw Signal*, July 14, 1841. For reprintings and reactions to the *Signal*'s report, see Untitled, *Manufacturers & Farmers Journal, and Providence and Pawtucket [RI] Advertiser*, Aug. 9, 1841, 1; "Baptism for the Dead," *[Hartford] Connecticut Courant*, Aug. 15, 1841, 3; and "Baptism for the Dead," *Weekly Messenger* (Chambersburg, PA), Sep. 29, 1841, 1. On Jones as proxy, see Black and Black, *Annotated Records of Baptisms for the Dead*, 2015–16.

72. Charlotte Haven, "A Girl's Letters from Nauvoo," *Overland Monthly*, Dec. 1890, 629–30.

73. "Baptism for the Dead," *Weekly Messenger*, Sep. 29, 1841, 1. See also "Journal of a Mormon," *Christian Observer*, Sep. 10, 1841, 146.

Indeed, the emergence of Mormon ritualism, including in the form of baptism for the dead, increasingly led many to associate Mormons with Catholics. Proxy baptism was so eccentric that suspicious Protestants classed it with the mélange of exotic rituals that Catholics were rumored to practice. Releasing the dead from spiritual prison, too, sounded suspiciously like an escape from purgatory. "[Mormons'] ceremonies," said one report, 'are said to be ... eclectic, being patchwork from the mummeries of old superstitions pieced together by new inventions of their own."[74] These liturgical resemblances augmented the common charge of ecclesiastical despotism, leveled at both Mormons and Catholics.[75] Because of widespread anti-Catholic prejudice, this linkage between Mormons and Catholics suited critical commentators, who pitted Mormons and Catholic priests in fiendish competition for souls. "This plan of competition [i.e., baptism for the dead] by the Mormons must be very dangerous to the Romish priests," gibed one article in the *Christian Secretary*, "for it operates quicker and cheaper than masses, and *just as good exactly*."[76] Another observer, after hearing Smith lecture and witnessing baptisms for the dead in 1843, opined that, in many ways, Mormons seemed to be "good orthodox Baptists." However, "in some of their forms they run close into Catholicism."[77]

"THE POWER OF GODLINESS IS MANIFEST"

Antebellum America was a hive of theological disputation, and water baptism was among the subjects of active debate. Most Christians in America regarded baptism as a holy act, grounded in the teachings of the Bible. And yet, like much of Christian theology in the period,

---

74. Untitled, *Manufacturers & Farmers Journal, and Providence and Pawtucket [RI] Advertiser*, Aug. 9, 1841, 1.

75. On the relationship between mainstream perceptions of Mormons and Catholics in the nineteenth century, as well their conceptions of each other, see Matthew J. Grow, "The Whore of Babylon and the Abomination of Abominations: Nineteenth-Century Catholic and Mormon Mutual Perceptions and Religious Identity," *Church History* 73, no. 1 (Mar. 2004): 139–67; and David Brion Davis, "Some Themes in Counter-Subversion: An Analysis of Anti-Masonic, Anti-Catholic, and Anti-Mormon Literature," *Mississippi Valley Historical Review* 47 (Sep. 1960): 205–24.

76. "Purgatory," *Christian Secretary* (Hartford, CT), Sep. 3, 1841, 3.

77. "Nauvoo—We Spent a Sabbath with the Mormons," *New York Spectator*, Aug. 23, 1843, 4.

the precise purposes and the proper execution of baptism were widely contested. At what stage of life should baptism be administered? Some traditional Christians still insisted, as the Puritans had, that baptism helped redeem even newborns from sin. Others, especially Baptists, asserted that only adult believers should participate in the ritual. Christians also disagreed about how baptism ought to be performed. Was there a particular method? Should initiates be sprinkled or immersed? Who ought to officiate? Contemporary ministers scoured scripture for insight and made their cases from biblical proof-texts.

Despite the intensity of debate on the subject, few American Protestants at the time believed that baptism was absolutely required for salvation. Baptism was a propitious act that Americans took seriously; it was the marker of a covenant life and an undertaking to be commended. It was not, however, a prerequisite or saving rite, as it was understood to be in Catholicism. To insist that it was essential would be to ascribe saving power to human works, something Protestants vehemently refused to do. Charles Buck's ubiquitous *Theological Dictionary* noted that "[baptism] is an ordinance binding on all those who have been given up to God in it. ... It is not however, essential to salvation." Indeed, baptism could not be a prerequisite to salvation, since "mere participation in the sacraments cannot qualify men for heaven." The act of baptism was important, but only as a marker of invisible spiritual transformation. It was this spiritual phenomenon—emphatically not the sacrament itself—that brought redemption. "To suppose [baptism was] essential," Buck noted, "was to put it in the place of that which it signifies."[78]

In contrast with most contemporary Protestants, Mormons *did* come to adopt the theological position that water baptism was obligatory for salvation. For Latter-day Saints, baptism was a necessary sacrament, the first of what would later become several ritual ordinances needed for ultimate redemption. While working on the Book of Mormon, Smith sought further inspiration about the rite of baptism and learned that it was indeed a central pillar of the Christian gospel. The Book of Mormon itself strongly condemned the baptism of infants (Moro. 8:10–21) and

---

78. Charles Buck, *A Theological Dictionary* (Philadelphia: William Woodward, 1830), s.v. "Baptism for the Dead"; emphasis removed. The dictionary was first printed in London in 1802 and became a definitive theological resource in England and America over the next half-century.

underscored baptism's necessity (3 Ne. 11:33–34). Invested with new priesthood authority, Smith not only reinforced the significance of water baptism, he also emphasized the necessity of its being performed under proper authority: baptism without authority was of no consequence.

A revelation received shortly after the organization of the new "Church of Christ" in 1830 made clear that authorized baptism was an inexorable commandment and would be required for church membership. Baptism was indeed a "dead work," it said—unless it was performed by virtue of the newly granted priesthood. When undergirded by that new authority, baptism became an essential sacrament, part of a paradoxically "new and an everlasting covenant" that God required of everyone. "Wherefore," the revelation directed, chiding skeptics, "enter ye in at the gate, as I have commanded, & seek not to counsel your God."[79] Doing so would open the way to salvation. To seekers like Smith, this was a tremendous realization. When his downtrodden father was baptized into the church about the same time, a gratified Smith exulted, "Oh! my God I have lived to see my own father baptized into the true church of Jesus Christ." He "covered his face in his father's bosom and wept aloud for joy."[80]

At odds with other Christians on this point, Mormons found themselves forced to persuade others of the absolute necessity of baptism—of the need for sacraments. Mormon missionaries reasoned with interlocutors and pointed doggedly to biblical passages that seemed to demand disciples to be baptized (e.g., John 3:5).[81] The strong current

---

79. Jensen, Turley, and Lorimer, *Revelations and Translations Books, Facsimile Edition*, 35, spelling modernized (D&C 22). The revelation, received on April 16, 1830, was given in response to inquirers who sought membership in the new church without being baptized or rebaptized by a church officer. The scope of the "new and everlasting covenant" that it referred to would expand over time to incorporate all of the faith's emerging sacraments, including "celestial marriage."

80. Anderson, *Lucy's Book*, 477. See also Bushman, *Joseph Smith: Rough Stone Rolling*, 111.

81. For LDS efforts to persuade others about the necessity of baptism, see "Can I Not Be Saved without Baptism?" *Millennial Star*, Sep. 1841, 120–23; "Baptism," *Times and Seasons*, Sep. 1842, 903–905; and Lorenzo Snow, *The Only Way to Be Saved* (London D. Chalmers, 1841). Although the doctrine of proxy baptism was reserved to Nauvoo, Mormon missionaries like George J. Adams occasionally taught and wrote about it. See, for instance, "Review of the Mormon Lectures," rpt. from the *Boston Bee* in *Times and Seasons*, Mar. 1, 1843, 126; and George J. Adams, *A Lecture on the Doctrine of Baptism for the Dead; and Preaching to Spirits in Prison* (New York: C. A. Calhoun, 1844).

of revivalism, however, with its emphasis on a conversion experience with the Holy Spirit, tended to undercut this logic. One layman who later converted to Mormonism felt that baptism, part of the original order of Christian discipleship, had been lost by evangelical Christianity. "I cannot see any religion of the Bible in it," he wrote. "The ancient Apostles said, 'Repent and be baptized for the remission of your sins' ... But these preachers say, 'Come to the anxious seat and we will pray for you, and you will get religion. No mater about baptism[;] that is nonessential.'" "I have read the scriptures too much," he concluded, "to be deceived with such stuff."[82] Smith spoke to the issue directly in 1842, teaching that "[baptism] is a sign, and commandment which God has set for man to enter into his Kingdom. Those who seek to enter in any other way will seek in vain; and God will not receive them, neither will the angels acknowledge their works as accepted; for they have not obeyed the ordinances, nor attended to the signs which God ordained for the salvation of man."[83] The necessity of authorized baptism became a familiar Mormon refrain.

As early as 1832, it was clear that for Mormons baptism was more than a mere formality, a test of compliance, or a tradition initiating new members into the church. In September of that year, Smith received a revelation regarding priesthood authority, and it taught a deeper purpose for rituals and ordinances. In such sacred acts, the revelation taught, "the power of godliness is manifest." Without the priesthood and its ordinances, on the other hand, "the power of godliness is not manifest unto man in the flesh."[84] Thus, unlike Protestants, who treated sacraments as formulae only, Mormons could expect the rituals to precipitate the power of God in their lives. In rituals like baptism and baptism for the dead, the Saints could expect God's healing, hope, and sanctification.

---

82. Warren Foote, Journal, May 24, 1841, 53, MS 1123, CHL. For the initial discovery of this source and as a finding aid generally, I am indebted to the Book of Abraham Project, http://www.boap.org. The "anxious seat" or "anxious bench" was a means of evangelization pioneered by revivalist Charles Grandison Finney, in which the unconverted were conspicuously called before the assembly (to sit on the "anxious bench") to become the object of special suasion and collective scrutiny.

83. Ehat and Cook, *Words of Joseph Smith*, 107–08.

84. Jensen, Woodford, and Harper, *Manuscript Revelation Books, Facsimile Edition*, 457 (D&C 84:19–22).

Indeed, as baptism for the dead was introduced into pestilential Nauvoo, many claimed to experience the "power of godliness." Joseph and Martha Hovey, for instance, arrived in Nauvoo on a cold, rainy night in November 1840. Formerly a carriage wright, but now poor in means and in health, Joseph Hovey had initially been eager to move his family to Nauvoo. However, the couple spent a good part of the ensuing winter in a tent on an unimproved lot loaned to them by the church. It was, Hovey recalled candidly, "cold and disagreeable."

Like other contemporary families, the Hoveys had lost children to disease: first, a daughter, Martha, and then Grafton, a son. Grafton, his father recalled, "was taken in the bloom of childhood when our hearts were set upon him as our first sun [son]. Our fond hopes were entwined about him and our future happyness and prosperity we should injoy in future days." Now, Hovey grieved, "He is gon. We cannot imbrace him more in this probation." Yet even as the family contended with weather, indigence, and loss, the Hoveys found staying power in the emerging principles of Mormonism. "We were taught by the Prophet Joseph those things that cheerd our souls," Hovey recorded, "especially that about our dead." When Martha became ill and miscarried in 1841, "she was heald," by being baptized for her own health and in behalf of her deceased relatives. Joseph Hovey was likewise baptized for his grandfather and grandmother.[85]

Several years later, in 1842, Hovey learned that his mother, not a Mormon, had died. The news came on the same day that yet another son, Thomas Josiah, died in infancy. The climate of Nauvoo was gradually improving, but the child was "taken varry sick with his teeth." "Truly I did feal to morn," Hovey conceded. By his account, however, Hovey and his wife tried not to complain about their son's death. Hovey felt confident that "we will meate him a gain in the reserection if we [are] faithfull and hold out until the end." And although Hovey's mother had not embraced the Mormon gospel ("for she did not have it presented to her[,] only as I wrote to her"), he was hopeful that he would eventually be reunited with her as well. This could happen "thrugh the provisions that God has made for those that had not the

---

85. Joseph G. Hovey, Journal, Oct. 6, 1839, MS 1576, CHL.

oppertunity to imbrace the Gospel of Christ." Hence even under the "exsisting sircomstances," Hovey wrote, "I have a most … gloryous hope of meeting my Dead friendes, to clasp handes in eternal felisety."[86]

Like the Hoveys, Sally Randall and her family endured death and bereavement in Nauvoo. Randall came to the city as a convert from Warsaw, New York, in September 1843, bringing two young sons to join James, her husband. Like many other Saints, she left behind a family of unbelievers, and her letters home reflect both contentment in her new life and sorrow at separation from her parents and siblings. Shortly after Sally arrived, she wrote to her family about the prospects of her new home: generally she was impressed with what she saw but noted that "it is verry sickly here at presant with fevers … and ague and measles, and a great many children die with them."[87] Less than a month later, her fourteen-year-old boy George was dead and her ten-year-old son, Eli, was feverishly ill. She wrote home again, "with a trembling hand, and a heart full of grief and sorrow," relating the child's dying spasms, the family' grief, and her own distress. "It seemed as though my heart would break," she lamented, "but the Lord hath given and he hath taken his own to himself."[88] This was pious, but disconsolate, wisdom.

Although Eli recovered, Randall was still mourning over George's death the next April. Rather than surrendering to her grief, though, she was starting to find reasons for hope and solace. Since George's death, she told her family, "his father has been baptized for him." "What a glorious thing it is, that we believe and receive the fulness of the gospel as it is preached now and can be baptized for all our dead friends." Feeling this consolation, Randall asked her family for the names of all their deceased relatives and invited their help.[89] If they would join the church and come to Nauvoo, she offered, they could help her in the work of redemption. "I intend to do what I can to save my friends," she said, "and I should be verry glad if some of you would come and help me for it is a great work to do alone." In particular, Randall wanted to

---

86. Hovey, Dec. 17, 1842.

87. Sally Randall to family, Oct. 6, 1843, typescript, MS 3821, CHL.

88. Sally Randall to family, Nov. 12, 1843.

89. Correspondence from Nauvoo requesting genealogical information for baptisms became common. Leonard, *Nauvoo*, 255n89. See also Ellen Wadsworth Parker to family, Feb. 1, 1843, MS 5539 8, CHL.

know from her mother whether a deceased sister had reached the age of eight—the age of accountability when children came to need baptism. If they did their part, she promised, both she and her mother could have their children "just as we laid them down in thare graves." She acknowledged, "I expect you will think this strange doctrine, but you will find it is true."[90]

As a new convert, William Appleby came to Nauvoo in May 1841, where he learned about vicarious baptism in a personal conversation with Joseph Smith. Visiting Smith in his home, Appleby inspected the written revelations for himself, along with Smith's curious Egyptian artifacts. After reading the revelation, hearing Smith explain proxy baptism, and "seeing the glorious principle of the Gospel, and what a plan has been devised for the salvation of man," Appleby went straight to the Mississippi River with William Marks, president of the Nauvoo Stake. There he was "buried six times in the 'likeness of my Saviour' beneath the liquid wave" in behalf of his grandparents, his father, a brother and two sisters. He was confirmed for each of them.

As Appleby experienced it, this was not just as the accomplishment of a necessary rite, but a deeply gratifying personal experience. "Oh! What a glorious time it was for me, to think I could become an instrument ... in the hands of God, in setting captive spirits free." He exulted, "Glory and honour be ascribed to God, for this privilege, the Glorious principles of the Gospel,—and for all I enjoy." A few days later, Appleby had a dream in which his dead father appeared to him. He often dreamed of his father, he wrote, but typically the settings were "situations, or attitudes that I would sometimes awake out of my slumber, and was glad to find it was but a dream." This time he dreamed that his father embraced him and comforted him with loving words. When Appleby kissed his father's cheek, he "manifested pleasure, and joy, and disappeared!" This seemed to Appleby a manifestation that his

---

90. Sally Randall to family, Apr. 21, 1844. A short biography and Randall's letters have been published in Kenneth W. Godfrey, Audrey W. Godfrey, and Jill Mulvay Derr, eds., *Women's Voices: An Untold Story of the Latter-day Saints, 1830–1900* (Salt Lake City: Deseret Book Co., 1982), 134–46. See also Jordan Watkins and Steven C. Harper, "'It Seems That All Nature Mourns': Sally Randall's Response to the Murder of Joseph and Hyrum Smith," *BYU Studies* 46, no. 1 (2007): 95–100.

proxy efforts had been effective. "Since the Baptism," he noted meaningfully, "I have dreamed but little concerning him."[91]

The doctrine of baptism for the dead also inspired church leaders. When they learned of the new teaching, apostles Wilford Woodruff and Brigham Young felt a similar sense of empowerment. Young said that he believed the doctrine even "before anything was done about it in this Church. … It made me glad," he said, "that I could go forth, and officiate for my fathers, for my mothers, and for my ancestors … who have not had the privilege of helping themselves."[92] Woodruff, who became perhaps the greatest champion of rituals for the dead, said that, upon learning the concept, his mind turned instantly to his mother, who had died while he was an infant. If he could help save her, he thought, "this alone would pay me for all the labors of my life." "Well might the Prophet say," he reflected, that "God has fulfilled His promise that in the last days He would raise up saviors upon Mount Zion." By the end of his life, Woodruff would perform or arrange proxy rituals for more than 4,000 dead relatives.[93]

A "GLORIOUS" DOCTRINE

For William Appleby and other theologically minded Mormons, the marvelous spiritual experience of baptism for their dead only served to heighten its logical appeal. If the initial strangeness of the idea could be set aside, Appleby thought, its deep rationality would be seen. "No

---

91. Appleby, Autobiography and Journal, 1, 74–79.

92. Brigham Young, "Speech Delivered by President B. Young … April 6, 1845," *Times and Seasons*, July 1, 1845, 953–55.

93. Wilford Woodruff, "Talks to the Sisters," *Deseret Weekly*, Feb. 24, 1894, 288; "Discourse," *Deseret Weekly*, Apr. 25, 1891, 554. Because of Woodruff's great enthusiasm for proxy baptism, Brigham Young commissioned him to dedicate the baptistry of the St. George temple when completed in 1877. Later, while Woodruff presided over that temple and then over the church generally, he placed great emphasis on the significance of proxy rituals and mindfulness of the dead. His influence helped rekindle Mormons' interest in the redemption of the dead and in temples generally. Richard E. Bennett, "Wilford Woodruff and the Rise of Temple Consciousness among the Latter-day Saints, 1877–84," in *Banner of the Gospel: Wilford Woodruff*, eds. Alexander L. Baugh and Susan Easton Black (Provo, Utah: BYU Religious Studies Center, 2010), 233–50. On the decline of baptism for the dead in the Reorganized Latter Day Saint tradition, see Roger D. Launius, "An Ambivalent Rejection: Baptism for the Dead and the Reorganized Church Experience," *Dialogue: A Journal of Mormon Thought* 23, no. 2 (Summer 1990): 61–84.

doubt but this Idea will meet with ridicule from many," he mused in his journal, "but let us first examine, and see if it is not rationable, and reasonable, and according to the Scriptures."[94] In nineteenth-century America, the prevalent standards of truth were common sense and congruence with scripture, and baptism for the dead was subject to both of these tests.

From the first, Joseph Smith had treated proxy baptism as if it were self-evident from the Bible. Although other scriptural analysts disagreed, he was unapologetic. To some in Nauvoo who evidently found it difficult to accept the doctrine based on its appearance in an obscure and singular verse, Smith reportedly answered, "If there is one word of the Lord that supports the doctrin, it is enough to make it a true doctrin." As a result of its presence in the Bible, vicarious baptism was, he insisted, "the burden of the scriptures."[95] When skepticism persisted, he retorted in frustration: "The doctrin of Baptism for the dead is clearly shown in the new testament & if the doctrin is not good then throw away the new testament. [B]ut if it is the word of God, then let the doctrin be acknowledged."[96]

Mormons quickly found additional scriptural evidence to corroborate the teaching. By the 1840 October general conference, instruction about the doctrine was adducing elements of 1 Peter for additional support. Alluded to in "The Vision" in 1832, the epistle made unclear references to "preaching" to dead spirits, which were "in prison." This preaching, supposedly performed by Jesus Christ, enabled these spirits to be "judged according to the flesh, but live according to God in the spirit" (1 Pet. 3:18–20, 4:6). Now, however, in light of baptism for the dead, these passages about evangelizing the dead took on new and more appreciable meaning: Mormons could see that they outlined the theological function of proxy baptism precisely. Spirits of the dead imprisoned in the afterlife did indeed receive instruction there in the restored Mormon gospel. The efforts of living kindred proxies, meanwhile, supplied the ritual mechanism by which they could meet the formal criteria for salvation. In this way the dead were fully "judged

---

94. Appleby, Autobiography and Journal, 76.
95. Appleby, 78.
96. Ehat and Cook, *Words of Joseph Smith*, 109, 178, 213.

according to the flesh," and yet could live "according to God in the spirit."[97] For the Latter-day Saints who contemplated the subject, there was no shortage of scripture that could be applied in favor of the new doctrine.[98] Baptism for the dead soon became enmeshed in a web of scriptural support.

Mormons also found baptism for the dead in the prophetic poetry of the Old Testament, intertwined with the language of Zion. According to the scripture, ancient Obadiah had envisioned that in future day of redemption, "saviours shall come up on mount Zion to judge the mount of Esau; and the kingdom shall be the Lord's" (Obad. 1:21). As the modern children of Zion, Mormons could evidently claim this ennobling title of "saviours." And indeed that was part of the grand vision that Smith articulated, a vision that incorporated the Spirit of Elijah, the gathering of the Saints, and the building up of Zion. As part of this, Smith said, the Saints must "come up as Saviors on mount Zion." Samuel Brown explains, "For the early Latter-day Saints, a savior on Mount Zion was an individual responsible for ensuring a place for his adoptive kindred in the society of the blessed at the time of final judgment. The Saints were human extensions of Christ."[99] "But how are they to become Saviors on Mount Zion?" Smith asked rhetorically in 1844. By giving themselves fully to the work of salvation for their dead. "By building their temples[,] erecting their Baptismal fonts & going forth & receiving all the ordinances, Baptisms, Confirmations, washings[,] anointings ordinations[,] & sealing powers upon our heads in behalf of all our Progenitors who are dead."[100] Baptizing for the dead

---

97. In 1918, LDS Church President Joseph F. Smith described a vision that offered further clarification of "preaching to the dead." His account of the vision "the Lord [Jesus Christ] went not in person among the wicked and the disobedient who had rejected the truth, to teach them; But behold, from among the righteous, he organized his forces and appointed messengers, clothed with power and authority, and commissioned them to go forth and carry the light of the gospel to them that were in darkness, even to all the spirits of men; and thus was the gospel preached to the dead" (D&C 138:29–30).

98. Appleby, Autobiography and Journal 76–78.

99. Brown, "Early Mormon Adoption Theology," 47.

100. Ehat and Cook, *Words of Joseph Smith*, 318. In the months before his assassination, Smith taught that all of the saving sacraments he had introduced while in Nauvoo would need to be performed for the dead as well as baptism. Ehat and Cook, 318, 363, 368, 379. Its implementation, however, did not occur in Nauvoo while church members were preoccupied with completing the temple and performing their own ordinances. The performance of the

and then seeing the work to its finish was the only way, he said, that the Saints could become worthy of the title.[101]

To be credible, baptism for the dead not only needed scriptural sanction, it had to make sense. Smith was confident that it did when he wrote to his apostles in late 1840. "I presume the doctrine of 'baptizm for the dead' has ere this reached your ears, and may have raised some inquiries in your mind respecting the same," he wrote. He explained that he was unable to expound at length in writing but assumed that even "without enlarging on the subject you will undoubtedly see its consistency, and reasonableness." The new revelation on baptism for the dead, he explained, merely "presents the gospel of Christ in probably a more enlarged scale than some have received it."[102] Having listened to him present the doctrine in person, Phoebe Woodruff attested that "Brother Joseph makes this doctrine look verry plain and consisten[t]."[103]

Not all were sure they saw the consistency. Baptizing for the dead ran against intuition in too many ways. Were the dead, whose mortal time of proving was over, really able to benefit from this act? "It is no more incredible that God should *save* the dead, than that he should *raise* the dead," Smith answered. "There is never a time when the spirit is too old to approach God."[104] Or, as another apologist for the doctrine reasoned: "Inasmuch then as the gospel is preached to the dead, they have a capacity and agency, to believe and in some way obey it, or the contrary."[105] Others balked at Smith's precept of surrogacy— the principle that one person could legitimately represent another in religious ceremonies. But Smith countered with more deductive logic about human agency. "If we can *baptize* a man in the name of the Father of the Son & of the Holy Ghost for the remission of sins," he

---

rest of the temple ordinances for the dead, including the endowment and sealing rituals that Smith introduced in Nauvoo, began after the Saints' migration to Utah and the dedication of the St. George temple in 1877. Richard E. Bennett, "'Line upon Line, Precept upon Precept': Reflections on the 1877 Commencement of the Performance of Endowments and Sealings for the Dead," *BYU Studies* 44, no. 3 (2005): 39–77.

101. Bennett, "Line upon Line," 77.

102. Joseph Smith to the Council of the Twelve, Dec. 15, 1840, The Joseph Smith Papers, http://josephsmithpapers.org (accessed Jan. 15, 2013).

103. Phoebe Woodruff to Wilford Woodruff, Oct. 6, 1840.

104. Ehat and Cook, *Words of Joseph Smith*, 77; emphasis in original.

105. G[ustavus] H[ills], "Baptism for the Dead," *Times and Seasons*, May 1, 1841, 397.

pointed out, "it is just as much our privilege to act as an agent & *be baptized* for the remission of sins for & in behalf of our dead kindred who have not herd the gospel or fulness of it."[106] In other words, if one could represent God in administering the ordinance, one could certainly represent another person in receiving it. Smith had complete confidence in the doctrine's coherence. "I have the truth," he once said, speaking of his insight into baptism, "& I am at the defiance of the world to contradict."[107]

Many of the Latter-day Saints could see that the idea of vicarious salvation and baptism for the dead supplied crucial pieces of a long-standing theological puzzle. For one thing, it addressed the inevitable injustice that had long been a problem in Christian schemes of salvation. In 1841, Smith illustrated the dilemma by offering a metaphor about "two men, brothers, equally intelligent, learned, virtuous and lovely, walking in uprightness and in all good conscience." One, he postulated, died unenlightened and unaware of "the gospel of reconciliation," while the other embraced it and became "the heir of eternal life. Shall the one become a partaker of glory," he asked, "and the other be consigned to hopeless perdition?" Contemporary religion would say so. But in fact such an idea was "worse than atheism," Smith declared, because it betrayed God's affections for the "honest in heart."[108]

This dilemma of the unbaptized dead was also captured by *Times and Seasons* associate editor Gustavus Hills, in one of several editorials published to expound and defend baptism fore the dead in the 1840s. Hills, a former Methodist preacher, urged his readers simply to compare baptism for the dead with "the horrible views of the partial [i.e, prejudiced] bigot," who could take pleasure in the thought of eternal felicity while other innocent people suffered. He agreed with English convert Joseph Fielding, who said that he found "a wide contrast" between the vision of vicarious salvation in Mormonism and the "narrow, contracted views" of other Christians.[109] But Hills also observed that proxy baptism exposed the heresy of Universalists, those "impartial

---

106. Ehat and Cook, *Words of Joseph Smith*, 109–10; emphasis mine.
107. Ehat and Cook, 354.
108. Ehat and Cook, 78.
109. Joseph Fielding to Ebenezer Robinson, *Times and Season*, Jan. 1, 1842, 649.

liberalist[s]" who rejected the reality of damnation and presumed to crowd "the pious and the profane" into heaven together.[110] For both exclusive sectarians and inclusive liberals, Mormons thought, baptism for the dead was the key to understanding Christian justice.

Although Mormons in Nauvoo were scarcely familiar with world religions, they sensed that the news of vicarious salvation had global significance. A long and remarkably broad-minded editorial published in 1842 acknowledged the deep religious conflict that divided the world. The "Mussulman [Muslim]," "the Heathen," "the Jew," and "the Christian" all held mutually exclusive systems of belief, it noted, which they guarded jealously. God, however, was not bound by "any of these contracted feelings that influence the children of men." "He knows the situation of both the living, and the dead, and has made ample provision for their redemption, according to their several circumstances, and the laws of the kingdom of God." Mormons were confident that a review of the Bible and insight into the doctrines of vicarious salvation would show that God would deal with all nations fairly. The people of the earth would be judged in their own terms, whether they lived in "England, America, Spain, Turkey, [or] India," a promise that seemed to overcome Christian exclusivism.[111] This great, even global, equity lay at the heart of the doctrine's appeal. "Is not this a glorious doctrine?" Vilate Kimball asked her husband. "You see there is a chance for all."[112]

Because it made clear precisely how God provided a chance for all, baptism for the dead also absolved God's character, enabling Mormons to throw off any lingering fears of a stern, capricious Puritan deity. Wilford Woodruff said he experienced baptism for the dead "like a shaft of light from the throne of God to our hearts. It opened a field wide as eternity to our minds. It enlightened my mind and gave me great joy. It appeared to me that the God who revealed that principle unto man was wise, just and true, possessed both the best of

---

110. H[ills], "Baptism for the Dead," 398. Hills also addressed the question of whether the salvation that baptisms for the dead brought about would be compulsory. "It may be asked, will this baptism by proxy necessarily save the dead? We answer no: neither will the same necessarily save the living. But this, with the other requisites will save both the living [and] the dead, and God will raise them up to glorify him together."

111. "Baptism for the Dead," *Times and Seasons*, Apr. 15, 1842, 759.

112. Vilate Kimball to Heber C. Kimball, Oct. 11, 1840.

attributes and good sense and knowledge. I felt he was consistent with both love, mercy, justice and judgment, and I felt to love the Lord more than ever before in my life."[113]

Likewise, in his editorial on the same topic, Gustavus Hills expressed his feeling that baptism for the dead was "perfectly consistent with reason, honorable to the divine character, and in accordance with the desires and wishes of every truly pious and benevolent mind."[114] Joseph Fielding reflected that "every step I take in surveying the plan of heaven and the wisdom and goodness of God, my heart feels glad. But when I have listened to the teachings of the servants of God under the new covenant and the principle of Baptism for the Dead[,] the feelings of my soul were such as I cannot describe."[115] These feelings, the perception that baptism for the dead ennobled God and revealed his essential benevolence, aligned with Smith's own experience. Having passed through his own crucibles and bereavements, Smith agreed that "this doctrine appears glorious, inasmuch as it exhibits the greatness of divine compassion and benevolence in the extent of the plan of human salvation."[116]

"THIS ORDINANCE BELONGETH TO MY HOUSE"

The commandment from God to build a temple in Nauvoo came in an omnibus revelation in January 1841, confirming plans that were already underway. As the revelation to Smith, given in the voice of God, explained, a temple was needed in Nauvoo for the same reasons that the church had needed one in Kirtland—to facilitate the restoration of additional knowledge, power, and ordinances, "even the fulness of the priesthood." But a temple in Nauvoo was also needed for an additional reason, one without precedent. The revelation specified that it must also be built because "a baptismal font there is not upon the earth; that they, my saints, may be baptized for those who are dead." Because of their poverty, the revelation said, Mormons in Nauvoo had been permitted to baptize for their dead in the river, but that was changing. After a "sufficient" period of time, river baptisms for the dead would

---

113. Wilford Woodruff, "Remarks," *Deseret News*, May 27, 1857, 91.

114. H[ills], "Baptism for the Dead," 399.

115. Fielding to Robinson, Jan. 1, 1842, 649.

116. Ehat and Cook, *Words of Joseph Smith*, 77–78.

no longer be recognized because, as the revelation explained, "this ordinance belongeth to my house." After that, only baptisms performed in a temple could be legitimate. If the Saints did not comply with the requirements, they would be "rejected as a Church with your dead."

The revelation made clear that the new ritual of proxy baptism, like other rituals that had previously been practiced in Ohio, was intended for sacred space. Indeed, as the revelation indicated, *all* that was sacred in Mormonism emanated from the temple. All of the revelations and teachings—everything necessary to establish Zion—was rooted there. And the temple was especially a house of rituals and ordinances. Washings, anointings, baptisms for the dead, and other rituals still to be revealed were all centered there—"ordained by the ordinance of my holy house, which my people are always commanded to build unto my holy name."[117] It was only natural that baptism for the dead should become a function of the temple since the temple was the seat of all of Mormonism's sacred enterprises.[118]

Temple construction began immediately, and once the excavation and foundational work were complete, and the cornerstones had been laid with great ceremony, a baptismal font was the first priority. A highly peculiar undertaking, the font was situated mostly below ground level, near the east end of the temple's cellar. The design for the structure, approved by Smith, was drawn by the young architect William Weeks, whose superb sketches had also been selected as the plans for the temple itself. The font was to be made of hand-carved wood, and over the course of the next two months, Weeks, woodworkers Elijah Fordham and John Carling, and others worked to execute the design. Weeks helped with the initial proportioning, then turned the effort over to Fordham and others for detail work. Construction of the structure lasted about two months, and then the woodcarvers continued to work on the baptistry's ornamentation.[119]

---

117. Jensen, Turley, and Lorimer, *Revelations and Translations, Volume 2*, 654–73 (D&C 124).

118. Despite the shift of two forms of baptism—baptism for the dead and baptism for health—to the temple, convert baptism and rebaptism were not absorbed into temple worship. On rebaptism in the Nauvoo era, see D. Michael Quinn, "The Practice of Rebaptism at Nauvoo," *BYU Studies* 18, no. 2 (1978): 226–32.

119. Smith's clerks, including William Clayton, kept a thorough record of the temple's construction in "History of the Nauvoo Temple," MS 3365, CHL. For modern histories, see

As the font took shape in the fall of 1841, the grace period that had been granted to the Saints in the temple revelation suddenly ended. During the October conference, after a sermon full of instruction on baptism for the dead and affirmations of its importance, Smith unexpectedly announced that baptisms for the dead would be suspended until the temple was complete, saying emphatically that it was the will of the Lord.[120] Some Saints were initially disappointed at what seemed to be a major delay. Helen Soby wrote to her father that she had intended to be baptized for his mother, "but the word of the Lord is unto us this day that we cannot be Baptized any more in the Mississippi River for our Dead." As she understood it, the temple wouldn't be done in less than a year; but when it was, "then we will be baptized in that."[121] Fortunately for the Saints, however, it soon became clear that baptisms for the dead could go forward before the rest of the temple was completed. Although the font simply sat in the unfinished temple's cellar, and the temple walls stood but a few feet tall, the arrangement evidently satisfied the commandment for the ritual to become part of the Lord's house.

The new font was dedicated November 8. Workmen dug a well in the opposite end of the temple cellar from which they drew water for the font, and Smith invited Reuben McBride, a young Latter-day Saint visiting Nauvoo, to act as the first proxy before he returned home to Ohio. During the evening ceremony, Smith conducted the dedication and Brigham Young entered the font and performed the baptisms.[122] Also present at the event was Samuel Rolfe, president of the quorum of priests in Nauvoo. Rolfe had a badly infected finger, and a doctor

Leonard, *Nauvoo*, 233–65; Don F. Colvin, *Nauvoo Temple: A Story of Faith* (Provo, Utah: BYU Religious Studies Center, 2002); and Matthew S. McBride, *A House for the Most High: The Story of the Original Nauvoo Temple* (Salt Lake City: Greg Kofford Books, 2002). J. Earl Arrington, "William Weeks: Architect of the Nauvoo Temple," *BYU Studies* 19, no. 3 (1979): 337–60.

120. "There shall be no more baptisms for the dead, until the ordinance can be attended to in the font of the Lord's House; and the church shall not hold another general conference, until they can meet in said house. *For thus saith the Lord!*" Ehat and Cook, *Words of Joseph Smith*, 79; emphasis original.

121. Helen S. Soby to her father, Oct. 3, 1841, MS 9159, CHL.

122. Alexander L. Baugh, "'Blessed Is the First Man Baptised in This Font': Reuben McBride, First Proxy to Be Baptized for the Dead in the Nauvoo Temple," *Mormon Historical Studies* 3, no. 2 (Fall 2002): 253–61.

had advised him that it need an operation. At the dedication, however, Smith directed Rolfe to step forward instead and wash himself in the font, promising him it would be healed. Rolfe did so, dipping in his hands, and, William Clayton recorded, "In one week afterwards his hand was perfectly healed. After this time," Clayton continued, "baptisms was continued in the font, and many realized great blessings, both spiritually and physically."[123]

With the font in operation, the experience of proxy baptism changed significantly. The new arrangements intensified focus on the rising temple. Rather than stepping into the silt of the Mississippi, proxies gathered to what was simultaneously a sacred edifice and a construction site. They descended into the cellar, a place "underneath where the living are wont to assemble" and symbolic of death.[124] Then they mounted the stairs, grasping a wooden handrail, and lowered themselves into the consecrated vessel. Sabbath-day crowds still gathered to watch and to participate, particularly while the baptistry level was still exposed. Proxy baptism in the river did not end completely, but communal baptisms, with many ordinances going on concurrently, fell off.[125]

The font itself heightened the experience. Weeks's design was redolent with the symbolism of ancient Israel and well suited to Smith's vision of a modern Zion. Taking a page straight from 1 Kings, the font featured twelve broad-shouldered oxen, standing two and four abreast

---

123. Clayton, History of the Nauvoo Temple, 21. See also Clayton's entry in Smith's personal record: Jessee, Ashurst-McGee, and Jensen, *Journals, Volume 1*, 73. Baptism and the temple font were widely associated with healing until well into the twentieth century. Jonathan A. Stapley and Kristine L. Wright, "'They Shall Be Made Whole': A History of Baptism for Health," *Journal of Mormon History* 34, no. 4 (Fall 2008): 69–112.

124. Andrew H. Hedges, Alex D. Smith, and Richard Lloyd Anderson, eds., *The Joseph Smith Papers: Journals, Volume 2: December 1841–April 1843* (Salt Lake City: Church Historian's Press, 2011), 147 (D&C 128:13).

125. Although the font became established as the designated site, baptisms for the dead in the Mississippi River continued until at least 1843, and likely for as long as the Saints were in Nauvoo. Records indicate that the river was used when the font was closed for maintenance and in other cases. See "Minutes of Elders' Conference in Nauvoo," *Times and Seasons*, Apr. 1, 1843, 158; Wilford Woodruff, *Wilford Woodruff's Journal, 1833–1898*, typescript, ed. Scott G. Kenney, 9 vols. (Salt Lake City: Signature Books, 1983–85), 2:455; Charlotte Haven, "A Girl's Letters from Nauvoo," *Overland Monthly*, Dec. 1890, 629–30; "Nauvoo— We Spent a Sabbath with the Mormons," *New York Spectator*, Aug. 23, 1843, 4.

in the cardinal directions. They bore on their backs a deep, oval basin like the scripture's "molten sea."[126] The twelve oxen, "copied after the most beautiful five year old steer that could be found in the country," represented each of the tribes of Israel; their orientation reflected the all-encompassing scope of the redemptive work.[127] For a place and people unused to such ornamentation, the whole structure, seven feet high, stood as if transported from Solomon's temple. If Smith wanted to dignify the ritual and reinforce to the Saints their identity as the modern Israel, the new font suited his purpose.

The peculiar font quickly became a visitors' attraction. After visiting Nauvoo in 1844, one correspondent acknowledged that the font intrigued him, suggesting that once the oxen and laver were gilded, as was intended, "this unique apparatus of the Church ... will be one of the most striking artificial curiosities in this country." The craftsmanship of the twelve oxen in particular revealed "a degree of ingenuity, skill, and perseverance that would redound to the reputation of an artist in any community." The baptistry as a whole was evocative, summoning images of Mormon priests in long robes, leading "a solemn procession of worshippers through the somber avenues of the basement story, chanting as they go."[128] Another visitor praised the temple's unfinished exterior and siting but criticized the design of the baptistry as tawdry and bizarre. It was one of the most "absurd and out-of-place contrivances, that human folly could have devised for man or mockery," he insisted. "Neither tasteful in design, nor in keeping," it was adorned with flimsy and ostentatious woodwork finishings—in all "a most perfect piece of ginger-bread workmanship and wasteful gimcrack."[129]

As the font and the temple attracted attention, the idea of baptism for the dead continued to settle in Mormons' minds. The Latter-day Saints were building not only a temple, but a vision of its meaning, and some of

---

126. The basin, sixteen feet long by twelve feet wide, was, as one visitor explained, "large enough for two priests to officiate at the rite of baptism, for which it is intended, at once." By 1843, a water pump had been devised to fill it. "The Prairies, Nauvoo, Joe Smith, the Temple, the Mormons, &c," *New York Weekly Express*, Sep. 29, 1843, 5.

127. Historian's Office, History of the Church, 1839–[ca. 1882], Addenda to Book C-1, 44, CR 100 102, CHL.

128. "The Mormon City," *New York Spectator*, Nov. 9, 1844, 2.

129. "Nauvoo and Joe Smith," *Hampshire Gazette* (Northampton, MA), Aug. 22, 1843, 1.

them attempted to do so through poetry. The hymnist Joel H. Johnson's piece "Baptism for the Dead," was printed in the *Times and Seasons* in October 1841. Its terse lines urged the Saints to recognize how their rite of proxy baptism gave them common cause with Jesus Christ:

> Now, O! ye saints, rejoice to day
> The Lord has to his saints revealed,
> That you can saviors be,
> As anciently he did.
> For all your dead, who will obey
> The gospel and be free.[130]

In 1842, Eliza R. Snow helped to copy revelations on baptism for the dead, and a month or two later she wrote "Apostrophe to Death." "What art thou, Death?" the poem demanded, rehearsing the universal terrors of mortality. The speaker claimed, however, to find a new change in Death's fearsome countenance:

> But thou art chang'd—the terror of thy looks—
> The darkness that encompass'd thee, is gone;
> There is no frightfulness about thee now. [...]
> Seen as thou art, by inspiration's light,
> Thou hast no look the righteous need to fear,
> With all thy ghastliness—amid the grief
> Thy presence brings. [...]
> Art thou a tyrant, holding the black reins
> Of destiny that bind the course
> Of man's existence? No: thou art, O Death!
> A haggard porter charg'd to wait before
> The Grave, life's portal to the worlds on high.[131]

---

130. J[oel] H. Johnson, "Baptism for the Dead," *Times and Seasons*, Oct. 1, 1841, 564. Johnson is best known for his later hymn, "High on a Mountain Top," composed in 1853.

131. Jill Mulvay Derr and Karen Lynn Davidson, eds., *Eliza R. Snow: The Complete Poetry* (Provo, Utah: Brigham Young University Press/Salt Lake City: University of Utah Press, 2009), 223. For more Nauvoo poetry related to baptism for the dead, see also W. W. Phelps, "The Temple of God at Nauvoo," *Times and Seasons*, June 15, 1842, 830; and Wilson Law, *Times and Seasons*, Jan. 15, 1844, 412–13. A poem attributed to Joseph Smith, a versified rendition of "The Vision" of 1832, also touched on the subject, "The Vision," *Times and Seasons*, Feb. 1, 1843, 84. Though attributed to Smith, scholars consider Phelps as the probable author. Michael Hicks, "Joseph Smith, W. W. Phelps, and the Poetic Paraphrase of 'The Vision,'" *Journal of Mormon History* 20, no. 2 (Fall 1994): 70.

The new revelations and the doctrine of baptism for the dead diminished Death, leaving it merely a shadow of its former self. Among those who fully understand God's designs for his people, death remained ghastly, but need not induce fear.

The relocation of proxy baptism to the temple also brought changes to the dynamics surrounding the practice. The ritual came more fully under church control and became part of the larger temple project. Smith had explained that, in building the temple, the Saints would be expected to tithe toward the project, giving materials and also laboring one day in ten. Not all contributed equally, however, and the apostles, with newly expanded authority in Nauvoo, broached the problem to the Saints in a circular to the church in December 1841. Acknowledging that baptism for the dead was "one of privileges which is particularly attracting the notice of the Saints at the present moment," the letter raised the question of the "propriety of baptizing those who have not been obedient, and assisted to build the place for baptism." The apostles went on to express their conclusion that it would be "unreasonable" to administer the ordinance to those who had not contributed to the temple. If the Saints failed to build the temple and the church was rejected "with her dead," the letter insisted, then all baptisms would be pointless anyway.[132] Those who wished to have the privilege of proxy baptism and to redeem their dead kindred, in other words, would have to contribute their fair share.

As a way of tracking contributions and regulating privileges, church authorities eventually began issuing certificates granting access to the font. This was a new variation of the practice of issuing documentation, as church leaders routinely did, to church members who were baptized, ordained, called to preach or deed property, or in other circumstances. The font certificates, small handwritten slips of paper, endorsed with a signature, indicated that bearer was "entitled to the privilege of the

---

132. Brigham Young et al., "Baptism for the Dead," *Times and Seasons*, Dec. 15, 1841, 625–27. In 1844, John Taylor preached that "a man who has not paid his tithing is unfit to be baptized for his dead." "Minutes of October Conference," *Times and Seasons*, Oct. 15, 1844, 685. Critic Reverend Daniel P. Kidder responded to the circular, accusing church leaders of using the baptismal font coercively. Kidder, *Mormonism and the Mormons: A Historical View of the Rise and Progress of the Sect Self-Styled Latter-Day Saints* (New York: Lane & Sanford, 1842), 249–51.

Baptismal Font, having paid his labor & property tithing in full."[133]
Hence, the font and its promised blessings became an incentive for
the Saints to heed the revelations and the instruction of church leaders
by gathering in Nauvoo. They were told to bring their materials and a
commitment to build the temple with them.

A "VERY PARTICULAR" ORDER

The transformation of baptism for the dead into a temple ordinance
was only the most prominent of many adjustments to the ritual during
the 1840s. When Jane Neyman became Joseph Smith's illustration in
teaching the doctrine and then one of the first to undertake the ordinance in September 1840, the practice had few protocols and little
oversight. In a deposition made to the Church Historian's office many
years later, Neyman recounted merely finding an ordained elder, Harvey Olmstead, to go with her to the river and perform the ordinance.
Hearing of it later, Smith asked how the ritual had been conducted,
then simply affirmed that "father Olmstead had it right." Vienna
Jacques, who also contributed to the deposition, remembered that
when Neyman was baptized, she (Vienna) rode her horse into the river,
and listened "to hear what the ceremony would be."[134]

In the ensuing years, the administration of proxy baptisms tightened
up dramatically. What began as a ritual available as desired to individual families quickly became a religious imperative carefully regulated
by the church. Within a few months of first being taught, even, the
ordinance was already becoming regimented as church leaders sought
to manage the saving work that the Saints were eager to do. Smith's
instructions on the practice in the October 1840 conference included

---

133. Font Certificate (Benjamin Brown, 1845), Benjamin Brown Family Collection,
1819–2002, MS 17647, CHL. One could say that the Nauvoo font certificates constitute
the origins of the modern LDS temple recommend. A number of such certificates survive
in archival holdings, dating from as early as March 1842. Initially these credentials were issued by scribes under Joseph Smith's imprimatur. See, for example, Font Certificate (Anson
Mathews, 1842), Sturdevant and Mathews Family Collection, 1807–53, MS 10304, CHL.
Later, the certificates bore only the signature of the temple recorder. See Font Certificate
(Shadrach Roundy, 1846), Shadrach Roundy Papers, 1840–57, MS 16912, CHL. For additional examples, see Leonard, *Nauvoo*, 256n93. I have not found any font certificates
issued to women.

134. Jane Neyman and Vienna Jacques, Statement, Nov. 29, 1854, CHL.

a set of parameters intended to guide the Latter-day Saints in their practice of the ritual. Conference attendees came away understanding that baptism for the dead was associated with "a particular order" that should be observed.[135]

Part of this initial order was the directive that the Saints were only to baptize for their dead relatives. So long as the proxy had "been personally acquainted" with the person for whom they wished to be baptized, the work could extend back to four generations—as far as grandparents and great-grandparents. Doing proxy baptisms for family was a privilege that rested with the heads of households and first-born children, but they could delegate if they chose. In line with the revelation that salvation was still available to those who had died without hearing and accepting the restored gospel but "who would have received it, if they had been permitted to tarry," the Saints were also taught that they should perform baptism for their kindred only if they believed that the person would have the disposition to accept the ordinance.[136] And although they could be baptized for family members, the Saints were generally not to be baptized for acquaintances. If an acquaintance wished for his or her baptism to be performed, he or she would send a messenger from the world of spirits to make it known. In any case, baptism should not be performed for murderers, for, as one Mormon paraphrased Smith's teaching, "the Lord had other ways of dealing with murderers."[137] The Saints were also cautioned to be careful that confirmation was performed for each of the baptismal ordinances. So that this order could be ensured, the Saints should not perform the ordinance away from Nauvoo.[138]

As the Saints caught the full vision of vicarious salvation over the next several years, however, some of these original stipulations broke down. The regulation limiting the Saints to four generations of their family gave way to a much more expansive view, in which the work reached "clear back to the apostles day," and even to the beginning of

---

135. Vilate Kimball to Heber C. Kimball, Oct. 11, 1840; Phoebe Woodruff to Wilford Woodruff, Oct. 6, 1840.

136. Jessee, Ashurst-McGee, and Jensen, *Journals, Volume 1,* 168.

137. Foote, Journal, Oct. 3, 1841, 57.

138. Foote; Phoebe Woodruff to Wilford Woodruff, Oct. 6, 1840.

time.[139] In addition, the general prohibition on baptizing for non-kin-
dred loved ones loosened up considerably. As early as 1841, hundreds
of Latter-day Saints were baptized for non-relatives they identified as
"friends," and celebrity baptisms of the kind that piqued popular interest were not uncommon. By 1844, Smith was teaching that "any man
that has a friend in eternity can save him," and that "we may be baptized for those we have much friendship for," though he still cautioned
the Saints to wait on special authorization to officiate for non-kin-
dred, "lest we should run too far."[140] Although the practice had been
confined to Nauvoo, it quickly spread to surrounding settlements, to
Kirtland, and possibly further.[141]

While restrictions changed on who was eligible to receive proxy
baptism, there was always a great deal of latitude in who could provide
it. In Kirtland and later in Nauvoo, Smith introduced "higher" temple-related rituals selectively among church members, but baptism for
the dead was always a democratic ordinance, accessible to all. It made
no distinctions based on class or standing; hence, the impoverished
Joseph and Martha Hovey had as much right to participate in the ordinance as anyone. Some of the most active proxies during the Nauvoo
period, such as a man named Nehemiah Brush, were Latter-day Saints
who are otherwise obscure.[142] Access to the ritual extended equally to
men and women. And, like ordination to the priesthood during the
period, baptism for the dead also extended to black church members.
Elijah Abel and Joseph T. Ball, African American converts, both were
baptized for the dead in 1840 and 1841.[143] Anyone with a human body
had something to offer those who did not.

Apart from being incorporated into the temple, the most profound
changes to proxy baptism came following new insights from Smith
in September 1842. Trying to avoid extradition to Missouri, Smith
had spent much of the summer in hiding, where he was lonely and

---

139. Sally Randall to family, Apr. 21, 1844.

140. Ehat and Cook, *Words of Joseph Smith*, 346, 368. The term "friend" could also
refer to family members in nineteenth-century parlance.

141. Baugh, "This Ordinance Belongeth to My House," 47–58.

142. Bishop, "What Has Become of Our Fathers?," 90.

143. On Elijah Abel as proxy, see Black and Black, *Annotated Records of Baptisms for the
Dead*, 9–10. For Joseph T. Ball, see Black and Black, 214–15.

had ample time for reflection. Anxious and melancholy because of the attempts to arrest and imprison him once again, his mind turned gratefully to the kindnesses of his friends and family, many of whom, like his father, had died. He found solace in having their names and deeds inscribed in his journal, "The Book of the Law of the Lord." "There are many souls, whom I have loved stronger than death," he wrote. Among them was his brother Alvin, whose virtues he recounted. "Shall his name not be recorded in this Book? Yes, Alvin; let it be had here, and be handed down upon these sacred pages forever and ever."[144] Writing the names and kindnesses of the righteous seemed to keep their worthy deeds from fading away.

Such thoughts evidently turned Smith's mind again to baptism for the dead. In exile it was that subject, he said, that "seems to occupy my mind, and press itself upon my feelings the strongest." His reflections brought new insights to the practice, and in two letters written from his places of concealment in early September, he related these new insights, "certifying" them as God's revelations to the Saints.[145] In effect, Smith's letters extended and formalized the work he had been doing in his journal, bestowing deep new theological significance upon records and record-keeping. Although Mormons had been self-conscious chroniclers from the beginning, and had endeavored to record their work in behalf of the dead, the revelations from Smith made it clear that their efforts were inadequate. Records they had kept of the baptismal work were incomplete and irregular, and when it came to the ordinances of salvation, casual documentation was not enough. "These are principles in relation to the dead and the living that cannot be lightly passed over," Smith wrote. Rather, they demanded painstaking precision.

To fix the problem, the revelation-letters laid out an elaborate method for how records of proxy baptism were to be produced and

---

144. Hedges, Smith, and Anderson, *Journals, Volume 2,* 117.

145. Smith's letters regarding the baptism for the dead, written in September 1842, were subsequently copied into his personal journal by Eliza R. Snow, who was then living in the Smith household and acting as a scribe. Jessee, Ashurst-McGee, and Jensen, *Journals, Volume 1,* 131–33, 143–50 (D&C 127, 128). Several months later, Snow penned the poem "Apostrophe to Death," which was evidently prompted by the experience (see above). The letters were subsequently published in the *Times and Seasons* in October 1842, then canonized in the 1844 edition of the Doctrine and Covenants.

maintained—a system that would involve an extensive network of witnesses, notaries, and clerks. Smith called for the appointment of a church general recorder, someone who would be formally responsible to keep track of the Saints' baptismal work. But to help deal with the logistical challenge such an assignment would present to a single individual, he also suggested that other recorders could be enlisted to help in the process. These should be attentive and meticulous clerks, in each of Nauvoo's wards, who would be present at the event and "very particular and precise in making his Record and taking the whole proceeding, certifying in his Record that he saw with his eyes, and heard with his ears; giving the date, and names &c. and the history of the whole transaction." The recorder should also specify several witnesses who could, if needed, attest to what they had seen.[146] When collected by the general recorder, these accounts—witnessed, certified, and notarized—could be incorporated into the church's institutional records. They would constitute a true and faithful record. Such a record would be worthy to be "put in the archives of my holy Temple, to be held in remembrance from generation to generation."

Smith recognized that the extensiveness of the system might be puzzling. "You may think this order of things to be very particular," he wrote, "but let me tell you that it is only to answer the will of God." The careful management and documentation of the ritual process only "conform[ed] to the ordinance and preparation that the Lord ordained … before the foundation of the world." It was this plan, with all of its particularities, which God had developed to redeem those who would die without access to his gospel. The great care embedded in the system was a reflection of God's love and divine design.[147]

As they stressed the need for documentation, the revelations also

---

146. Smith also gave instructions about the need for a recorder in a Relief Society meeting on August 31, 1842, the day before writing the first letter to the Saints. Ehat and Cook, *Words of Joseph Smith*, 131.

147. After the second letter (September 7, 1842) was copied into Smith's journal, Clayton added a note stating, "The important instructions contained in the foregoing letter made a deep and solemn impression on the minds of the saints, and they manifested their intentions to obey the instruction to the letter." Church members indeed responded to the letter by creating a system of record-keeping that captured crucial dates, names, and other information. Hedges, Smith, and Anderson, *Journals, Volume 2*, 150–51n507.

showed that records did far more than keep order or even to help insure that the ordinances were not forgotten. The act of recording, they
taught, was an essential part of the ritual itself. Indeed, to "bind" or
"seal," wrote Joseph, also meant to "record." Sealing and recording in
other words, were actually synonymous, one and the same. To perform baptism authoritatively was one dimension of the ordinance;
to inscribe and record that act was another. The ordinance could not
truly be accomplished without a proper account. Hence the Saints'
dilemma: without a record of their rituals to anchor them in reality,
they did not exist.

Smith's revelations also taught that the records the Saints kept could
do still more than embody the saving rituals—ultimately they would
become instruments of judgment. Smith reminded readers of the Book
of Life discussed in St. John's Revelation. In the day of final judgment
this book, containing all the deeds of humankind, would be opened
and the dead would be "judg'd out of those things which were written
in the books, according to their works."[148] What was needed, Smith
wrote, was such a book, a ledger that chronicled the deeds of humankind and could serve as a second testament, when the time came, that
each person had received baptism, whether in the flesh or vicariously.
Multiple records, one kept by the Saints on the earth and one kept by
angels in heaven, would triangulate the truth and corroborate God's
judgment. This was, in one sense, what it meant for the priesthood to
bind on earth and in heaven.[149]

---

148. Hedges, Smith, and Anderson, 146. See also Rev. 21:12.

149. On the meanings of records, see also Leonard, *Nauvoo*, 238–39. Changes to the
administrative order of proxy baptism continued in Nauvoo after Smith's death. Baptisms
for the dead were suspended from his murder until August 24, 1844. Historian's Office, History of the Church, Aug. 9, 1844–June 30, 1845, 18–19. During the winter of 1844–45, at
Brigham Young's direction, cross-gender baptisms were discontinued. Young saw the baptism
of women for men as incongruous, since proxies for male persons were now being ordained vicariously to the priesthood. He was concerned that cross-gender baptisms might lead women
to seek ordination as well. "Speech Delivered by President B. Young ... April 6, 1845," *Times
and Seasons*, July 1, 1845, 956. (Young's history is interrupted in its serialized form by Wilford Woodruff's, before returning to Young's.) Moreover, cross-gender baptisms that had been
performed previously were required to be done over again. "Speech Delivered by President
Wilford Woodruff ... April 6, 1891," *Deseret Weekly*, Apr. 25, 1891, 554. Young also oversaw
the removal of the wooden font from the temple and the construction of a more sanitary stone
replacement, also designed by William Weeks. To those inquiring about the change, Young

Although Neyman heard Smith say in 1840 that "I have laid the subject of baptism for the dead before you. You may receive or reject it as you choose," over time it became clear that the offering was not optional.[150] It was a privilege to save the dead, but it was also a necessity and a commandment. The 1842 revelation letters showed it to be an imperative; they adopted the teaching of Paul, asserting that the dead, righteous predecessors of the past could not "be made perfect" without the faithful Saints of the present. But Smith also added the clause "neither can *we without our dead* be made perfect."[151] This injunction suggested that the generations—the fathers and the children—were mutually dependent on each other to attain salvation. In 1844 Smith underscored the point with a superlative, teaching the Saints that "the greatest responsibility in this world is to seek after our dead."[152]

Responsibility stemmed from the fact that through the ordinance of baptism for the dead, "welding links" had to be forged between the generations, each one connecting to the one past. Together these links would form a perpetual chain stretching back through all of human history. Once it was completed, it would lift the entire human race to salvation. This was the phenomenon foretold by Malachi, the way that the affections and interests of the children and the fathers would be "turned" to each other. To fail would be to suffer Malachi's curse—the damnation of all the earth's people. It was, increasingly, a vast enterprise that would involve the entire community of believers. Each baptism would forge a link, one by one. Smith thought it would take "at least a thousand years."[153]

---

explained: "We will have a fount that will not stink and keep us all the while cleansing it out: and we will have a pool wherein to baptise the sick, that they may recover. And when we get into the fount we will show you the priesthood and the power of it." "Speech Delivered by President B. Young ... April 6, 1845," *Times and Seasons*, July 1, 1845, 986.

150. Neyman and Jacques, Statement, Nov. 29, 1854.

151. Hedges, Smith, and Anderson, *Journals, Volume 2*, 148 (D&C 128:15); emphasis mine. See also Heb. 11:40; Ehat and Cook, *Words of Joseph Smith*, 329, 333, 346.

152. Ehat and Cook, *Words of Joseph Smith*, 369; also 353, 346.

153. Apostle George A. Smith recounted that, in Nauvoo, "it soon became apparent that some had long records of their dead, for whom they wished to administer. This was seen to be but the beginning of an immense work, and that to administer all the ordinances of the Gospel to the hosts of the dead was no light task. The Twelve asked Joseph if there could not be a shorter method of administering for so many. Joseph in effect replied—'The laws of the Lord are immutable, we must act in perfect compliance with what is revealed to us. We need not expect to

CONCLUSION

By the spring of 1844, nearly four years after the funeral of Seymour Brunson, Nauvoo had become a thriving city. Swollen by a steady stream of converts, it challenged Chicago as the largest city in Illinois. The temple was still not finished, but Nauvoo had many fine homes and public buildings, as well as a flourishing civic culture.[154] The women's Relief Society, the arrival of international converts, polygamy, and other developments had given Mormonism a markedly different character. Simultaneously, baptism for the dead, initiatory rituals, the new endowment, and marital sealings had transformed Mormonism into a fully sacramental faith. In the Mormons' final years in Nauvoo, they were beginning to look to these ritual ordinances as the rubric of their lives.

Improvements had made the city more salubrious, too. The rate of death that characterized the place earlier had slowed, and sickness—though still prevalent—was much abated. Still, Smith continued to speak at funerals, and funerals still found him at his most profound. On April 7, 1844, he spoke to ten thousand Latter-day Saints shortly after the death of King Follett, a church member killed while digging a well. Smith's sermon, widely known as the "King Follett Discourse" and given less than three months before Smith's assassination, is often seen as the apex of Smith's prophetic teaching and the culmination of his rich Nauvoo theology. In it Smith publicly taught his divine anthropology, the "plurality of Gods," and the coeternity of humanity with God.[155]

While these themes emerged, however, death—the condition of the dead, the resurrection of the dead, the baptism for the dead, and triumph over death—continued at the core of Smith's orations. It was chiefly for the consolation of mourners that he taught these new ideas, he explained.[156] In the final years before his assassination, he returned to the subject of baptism for the dead frequently, reiterating again and

---

do this vast work in a short time. I expect it will take at least a thousand years.'" Quoted in James G. Bleak, "Christmas Assembly in St. George," *Deseret News*, Jan. 13, 1875, 799.

154. On Nauvoo's civic culture, see Leonard, *Nauvoo*, 173–99.

155. For the King Follett Discourse, see Ehat and Cook, *Words of Joseph Smith*, 340–62; or Stan Larson, "The King Follett Discourse: A Newly Amalgamated Text," *BYU Studies* 18, no. 2 (1978): 193–208.

156. Ehat and Cook, *Words of Joseph Smith*, 344; see also 357, 458.

again how proxy ordinances removed the pain of mortality. The bonds of sealing they created were so strong that they rendered death as inconsequential as the passing of a single night. Human death was only, Smith said, like affectionate friends who, absorbed in the warmth of their conversation, did not separate in the evening, but lay down together to sleep, "locked in each others embrace." When they awakened, they could immediately "renew their conversation of love," and "readily salute each other," uninhibited even by the separation of walls or space. Death would come and go, but sacred relations would endure unaffected. Parties to these relationships would continue in them, "never suffering loneliness," a fact that Smith himself found comforting.[157]

Ultimately, it was this prospect of eternal family unity and perpetual friendship that appealed most deeply to contemporary Mormons, more than the soaring theology about the nature of God. Because their lives were difficult and death was fearsome, Latter-day Saints hailed proxy baptism and Nauvoo's doctrines for the dead as a form of deliverance, both for their families and themselves. Mormons flourished under the knowledge that they were not helpless before the ravages of mortality. As agents for the race, they could take an active part in achieving God's grand designs.

For Mormons in Nauvoo, it was as one old and ailing Mormon had said, scratching out his thoughts at the close of October 1840, the month when baptisms of the dead began: "We have had much sickness this month. It has been a scene of sorrow that I do not wish to pass through again. Such scenes of poverty & distress, I hope not to pass often. Human life and misery go hand in hand through life's uneven path. But there is a hope [that] inspires the breath with joy & lights the dreary path & render[s] life pleasant as we pass to worlds unknown. ... Thank the Lord for the Great things Revealed to the children of men, even glory honor immortality and eternal life[—]the hope of which cheers our Spirits in midst of the greatest trials. And thus we pass along."[158]

---

157. Ehat and Cook, 198. Smith acknowledged that he would rather experience a "cessation of being" than perpetual separation from friends and family. Ehat and Cook, 240. See also Bushman, *Joseph Smith: Rough Stone Rolling*, 473.

158. John Smith, Journal, Oct. 30, 1840, MS 13265, CHL; terminal punctuation and initial capitals added.

FOUR

"THE UPPER ROOM"
THE NATURE AND DEVELOPMENT OF
LATTER-DAY SAINT TEMPLE WORK, 1846–55

RICHARD E. BENNETT

Several years ago, Gordon B. Hinckley, president of the Church of Jesus Christ of Latter-day Saints, uttered the following words:

> Today facing west, on the high bluff overlooking the city of Nauvoo, thence across the Mississippi, and over the plains of Iowa, there stands Joseph's temple, a magnificent house of God. Here in the Salt Lake Valley, facing east to that beautiful temple in Nauvoo stands Brigham's temple, the Salt Lake Temple. They look toward one another as bookends between which there are volumes that speak of the suffering, the sorrow, the sacrifice, even the deaths of thousands who made the long journey from the Mississippi River to the valley of the Great Salt Lake.[1]

The purpose of this essay is to discuss the nature, survival, and development of LDS temple work in the western wilderness from 1846 to 1855, between the one "bookend" of their abandoned Nauvoo temple and the other "bookend" of LDS temple work as it had developed in the Salt Lake Valley as of May 1855.

While "volumes" have indeed been written about the exodus of the Latter-day Saints to the valleys of the Rocky Mountains beginning in 1847 and of emigration, colonization, economics, frontier violence, and plural marriage, far less attention has been devoted to the topic of temple worship itself. Ironically, that which explains so much of what it meant to be a Latter-day Saint, and what it now means to a religion that places so high a premium on temples and temple-building throughout

---

1. Gordon B. Hinckley, "O That I Were an Angel and Could Have the Wish of My Heart," *Ensign*, Nov. 2002, 6.

the world, has not been discussed, at least not in a public or profane way. As new sources continually come to light, this period of time—1846–55—is no longer a vacant room in Mormon history. Though very much still in its infancy during that decade, temple practice and worship transcended place and personality and played an integral role in building and deepening the faith and devotion of a despised and suffering people in their errand into the American wilderness.

Without trespassing upon the sacred precincts of temple ordinances themselves, I will examine three major temple-related practices that were begun in Nauvoo and continued in one degree or another during the following decade: baptisms for the dead; endowments for the living; and sealings in all their various expressions, for both the living and the dead, including spiritual adoptions. What I hope to show is the continuity, vitality, creative adaptability, and robust flexibility that contributed to maintaining a lively temple consciousness among the Latter-day Saints during a time when, as a people, they were preoccupied with wresting a living from their new and oft-times harsh and unforgiving Great Basin Kingdom. If temple work along the Mormon trail and in the early years of settlement in the Salt Lake Valley lacked the urgency of Nauvoo when over 5,600 people crowded into the yet-to-be-completed temple for their endowments and other blessings, nevertheless, the Latter-day Saints eagerly sought temple-related ordinances in the wilderness, particularly for the living. These ordinances inspired the Saints to prepare for and endure the rigors of the exodus. Brigham Young and other church leaders could hardly resist providing these blessings, with or without a formal temple structure. While the edifice of the temple itself was by far the preferred sanctuary for performing saving ordinances for the dead, the urgency and demand for temple ordinances for the living transcended sacred space and were performed quietly by invitation and on demand from Kanesville in the east to Springville in the west.

The topic of temple work has been a contentious and divisive subject for many years. The performance of baptisms for the dead died a rather slow and uncertain death among the early ranks of the Reorganized Church of Jesus Christ of Latter Day Saints (after 2001, the Community of Christ). While at first recognized, by 1865 the

RLDS Church was fast retreating from it. Said Apostle William Marks in 1865, "When Joseph [Smith] stopped the baptism for the dead he stated that he did not believe it would be practiced any more until there was a fountain built in Zion or Jerusalem. Resolved [by the council] that it is proper to teach the doctrine of baptism for the dead, when it is necessary to do so in order to show the completeness of the plan of salvation, but wisdom dictates that the way should be prepared by the preaching of the First Principles."[2]

Joseph Smith III (1832–1914), however, as president of the Reorganization, never warmed up to the practice and, as Mark Scherer has pointed out in his history of the movement, may have seen it more of a works-based, rather than a grace-centered, expression of Christian faith.[3] In his series of articles titled "The Situation," written in the early 1870s, Smith implied that, because the Nauvoo temple was never fully completed, certainly not as originally designed, therefore temple work, at least of the kind practiced there by Brigham Young, was rejected by the Lord. He went on to state the position of the Reorganized Church at that time as having "positive and continued antagonism" to polygamy or a plurality of wives and "the doctrine of sealing as applied to the marriage covenant [and] the train of evil teachings and consequent evils resulting from the teaching, practicing, and defending these doctrines."[4] Robert Flanders, in his well-known study of Nauvoo, summed it up this way: "Dissenters who broke with the [LDS] Church over the radical innovations in doctrine tended to view the [Nauvoo] temple as a symbol of apostasy, and its destruction as a righteous judgment."[5] Today the Community of Christ, in addition to restoring, refurbishing, and maintaining the temple or "House of the Lord" in Kirtland, Ohio, has erected a temple in

---

2. Council Minutes, Reorganized Church of Jesus Christ of Latter Day Saints, May, 1865, Archives, Community of Christ, Independence, Missouri. I thank Mark Scherer, Historian of the Community of Christ, for bringing this source to my attention.

3. Mark A. Scherer, *The Journey of a People: The Era of Restoration, 1820–1844,* (Independence, MO: Community of Christ Seminary Press, 2013), 1:394–409.

4. Joseph Smith III and Heman C. Smith, *History of the Reorganized Church of Jesus Christ of Latter Day Saints, 1805–1890,* 4 vols. (Independence, MO: Herald House, 1896), 3:684.

5. Robert Bruce Flanders, *Nauvoo: Kingdom on the Mississippi* (Urbana: University of Illinois Press, 1965), 209–10.

Independence, Missouri, with its special emphasis on the first principles, gospel education, and worldwide Christian community service.[6]

Melvin C. Johnson, in his fine study *Polygamy on the Pedernales,* offers convincing evidence that Lyman Wight's Zodiac Community near San Antonio, Texas, completed a two-story log temple in February 1849. Ordinances performed in the Zodiac temple from 1849 to 1851 included baptisms for the dead, washing of feet, a general endowment, adoption, and the marriage sealing of men and women for time and eternity. Wight (1796–1858) believed that all ordinances performed in the Nauvoo temple after Joseph Smith's death were unauthorized and that he, Wight, "not Brigham Young, was the Lord's appointed messenger" and that his temple at Zodiac was the only "acceptable" place for such ordinances.[7]

Alpheus Cutler (1784–1864) and his small group of believers broke with Brigham Young at Winter Quarters and established their headquarters, first in Manti, Iowa, and later in Clitherall, Minnesota. They also performed washings and anointings, endowments, sealings, and baptisms for the dead.[8] On the second floor of their two-story log church in Clitherall, dedicated in 1867, "windows were covered with curtains and space set aside" for what historian Biloine Whiting Young has described as "the secret temple ordinances they had learned in Nauvoo." The Cutlerites believed—and still do—in reclaiming the original purity of such temple ordinances as "blessings, sealings, baptisms for the dead, ordinations and other secret rituals of Nauvoo Mormonism."[9]

6. For more on the experience of the Reorganized Church of Jesus Christ of Latter Day Saints and the ordinance of baptism for the dead, see Roger D. Launius, "An Ambivalent Rejection: Baptism for the Dead and the Reorganized Church Experience," *Dialogue: A Journal of Mormon Thought* 23, no. 2 (Summer 1990): 63–85.

7. Melvin C. Johnson, *Polygamy on the Pedernales: Lyman Wight's Mormon Villages in Antebellum Texas, 1845–1858* (Logan: Utah State University Press, 2006), 139–47. It is important to note that Wight's involvement and belief in temple work owed everything to Joseph Smith and not to Brigham Young.

8. Danny L. Jorgensen, "The Fiery Darts of the Adversary: An Interpretation of Early Cutlerism," *John Whitmer Historical Association Journal* 10 (1990): 67–83. See also Biloine Whiting Young, *Obscure Believers: The Mormon Schism of Alpheus Cutler* (Kansas City: Pogo Press, 2002), 177–78.

9. Young, *Obscure Believers*, 109. See also Christopher James Blythe, "'The Upper Room Work': Esotericism in the Church of Jesus Christ (Cutlerite), 1853–1912," *Journal of Mormon History* 40, no. 3 (Summer 2014): 43–92.

Even James Strang (1813–56) and his followers drew up plans for the construction of a temple at Voree, Wisconsin, presumably to continue ordinances similar to those performed in Nauvoo. He and William Smith, Joseph Smith's younger brother, for some time concentrated their efforts on seizing the Nauvoo temple once the Saints had departed, but such efforts came to naught.[10] More recently, the Fundamentalist Church of Jesus Christ of Latter Day Saints erected a temple in Eldorado, Texas. Thus, temples and temple ordinances have taken on a wide assortment of different meanings and priorities within the Restoration movement. This essay, however, will concentrate on the place of temple ordinances among the Latter-day Saints who followed Brigham Young (1801–77) across the Mississippi in 1846 on their way west to the Rocky Mountains.

"PILLARS IN THE TEMPLE OF GOD": BAPTISMS FOR THE DEAD

Well known in the history of Nauvoo was Joseph Smith's initiation and performance of vicarious salvific work for the dead, specifically baptisms for the dead, which he announced on August 15, 1840, at the funeral of Seymour Brunson. Baptisms for the dead were first performed in the Mississippi River, often men for women and women for men in their almost child-like enthusiasm for assuring the salvation of their deceased loved ones and friends. Later, on November 8, 1841, a temporary wooden baptismal font in the basement of the Nauvoo temple was dedicated; and beginning on November 21, baptisms for the dead were conducted there under the direction of Brigham Young, Heber C. Kimball, and John Taylor. On December 28, 1841, Joseph Smith wrote in his journal, "I baptized Sidney Rigdon in the font for and in behalf of his parents; also baptized Reynolds Cahoon and others."[11] Susan Easton Black and Harvey Black, in their comprehensive compilation, show

---

10. Richard E. Bennett, *We'll Find the Place: The Mormon Exodus, 1846–48* (Salt Lake City: Deseret Book Co., 1997), 55–56. I have found no evidence that the LDS Church ever accepted as valid or binding any of the temple-related ordinances performed by Wight, Cutler, Strang, or the RLDS Church.

11. Joseph Smith et al., *History of the Church of Jesus Christ of Latter-day Saints*, ed. B. H. Roberts, 7 vols. (Salt Lake City: Deseret Book Co., 1902–12, 1932; 1970 rpt.), 4:486; qtd. in Flanders, *Nauvoo*, 98.

that, between 1841 and 1845, a minimum of 11,530 baptisms for the dead were performed in the river and in the temple.[12]

In sharp contrast to the numbers of baptisms for the dead performed in Nauvoo was their virtual disappearance among the Latter-day Saints between 1846 and 1855. Save for Wilford Woodruff's performing this ordinance for a handful of people at Winter Quarters, another in City Creek in Salt Lake City in August 1853, and a scattered few in 1865 and 1866, this ordinance did not reappear on the Mormon celestial radar scope until 1867. It was as if the practice had gone into a long desert hibernation.[13] The Wightites and the Cutlerites performed far more baptisms for the dead than did the Latter-day Saints in this twenty-year period.

Among the early Mormon pioneers, the emphasis was not on baptisms for the dead but rather on rebaptisms of the living, which began in their new valley home on August 6, 1847, at City Creek when Brigham Young rebaptized or "recovenanted" the other members of the Twelve Apostles, and Heber C. Kimball rebaptized Young. Of the over 4,000 baptisms performed between 1847 and 1852, approximately 75 percent were rebaptisms.[14] Not only were all hands needed in the fields and in assisting emigrants to cross the plains, but Young insisted on recovenanting the faithful in their new Zion by instructing everyone, himself included, to be rebaptized for the remission of their sins. Not only were the Twelve Apostles rebaptized (Parley P. Pratt, Orson Hyde, and John Taylor were away at the time), but Wilford Woodruff stated that Young at the same time also "confirmed us and sealed upon us

---

12. Susan Easton Black and Harvey Bischoff Black, comps., *Annotated Records of Baptisms for the Dead, 1840–1845, Nauvoo, Hancock County, Illinois*, 7 vols. (Provo, Utah: Center for Family History and Genealogy, Brigham Young University, 2002), 7:ii. See also M. Guy Bishop, "'What has Become of Our Fathers?': Baptism for the Dead in Nauvoo," *Dialogue: A Journal of Mormon Thought* 23, no. 2 (Summer 1990): 87–100. Baptisms for the dead were also performed in Quincy, Illinois, and Kirtland, Ohio. See Alexander L. Baugh, "'For This Ordinance Belongeth to My House': The Practice of Baptism for the Dead outside the Nauvoo Temple," *Mormon Historical Studies* 3, no. 1 (Spring 2002): 47–58.

13. Endowment House Baptism for the Dead Record Books, Book A–G, 1–12, Church History Library, Church of Jesus Christ of Latter-day Saints, Salt Lake City; hereafter CHL. Used with permission.

14. "Rebaptisms," Record Book, Salt Lake Stake, LR 604 78, CHL. Used with permission. For a good introductory study on this topic, see D. Michael Quinn, "The Practice of Rebaptism at Nauvoo," *BYU Studies* 18, no. 2 (Winter 1978): 226–32.

our Apostleship and all the keys, powers and blessings belonging to that office."[15] Baptisms for the healing of the sick and the restoration of health were also frequently performed.[16] There were, of course, also convert baptisms during this period. Francis Burr, "a black man," was baptized by Tarleton Lewis on August 8, 1852, in the Salt Lake Valley, and Sabino Hierro was the "first Mexican" to be baptized, again in the valley, on June 25 of that same year.[17]

A strong sentiment prevailed among most of the Twelve for restricting ordinances for the dead to the temple, or, at least, to a "temple pro tem," and baptisms for the dead to a specially constructed font dedicated for such purposes. At Winter Quarters in early 1847, Brigham Young said that "the use of the Lord's house is to attend to the ordinances of the Kingdom therein; and if it were lawful and right to administer these ordinances out of doors where would be the necessity of building a house? We would recommend to the brethren to let those things you refer to, dwell in the temple, until another house is built."[18]

Joseph Young of the Seventy seconded his brother's sentiments when he said in conference in 1852: "There are other things [than living temple endowments] that never will [be performed] until the temple is built—of which are the baptism for the dead and our endowments by proxy for our dead friends. Are they going on? No. Will they before the house is built? No, not that I know of."[19] Orson Pratt was even more to the point: "There are certain appointed places for the ministration of these holy ordinances. Temples must be built. ... But in what apartments in the temple shall the baptism for the dead be administered? It

15. Church Historian's Office, Journal History of the Church of Jesus Christ of Latter-day Saints (chronological scrapbook of typed entries and newspaper clippings, 1830–present), Aug. 6, 1847, CHL (hereafter Journal History, by date). Also available online at catalog.churchofjesuschrist.org, and in Richard E. Turley Jr., ed., *Selected Collections from the Archives of the Church of Jesus Christ of Latter-day Saints*," 2: DVDs 1–36 (hereafter *Selected Collections* by volume and DVD number).

16. See Kristine L. Wright and Jonathan A. Stapley, "'They Shall Be Made Whole': A History of Baptism for Health," *Journal of Mormon History* 34, no. 2 (Fall 2008): 83–88.

17. "Rebaptisms," Record Book, Salt Lake Stake.

18. Brigham Young to George Miller, Sep. 20, 1846, Brigham Young, Office Files, CR 1234, CHL, hereafter Young Papers.

19. Joseph Young, Apr. 8, 1857, *Journal of Discourses*, 26 vols. (London: LDS Booksellers Depot, 1854–86), 6:242.

will be in the proper place—in the lowest story or department of the house of God. Why: Because it must be in a place underneath where the living assemble, in representation of the dead that are laid down in the grave ... and in such a font this sacred and holy ordinance must be administered by the servants of God."[20]

The font, therefore, was more than a metaphor; as perhaps the most unique and holy place and often separately dedicated from the temple itself, the font or "fountain," to borrow William Marks's terminology, laid claim to the performance of all baptisms for the dead. As early as 1851, Brigham Young planned to erect a font in Temple Square. "The President directed Truman O. Angell to get up a font for the baptisms for the dead on the temple block and another font to be baptized in for sickness."[21] When the Salt Lake Endowment House was completed in 1855, it featured an outdoor stone font and later an indoor font dedicated on October 1, 1856. It appears, however, that both of these fonts were used primarily, if not exclusively, for baptisms for the living and rebaptisms until 1867.[22]

Above and beyond these reasons for not performing baptisms for the dead was the simple matter of lacking a sufficient number of trust-worthy family genealogies and other reliable ancestral records. Said Parley P. Pratt in conference in April 1853: "Our fathers have forgotten to hand down to us their genealogy. They have not felt sufficient interest to transmit us their names, and the time and place of birth, and in many instances they have not taught us when and where ourselves were born, or who were our grandparents, and their ancestry." Blaming it all on that "veil of blindness" cast over the earth by the apostasy, Pratt lamented the lack of "sacred archives of antiquity" with the resultant lack of knowledge of "the eternal kindred ties, relationship or mutual interests of eternity." He pointed out that the "spirit and

---

20. Orson Pratt, Aug. 28, 1859, *Journal of Discourses*, 7:86.

21. Church Historian's Office, Historian's Office Journal, Dec. 7, 1851, CHL. Also available at catalog.churchofjesuschrist.org, and *Selected Collections,* 1:17. I thank Randall Dixon for this and related references.

22. Historian's Office Journal, Oct. 2 and Dec. 30, 1856; Wilford Woodruff, *Wilford Woodruff's Journal, 1833–1898,* typescript, ed. Scott G. Kenney, 9 vols. (Salt Lake City: Signature Books, 1983–85), 6:173. See also Brigham Young to Cyrus Smith, Oct. 4, 1856, Letterpress Copybooks, Young Papers, CHL.

power of Elijah" had only begun "to kindle in our bosoms that glow of eternal affection which lay dormant" for so many centuries. "Suppose our temple was ready?" he asked. "We could only act for those whose names are known to us. And these are few with most of us Americans. And why is this? We have never had time to look to the heavens, or to the past, or to the future, so busy have we been with the things of the earth. We have hardly had time to think of ourselves, to say nothing of our fathers."[23] Thus they did as much as their immediate memories and available records allowed.[24]

Twenty-three years later, Wilford Woodruff, later founder of the Utah Genealogical Society, spoke of this same impediment to temple work for the dead, although by then in more encouraging terms:

> If there is anything I desire to live for on this earth, or that I have desired, it has been to get a record of the genealogy of my fathers, that I might do something for them before I go hence into the spirit world. Until within a few years past, it has seemed as if every avenue has been closed to obtaining such records; but the Lord has moved upon the inhabitants of this nation and thousands of them are now laboring to trace [their] genealogical descent. … Their lineages are coming to light, and we are gradually obtaining access to them, and by this means we shall be enabled to do something towards the salvation of our dead.[25]

In their rush to leave Nauvoo, the Saints brought more tools than they did records, and this may have been the primary reason Brigham Young pointed repeatedly to the Millennium as a time when the needed records would be revealed for the work to be done. Said he in private at Winter Quarters in early 1848, "We had the promise to have something if we built the temple in Nauvoo—we have now the privilege

---

23. Parley P. Pratt, Apr. 7, 1853, *Journal of Discourses*, 1:13.

24. A related concern was that of accurate record-keeping to meet the requirements of Doctrine and Covenants 128. Glen Leonard, in his bountiful study of Nauvoo, writes that when Joseph Smith discovered, in the fall of 1842, an "inconsistent pattern" in the records of proxy baptisms, he explained that the "record itself had legal standing in the next life and therefore had to be accurately presented and preserved." Glen M. Leonard, *Nauvoo: A Place of Peace, A People of Promise* (Salt Lake City: Deseret Book Co./Provo, Utah: BYU Press, 2002), 238. It would appear that in early Salt Lake City the difficulty of gathering and keeping accurate records put a temporary brake on performing baptisms for the dead.

25. Wilford Woodruff, Apr. 6, 1876, *Journal of Discourses,* 18:191.

of acting for our dead; we have grandparents and ancestors whom we have to act for—it can't be done in five or ten years—we can get our own ordinances and as many of our ancestors as we can—this will have to be done in the Millennium by saviors who will be on Mount Zion ... pillars in the temple of our God."[26]

The eventual solution to the problem of the scarcity and incorrectness of human records would be revelation of a most unusual kind: "About the time that the temples of the Lord will be built and Zion is established," said Young in 1852,

> there will be strangers in your midst, walking with you, talking with you; they will enter your houses and eat and drink with you, go to meeting with you and begin to open your minds as the Savior did the two disciples who walked out in the country in days of old.
>
> ... They will then open your minds and tell you principles of the resurrection of the dead and how to save your friends. ... You have got your temples ready: now go forth and be baptized for those good people.
>
> ... Before this work is finished, a great many of the Elders in Israel in Mt. Zion will become pillars in the temples of God to go no more out and [will] ... say "Somebody came into the temple last night; we did not know who he was, but he gave us the names of a great many of our forefathers that are not on record, and he gave me my true lineage and the names of my forefathers for hundreds of years back. He said to me ... take them and write them down, and be baptized and confirmed ... and receive of the blessings of the eternal priesthood for such and such an individual, as you do for yourselves.[27]

Until such a time, Young believed, baptisms for the dead would not be performed.

It is true that there were other scattered and isolated references in the period of 1846–55 to baptisms for the dead. For example, Young instructed Addison Pratt before his return as a missionary to the islands of the South Pacific in 1849: "When you get to [the] Islands build a

---

26. Church Historian's Office, General Church Minutes, Feb. 13–Mar. 31, 1848, CR 100 318, box 2, fd. 2, CHL. Again, in 1854, he declared: "As I have frequently told you, [salvation of the dead] is the work of the Millennium. It is the work that has to be performed by the seed of Abraham, the chosen seed, the royal seed, the blessed of the Lord." Brigham Young, Dec. 3, 1854, *Journal of Discourses*, 2:138.

27. Brigham Young, Aug. 15, 1852, *Journal of Discourses*, 6:294–95.

tabernacle for baptizing for the dead and for the endowments for the Aaronic P[riesthood]."[28] But so far as is yet known, no such ordinances were ever performed there.

Thus the ordinance of baptisms for the dead did not recommence in a serious way among the Latter-day Saints until 1867, well after the Civil War and when expectations of a return to their Missouri Zion were on the wane. Seventy-one such ordinances were performed in the Endowment House in Salt Lake City in 1867, 434 in 1868, and 5,527 the following year.[29] Thus, the ordinance was an uncommon practice among the Latter-day Saints for almost twenty years. The lack of a proper place, the scarcity of accurate and reliable records, and the press of so many other urgent tasks delayed its reappearance for a generation, despite Wilford Woodruff's best and repeated efforts.[30]

"MERELY BY PERMISSION": ENDOWMENTS IN THE WILDERNESS

In a circular dated October 8, 1845, the Quorum of the Twelve invited as many as possible to flock to Nauvoo "to see the beauty of the Lord and enquire in his holy temple. ... Wake up, wake up dear brethren, we exhort you, from the Mississippi to the Atlantic, and from Canada to Florida, to the present glorious emergency in which the God of Heaven has placed you, to prove your faith by your works, preparatory to a rich endowment in the temple of the Lord, and the

---

28. Church Historian's Office, General Church Minutes, Apr. 8, 1849, box 2, fd. 10.

29. Endowment House Baptism for the Dead Record Books. For baptisms for the dead performed at Winter Quarters, see Elijah F. Sheets, Journal, Jan. 24 and Apr. 6, 1847; Trustees Minutes, Nov. 21, 1847, Young Papers; and Woodruff, *Wilford Woodruff's Journal*, 3:356, 6:240, and 6:286. See also Richard E. Bennett, *Mormons at the Missouri: Winter Quarters, 1846–1852* (Norman: University of Oklahoma Press, 2004), 187–90. One cannot state with authority that there were not more—perhaps many more—such baptisms performed during these years. However, the lack of available records prohibits such a conclusion. The systematic recording of proxy baptisms did not resume after Nauvoo until 1867; and when it did, clerks in the Church Historian's office could find only a handful of records of such ordinances after 1847. I have found very few private journals in this period that mention the ordinance.

30. Listed in the Endowment House Baptisms: Dead: Male and Female Record Book, CR 334 9, CHL, are one baptism for the dead for 1855, two for 1857, 2 for 1866 (August 18, October 9), with the first for 1867 being June 14 (see pp. 1–12). Woodruff, *Wilford Woodruff's Journal*, 6:240, 286, references one baptism for the dead on August 19, 1865, and at least two others on May 19, 1866.

obtaining of promises and deliverances, and glories for yourselves and your children and your dead."[31]

And come they did. Believers accepted the endowment as a surety or promise of power and authority in the present life and of eternal blessings hereafter contingent upon their faithfulness. They also saw it as a promise of physical safety and health during the pending trial of the exodus. As one official church declaration phrased it, "If they [the Saints] do not receive their endowments, they can never attain unto that salvation they are anxiously looking for."[32] Little wonder that the temple and its ordinances were Nauvoo's spiritual magnet. In a ten-week frenzy of activity lasting from early December 1845 to the eve of their departure in early February 1846, Brigham Young, Heber C. Kimball, and others of the Twelve took the lead in administering this ordinance day and night to some 5,600 faithful followers, so much so that "in consequence of close application" some of the Twelve had to leave the temple temporarily "to rest and recruit their health."[33]

In sharp contrast, the total number of living endowments performed in all ten years following amounted to only 2,222, all but one of which were performed in the Salt Lake Council House.[34] If not in hibernation, the performance of endowments—and note that these were strictly for the living and not for the dead, which did not begin until January 1877 and the dedication of the St. George temple—were administered in a far more selective, measured, and intermittent manner than they were in Nauvoo, less on demand and far more often by invitation.[35]

Save for Addison Pratt, who received his endowment atop Ensign

---

31. "To the Brethren of the Church of Jesus Christ of Latter Day Saints Scattered Abroad through the United States of America" in "History of the Church," CR 100 102, Vol. 14:8, Oct. 1845, CHL; also *Selected Collections*, 2:16.

32. Historian's Office Journal, Apr. 7, 1851.

33. Historian's Office Journal, Jan. 12, 1846. See also James B. Allen and Glen M. Leonard, *The Story of the Latter-day Saints* (Salt Lake City: Deseret Book, 1976), 169–70.

34. Endowment and Sealings, Book A, 1851–1855, CR 334 14, vol. 2, CHL. See also Devery S. Anderson, ed., *The Development of Latter-day Saint Temple Worship, 1846–2000: A Documentary History* (Salt Lake City: Signature Books, 2011), xxvii.

35. For a thorough study of the beginning of endowments for the dead, see Richard E. Bennett, "'Line upon Line, Precept upon Precept': Reflections on the 1877 Commencement of the Performance of Endowments and Sealings for the Dead," *BYU Studies* 44, no. 3 (2005): 38–77.

Peak on July 21, 1849,[36] the other 2,221 endowments were administered in the Salt Lake City Council House, often called the State House, located on the southwest corner of the intersection of South Temple and Main Streets, kitty-corner from the present Joseph Smith Memorial Building. Patterned and named after the Council House in Winter Quarters, the Salt Lake Council House was a forty-five-foot square, two-story, adobe edifice that was built by a poll tax of $1.00 and/or by tithing of one day's labor per week donated by craftsmen and laborers from the nineteen Salt Lake City wards under the direction of Daniel H. Wells.[37] Brigham Young himself worked several days as a "common laborer."[38]

Work began on the foundation November 7, and the structure was above ground in March 1849 after a very intense winter which some described as "equal to the climate of New York." That same spring, many of the early pioneer settlers abandoned their apartments in the city forts in favor of houses on city lots.[39] While construction slowed due to such problems as the cricket infestations of June 1849, the Council House remained a pioneer priority. As John Taylor declared to the church in 1848, "The first thing to build up Zion is to build a Council House."[40]

Unlike its successor building, the better known Endowment House, which opened in May 1855, the Council House, built at a cost of approximately $45,833, was also called the State House or Representatives Hall and had a dual secular and religious purpose. Its first floor was given over to meetings of the original territorial legislature, classes of the University of Deseret, sittings of territorial and city courts, the territorial library, and socials. It also housed such church functions as meetings of the Salt Lake Stake bishops, high council, and other

---

36. Historian's Office Journal, July 21, 1849. "Addison Pratt received his endowments on Ensign Hill on the 21st, the place being consecrated for the purpose. 10 others participated."

37. Salt Lake Stake Manuscript History and Historical Reports, Oct. 29, 1848, CHL.

38. Thomas Bullock, Journals, Apr. 2 1849, box 65, MS 2737, CHL.

39. Bullock, Mar. 9, 1849. By Apr., 450 houses had been erected in "Great Salt Lake City" with another forty-seven in North Mill Creek (Farmington) and fifty-three in South Cottonwood. Bullock, Apr. 2, 1849.

40. Salt Lake Stake, Minutes, Oct. 29, 1848, 41, CHL.

ecclesiastical purposes.[41] Not a hotel in the envisioned sense of the Nauvoo House, the Council House was also a place for occasional meals, banquets, and socializing for guests and travelers, though not a place for lodging. The second floor or "upper room" was dedicated, reserved, and divided into rooms separated by partitions for the performance of endowments, prayer circles, sealings, and other temple-related ordinances. The Council House, which had no baptismal font, opened for gatherings early in June 1849.[42]

For four years, the Council House served as Salt Lake City's first "temple pro tem." With carpets laid and partitions, furnishings, two stoves, washing tubs, and other necessary accoutrements finally in place "in the upper room" of the Council House by mid-February 1851,[43] all was in readiness for the restoration of the performance of endowments. The first took place on the morning of a cold and frosty February 21, 1851, when twenty-nine-year-old Francis A. Hammond and his twenty-year-old wife, Mary Jane Dilworth Hammond, received this ordinance prior to embarking just days later on their mission to the Sandwich Islands.[44] Of the next fifteen persons, endowed on February 25 and 26, at least three of them were about to depart Addison Pratt-like on faraway missions. This pattern underscores the fact that a primary reason for Council House endowments was preparation required for mission service, including that of fifteen-year-old Taylor Crosby who received his endowment on February 26, 1851.

The pending missionary service of Parley P. Pratt to the "Pacific Mission" may also explain why two of his plural wives—Phoebe Eldred Soper Pratt (married February 1846) and Ann Agatha Walker Pratt (married April 1847)—were also endowed. Such was also the case with Sarah Zufelt Murdock (married March 1846) whose husband, John Murdock, resigned from his calling as bishop to serve in the Pacific Mission, with the specific assignment of Australia. Harriet Sargent

---

41. Woodruff, *Wilford Woodruff's Journal,* 4:114.
42. Gil Bradshaw, "The Council House as a House for Sacred Ordinances in the Early Church," cited in Lisle G Brown, "'Temple Pro Tempore:' The Salt Lake City Endowment House," *Journal of Mormon History* 14, no. 2 (Fall 2008): 5n16.
43. Historian's Office Journal, Feb. 15–19, 1851.
44. Endowment and Sealing Book A, 1851–55, 1.

Rich, sixth wife of Apostle Charles C. Rich, whom she married at Winter Quarters in March 1847, was also among the first endowed prior to their moving to San Bernardino with Amasa Lyman. Thomas E. Broderick, having been called on his mission to England, was endowed on April 24, 1852.

These early Council House endowments were also administered to those long-faithful and worthy members who, for one reason or another, had never received this blessing in the Nauvoo temple and who were now getting on in years. Such endowments were given almost as a reward for their many years of faithful service. Said Brigham Young: "I wish to say to the old brethren who were in Missouri, and in Nauvoo, we choose to give you your blessings first, and when any such [others] present themselves, we give you the preference; you have borne the heat and burden of the day and are entitled to these blessings first."[45] Among these were Daniel H. Wells, leader in the Battle of Nauvoo; Aphek Woodruff, Wilford Woodruff's father; Eleazer Miller, who had baptized Brigham Young; and at least three members of the 1834 Zion's Camp, including Reuben McBride and Solomon Angel, older brother of Truman O. Angel.

Those being called to colonize far-distant places in the new and expanding Mormon territories were also high on the priority list.[46] As in the Nauvoo temple, some particularly busy days ended in a season of rejoicing as the following account of April 1, 1852, indicates: "Afterwards all met in the celestial room. ... Sister [Elizabeth Ann] Whitney sung in tongues. Bro. [Samuel S.] Sprague danced while singing in tongues and received the blessing of President Young when we all separated greatly rejoicing in the presentation of the Lord."[47]

During its four years of service, 966 men and 1,256 women were endowed in the Council House for a total of 2,222.[48] Put in perspective, more than twice this number had been endowed in the Nauvoo temple in the three months between December 1845 and February 1846. For Council House endowments, the busiest months of the

45. Journal History, Apr. 8, 1852, 5–6.
46. General Church Minutes, Oct. 7, 1852, box 2, fd. 41.
47. Endowment and Sealings Book A, Apr. 1, 1852.
48. This number likely included Addison Pratt's endowment on Ensign Peak.

year were March, April, and July, with most sessions beginning at 10:00 a.m. Reflecting the rapidly changing emigration patterns of those newly arriving in the valley, many of whom had never known Nauvoo, 39 percent were from the British Isles, 4 percent from Canada, 2 percent from Europe, less than 1 percent (one each) from Jamaica and West Indies, one not designated, and the remaining 55 percent from New England, the Atlantic seaboard, and southern states (see Table 1).[49] Among those officiating in these ordinances were W. W. Phelps, W. C. Staines, S. S. Sprague, Albert P. Rockwood, and Wilford Woodruff. Among female officiators, the busiest three were Elizabeth Ann Whitney, Prescinda Huntington Buell Kimball, and Eliza R. Snow.

A look at the numbers of endowments per year shows that more than twice as many were performed in 1852 as in 1851. According to Council House records, Brigham Young stopped the performance of all such ordinances in November 1852 and did not resume them until February 3, 1854—a period of over fourteen months—apparently on account of "inferior oil brought by merchants," but which the original records say "for some reason now unknown."[50] Other factors, however, were likely at play such as flooring problems, the issue of needed privacy in what was a very crowded, oft-times noisy building where the floor separating church and state was thin indeed, and a somewhat troubling sentiment that such endowments would likely have to be repeated later anyway, once a temple was built. Of this Young said at the October 1852 conference: "There are many in this congregation who are aware that we do not give all the endowments, neither can we, legally, until we build a temple. Again, those

---

49. In 1851, 30 percent of those endowed were from the British Isles. In 1852 the percentage grew to 37 and by 1854, it was 53 percent.

50. Historian's Office Journal, Oct. 31, 1852, and Feb. 3, 1854. See also Endowment and Sealings Book A, handwritten title page. The down-turn in tithing contributions may have been another factor. As early as August 1851, Brigham Young was prohibiting persons from receiving their endowments "until they can show a certificate of settlement from the Tithing Office." William Clayton to Bishop Elias Blackburn, Oct. 14, 1851, Letterpress Copybook: "President Young gave orders for no man to receive his endowments … unless he first presents his receipts from the tithing office showing that he has paid his tithing up." See also Endowments and Sealings Book A, Aug. 11, 1851; Brigham Young, Dec. 3, 1854, *Journal of Discourses*, 2:144.

TABLE I. Regional Origins of Those Endowed, 1851–54	
Region	*Percentage of Endowed*
British Isles	39
Mid-Atlantic	19
South	13
New England	12
Midwest	11
Canada	4
Other	2
Scandinavia	1
Europe	1
Jamaica	0
West Indies	0

parts that are already given, and will be given, in the place we at present use, will be given over again in the temple, when it is finished. The endowments we now give, are given merely by permission, as we have not a house in which to officiate in these ordinances of salvation, that is legal, though we have got a comfortable place, which we have dedicated to the Lord."[51]

Counter-balancing repeated statements about the importance of the endowment was a somewhat contrasting sentiment that, for those who wanted them but who could not for one reason or another obtain them, all would work out well regardless. Speaking in 1857 to those men preparing to fight against the Utah Expedition or "Johnston's Army," Young said:

We work one day in a week [giving endowments] in order to stir-up the devil, that's all. The brethren that are going out, if they have not had their endowments, if they will keep the commandments of God, and do as well as [they] know, they shall live and be protected just the same as those that have had them. Bless your souls. ... If you do right you shall have your

---

51. Journal History, Oct. 6, 1852. See also General Church Minutes, Oct. 6, 1852. It was later made clear, however, that such ordinances would be "valid" if recipients died before a future temple was constructed. General Church Minutes, Nov. 5, 1852.

endowments, and God shall bless you just the same; and men and women that do not honor and magnify their callings, their endowments will do them no good, but only add sorrow to them.[52]

The last endowments administered in the Council House were on a very rainy Monday, April 29, 1854, when thirty-one people crowded their way through a building that had served its purposes. Included in that number was fifteen-year-old Joseph F. Smith who was about to serve his mission to the Sandwich Islands and whose 1918 "Vision of the Redemption of the Dead" would later have such a profound impact on LDS temple work.[53]

To summarize, temple endowments in early Salt Lake City were performed without a temple and "merely by permission," in a Council House that proved not entirely adequate, on a highly selective basis primarily for those about to serve missions or colonize far-distant places, as a reward for lifelong service to the church, and for emigrant converts arriving in ever-increasing numbers. The word was "be patient," remain faithful, and all will work out as well as if you had been endowed. If the endowment promised, and not merely portended, eternal glory, such glory, Brigham Young seemed to indicate, would come their way sooner or later by virtue of this ordinance whether received now or at another time. Thus, Young tried to remove the urgency of receiving the endowment, without sacrificing the need for it, thereby buying time in the hearts and minds of his faithful followers to build a more suitable temple or temple-like place for its performance. As he put it years later: "I want to see the temple finished as soon as it is reasonable and practicable. Whether we go in there to work or not makes no difference; I am perfectly willing to finish it to the last leaf of gold that shall be laid upon it, and to the last lock that should be put on the doors, and then lock every door, and there let it stand until the earth can rest before the Saints commence their labors there. They receive more in the House of the Lord now than is their due."[54]

---

52. Historian's Office Journal, Aug. 16, 1857, box 3, fd. 17.
53. Endowments and Sealings Book A, 78.
54. Brigham Young, Apr. 8, 1867, *Journal of Discourses*, 11:372.

"FOR TIME AND ETERNITY": SEALINGS

In contrast to the limited number of endowments and the virtual absence of baptisms for the dead, by far the most prevalent of temple-related ordinances was sealings in all their varieties. This study concentrates on the marriage sealings of living partners for "time and eternity" as well as for "time" only; proxy sealings in which one of the marriage partners was deceased at the time of the sealing ceremony; and the sealing adoptions of men and women to prominent priesthood leaders. In very few cases were children being sealed to their parents.

At least three factors complicate the accurate study of this practice: first, the incompleteness and scattered nature of the records; second, the lack of clear governing control over the practice until the reestablishment of a new First Presidency under Brigham Young in December 1847; and third, the obvious struggles of moving an entire people over several years to their new Rocky Mountain Zion.

Back in Nauvoo, during the three-month period between December 1845 and February 1846 when so many endowments were being performed, approximately 2,682 sealings of all different kinds—spousal marriages, children sealed to parents, and adoptions—were performed in the Nauvoo temple, of which over 80 percent (2,000) were marriage sealings. Almost all of these were done by members of the Quorum of the Twelve. In addition, a limited number of marriage sealings had been performed in private homes, including the homes of Presiding Bishop Newel K. Whitney and Patriarch John Smith, since 1843. Most cases of children being sealed to their parents were of living children being sealed to living parents. Such was the case, for example, of Newel and Elizabeth Whitney whose eight grown, living children were sealed to them at noon on January 12, 1846, by Brigham Young.[55] Less common were family sealings in which one of the parents was deceased. Also uncommon were adoption sealings or the spiritual adoption of children to parents.[56] There were few, if any, sealings of deceased children

---

55. Nauvoo Temple Sealings and Adoptions of the Living and Index, Book A, 561.

56. An exception was the sealings and adoptions of George Miller (b. 1794) to his three wives and fifteen "natural" and "adopted" children. Nauvoo Temple Sealings, 415–16. On January 31, 1846, Brigham Young also sealed to Alpheus Cutler and Lois Cutler their three sons and five daughters. Nauvoo Temple Sealings, 227.

to parents in Nauvoo, likely because of the blizzard of temple activity for the living in preparation for their pending exodus. Nor did such ordinances occur during the next nine years.

Nauvoo also provided the precedent for performing marriage sealings outside of a temple and prior to receiving one's endowment. Joseph Smith himself performed several such sealings in the Red Brick Store. Hyrum Smith likewise sealed several couples—for example, marrying and sealing Erastus Snow and Artemisia Beman in February 1844.[57] And what began in Nauvoo continued at Winter Quarters where 153 sealings were conducted, two in 1846, 49 in 1847, and 102 in 1848.[58] Many are the accounts of marriage sealings being conducted in Willard Richards's octagon house, the Recorder's House, the Council House, and in at least twenty different cabins in Winter Quarters. Two of only three such sealing ceremonies in Iowa occurred at Henry Miller's home in Kanesville.[59] Parley P. Pratt, who in July 1846 was about to leave for England, records that, on July 27, George Whitaker and Eveline Parsons "were by me sollemnly [sic] united in a Covenant of Matrimony for time and for all eternity according to the laws of God and by permission of President Brigham Young."[60]

Some of the Twelve, like Pratt, were convinced that they held as much authority and priesthood keys as Brigham Young who, though president of the Quorum of the Twelve, was not yet president of the church. Therefore, they acted independently in such matters whether on-board ship, in far-distant communities, or along the trail. Although Pratt had carefully spelled out the authority granted by Young in the 1846 sealing of Whittaker and Parsons, a year later he was rather defiantly telling his quorum leader, "We hold the keys as well as yourself and I will not be judged by you but by the Quorum."[61] For this reason and

---

57. Erastus Snow, Journal, Feb. 15, 1844, CHL.

58. For 1847 and 1848, most sealings occurred in April, just prior to Brigham Young's departure for the West. Nauvoo Temple Sealings and Adoptions of the Living, Book A, 691–800. See also "Pre-Endowment House Records, 1842–1854," CR 334 13, CHL.

59. Nauvoo Temple Sealings and Adoptions of the Living, Book A, 691–800. See also "Pre-Endowment House Records, 1842–1854."

60. Parley P. Pratt to Willard Richards, July 27, 1846, Willard Richards Papers, CHL.

61. General Church Minutes, Sep. 4, 1847. Almon W. Babbitt, an elder but not an apostle, also performed sealings without authority.

a variety of others, not all such ceremonies were properly recorded or faithfully reported to Thomas Bullock who, as chief clerk, was responsible for keeping the master record. Pratt made this statement in apparent self-justification after he had sealed one couple in the summer of 1847 at the Elkhorn River and another couple, Mary Brockway and Vinson Shirtleft, at the Sweetwater.[62] No records are lacking, however, for when Heber C. Kimball married two women to one man "by moonlight" on June 17, 1848, on the prairie on the south side of Loup Fork, or when Young sealed a couple earlier that same month "in a carriage at the [the] Elkhorn and [the] Platte."[63] Nevertheless as much care as reasonably possible was taken to have each sealing witnessed by at least one party and to record the names of the parties, date, place, and precise time the ordinance was performed and any unique circumstances involved.

While Young roundly criticized Pratt for acting without authority, he himself could hardly deny the entreaties of his people. Many who were sick and diseased sought special exemption. One man, J. W. Fox, begged Young to seal his dying daughter-in-law, Caroline, to his son, David, for time and eternity.[64] Fox's request was one of several from families in similar conditions. Men in the Mormon Battalion, such as George P. Dykes, apprehensive about their immediate future, wrote imploring letters like the following: "Shall my days be numbered and my pilgrimage ended and I go to the silent tomb without a Father to call me forth from the deep sleep of death? Or shall I enjoy in common with other citizens of the commonwealth of Israel the legal rights to adoption … I who have spent the prime of life in defending the truth … in the sacred death, or on the Battlefield shall I be forgotten in the day of choosing[?]"[65]

Finally scores of engaged couples were requesting celestial marriage with or without a temple. It was clear to them that their delay at Council Bluffs and the uncertainty of future events would postpone indefinitely the erection of another temple in the West. Joseph Smith had made exceptions; why could not Brigham Young?

---

62. General Church Minutes, Sep. 7, 1847.

63. Pre-Endowment House Records 1842–54, fd. 1.

64. J. W. Fox to Brigham Young, Mar. 23, 1847, Young Papers.

65. George P. Dykes to Brigham Young, Aug. 17, 1846, Young Papers. Dykes was seeking spiritual adoption into the Brigham Young family. For more on adoption, see below.

TABLE 2. Number of Sealing Groups per Year, January 1847–April 1855

Year	Number of Sealings
1847	48
1848	112
1849	38
1850	72
1851	222
1852	739
1853	506
1854	406
1855	58

TABLE 3. Sealers by Percentage of Sealings, 1847–55

Sealer	Percentage
Brigham Young	41
Heber C. Kimball	30
George A. Smith	12
Willard Richards	6
Orson Pratt	4
Ezra T. Benson	5
Others	2

The reorganization of the LDS First Presidency and the resettlement of the Saints in the Salt Lake Valley brought greater order to, and tighter control over, the practice. While there was at least one sealing performed in the "old Salt Lake Fort" on January 2, 1848, the largest number of sealings occurred once the Council House was in full operation, beginning in 1851 (see Table 2).

Of the 2,201 marriage sealings recorded by Thomas Bullock between February 9, 1847, and April 24, 1855, 881 (41 percent) were performed personally by Brigham Young with Heber C. Kimball and Willard Richards, his counselors, performing 780 (36 percent) more.

TABLE 4. Locations of Sealings, 1847–55

Location	Percentage
Council House and Church Offices	61
Not Available	13
Outside Salt Lake Valley	10
Other	10
Utah County	10
Iron County	2
San Pete County	1
Juab County	0
Other Counties	0
Winter Quarters and Pioneer Trail	6

As Table 3 shows, Brigham Young and his counselors performed a total of 76 percent of all sealings. The only non-apostles to do sealings were Isaac Morley and John Smith (three between them). Most were performed in March, April, February, and July coinciding with the cycles of planting and harvesting.

While the majority were performed in the Salt Lake Council House—whether in Brigham Young's office, the East Room, or elsewhere in that edifice—well over 400 were performed in private homes, not only in Salt Lake City, such as in Brigham Young's "log house," and the homes of W. W. Phelps, Heber C. Kimball, Benjamin Rolfe, and Rhonda Richards, but also in several other cities and towns all over Utah Territory (see Table 4). Care was taken to perform such sacred ceremonies privately and not under the gaze of "too many people." In a situation where Brigham Young again listened to the cries of his people, most of whom he had sent out on one kind of mission or another, he authorized taking this temple-based ordinance to his people—a case of the temple going to the people and not the other way around.

In several cases, sealings were performed for those suffering with consumption or so ill they were considered on their death beds.[66] For

---

66. Brigham Young likewise authorized the cancellations of some previous sealings in cases of abuse, lack of financial support, disharmonies of a serious nature, and severe incompatibility.

example, E. T. Benson sealed John Wood of Salt Lake City at 9:00 p.m. on September 7, 1851, to his thirty-year-old wife Ann Leigh, who died the next day.[67] Erastus Snow conducted one marriage sealing in Danish in 1854, the first occasion of a temple-related ordinance being given in a language other than English.[68] Apostle George A. Smith was particularly busy performing sealings in southern Utah. For instance, on May 30, 1854, the Historian's Office Journal records, "George A. Smith crossed Provo River on horseback, found water deep and rapid but got over safely by assistance of President Higbee and came to Dry Creek. Attended to sealing several couples."[69] Between 1851 and 1855, this intrepid traveling sealer conducted 255 such ceremonies, as many as all his fellow apostles (excluding the First Presidency) combined, and in other Utah towns such as Payson, Lehi, Springville, Parowan, and Fillmore, though always "by permission of President Young."[70]

In what is a reflection of the changing demographics of the Latter-day Saints in Salt Lake City in particular, which by 1855 numbered close to 7,000, the origins of those sealed from 1851 to 1854 show that 12 percent were from New England, 25 percent from the Atlantic States (mostly New York), 10 percent from the Midwest, 13 percent from the southern United States, 33 percent from Great Britain, 4 percent from Canada, and 3 percent from Europe (see Table 5). Many of these were recent immigrants and had never set foot in Nauvoo. Likely a large number of the British couples had been converted by the Twelve during their 1839–42 mission there. Clearly the decision to restrict the performance of sealings to the Twelve Apostles, like their earlier missions, bonded the Saints to their apostolic leaders in a way not otherwise attainable. Thus, the carefully guarded control of sealings insured order, inspiration, loyalty, and allegiance to church leaders and to priesthood authority and direction.

In the matter of personal worthiness, whether for sealings or more particularly for endowments, church leaders also found a way to bind their people to the teachings and expectations of membership,

---

67. Familyseach.org, ID # KWJT-DWM.
68. Historian's Office Journal, July 2, 1854.
69. Historian's Office Journal, May 30, 1854.
70. Historian's Office Journal, Feb. 22, 1856.

TABLE 5. Origins of Participants in Sealings, 1851–54

Place of Origin	Percentage
British Isles	33
Mid-Atlantic	25
South	13
New England	12
Midwest	10
Canada	4
Europe	3

particularly tithing. As already noted, on August 11, 1851, Young gave orders "for no man to have his endowment after that date unless he first presents his receipts from the tithing office showing that he has paid his tithing up."[71] Though formal temple recommends were not in use, sealings carried with them the expectation of improved behavior. That church leaders accepted repentance, however, is evident from an 1853 entry, "The girl has a child in her arms which he is the father of and they have not been previously married."[72]

This effort to perform sealings where the people were, in their own language, in their less than perfect behaviors, and in times of severe illness and incapacitation manifests a surprising flexibility and adaptability to meet needs and special circumstances. These exceptions to the rule of sacred space were endearing to the people and, while not surrendering the importance of restricting ordinances to a temple or temple-like place, signaled understanding and compassion, thus bringing church leaders into the hearts and homes of their followers.

The vast majority of marriage sealings were for "time and eternity," meaning the hope and promise that a marriage would last not only for the couple's lives but endure beyond the grave and into the resurrection. While there are instances of "divorces" and of unions being broken or "dismissed," the records show that most were for "time and eternity" with far fewer for "time in eternity" or, in other words, "time" only. For the period of my study, 95 percent of all marriages were for

---

71. Endowments and Sealings Record Book A, Aug. 11, 1851.
72. Endowments and Sealings, Apr. 16, 1853.

"time and eternity" and only the remaining 5 percent were for "time." An unusual case occurred in April 1853 when a woman was sealed to her second husband "for time" with the notation, "Her former husband ... was not baptized, to whom she wishes to be sealed for eternity, when the temple is built."[73]

Note also that the great majority of these marriage sealings were for living couples. In fact, for the decade of the study (1847–55), fully 95 percent fall into this category. This figure remains constant for both Winter Quarters and early Salt Lake City. Nevertheless, not a few were for a living spouse to a deceased partner, even on at least one occasion to a non-member such as Henry Howland, who began his trek to Zion but died of cholera after crossing the Missouri River before he could be baptized.[74] On very rare occasions, a deceased couple were sealed as a married unit, as long as both were well-remembered and their marriage certified by living posterity. I have found no cases as yet that reconstruct and seal ancestral marriages more than one generation in the past, likely for the same reasons already given for the absence of baptisms for the dead. These "proxy sealings" are, nevertheless, the only clear evidence of a substantial amount of work for the dead being done outside of a temple within the period of study. If nothing else, they point to a later time when such activity would become prominent.

The vast majority of marriage sealings were monogamous, from as low as 52 percent in 1849 to as high as almost 90 percent in 1855, 88 percent being between one man and one woman. While not downplaying plural marriage sealings, what seemed more important was the eternality of the marriage covenant—the "time and eternity" component alluded to earlier. Inherent in that covenant was an eternal binding—not just one to another, but also an attachment to God forever that made the ordinance so compelling to so many. The ceremony itself was attended to "by a form of words most sublime," as one woman described the giving of her husband in plural marriage to another woman. When done she said, "My destiny

---

73. Endowments and Sealings, Apr. 9, 1853.
74. Endowments and Sealings, Dec. 31, 1852.

has taken its bent and I am satisfied in the man the Lord has given me for a husband."[75]

Still, these plural marriage sealings are very revealing. For instance, in single sealing ceremonies, the average age of the male spouse was forty-one, thirteen years older than his female partner. Such older ages than what then was the national average might be attributed to the fact that many had been civilly married before, in some cases long before their conversions to Mormonism. The average age of the second and later plural wives at the time of sealing was considerably younger than the first wife's age at marriage—eleven years younger in the case of plural sealings performed in 1847 alone. What might come as a surprise, however, is that of those sealings performed in 1854, when the average age of the second and later wives was slightly greater than the husband's, suggesting what appears to be plural marriage sealings to sisters and even to the mother of the first wife. The important point is that plural marriages were becoming a part of the Mormon cultural and family life pattern. They never constituted a majority of sealings even after the 1852 public announcement embracing the plurality of wives, but they were becoming a fixture in Mormon life.

Finally, with respect to the law of adoption and the sealing of priesthood holders and heads of their families, often along with their wives and children, to a prominent church leader holding priesthood keys and authority, Gordon Irving, Brian Hales, Jonathan Stapley, Jennifer Ann Mackley, and I have discussed the doctrinal reasons for this practice.[76] Space does not permit a full doctrinal examination of the topic save to say that it was seen as a "grafting" in of one family without priesthood keys to another with such saving powers. In the same sense that believing gentiles were seen as wild branches being grafted into the tame olive tree of Israel (Jacob 5), for the period of this study, the emphasis was on faithful families and individual men being sealed to a living apostle who, in turn, was sealed to the Prophet Joseph Smith. It

---

75. Joyce Kinkead, *A Schoolmarm All My Life: Personal Narratives from Frontier Utah* (Salt Lake City: Signature Books, 1996), 23–24.

76. For the most recent study of this and related temple topics, see Jennifer Ann Mackley, *Wilford Woodruff's Witness of the Development of Temple Doctrine* (Seattle: High Desert Publishing, 2014).

was the essential chain of reconstructing and sealing together all past generations back to Father Adam, as was so often discussed in Nauvoo and in Winter Quarters.

In what was clearly a temple-related ceremony, many such adoption sealings occurred in Nauvoo and, to a lesser extent, in Winter Quarters and in early Salt Lake City. A total of 320 men and women (a small number of who were deceased), many with their children, were adopted to Brigham Young alone between 1847 and 1854.[77] The available records, however, show a definite tapering off of this ordinance toward the end of the study period. The practice of sealing adoptions was all but terminated in 1893 when Wilford Woodruff, as church president, issued a statement ending it in favor of families and individuals being sealed to their parents and ancestors in direct family lineages, a remarkable change in policy that led to the formation of the Genealogical Society of Utah and the modern emphasis on family history.[78]

CONCLUSION

Between what President Gordon B. Hinckley referred to as the bookends of the Nauvoo and Salt Lake temples and, more narrowly in this study, to the Salt Lake Council House, temple work as understood by the "Brighamites" or Latter-day Saints who fled to the Rocky Mountains, stayed in line with leadership policy, interpretations, and expectations on the one hand, while keeping pace with the needs of the people on the other. The temple in many instances came to where the people were—in their homes, in their languages, and to meet their particular needs. It showed surprising flexibility and adaptability and laid the groundwork for modern LDS temple building in which temples have sprung up all over the world where the Saints can be found. This blend of the spiritual and the practical in temple work and worship gave the rigidities of the doctrine a softer, gentler embrace.

We have also seen that the emphasis was clearly on the living and not on the dead. The many prayer circles, which abounded in Winter Quarters, all across the plains, and in early Salt Lake City, were

---

77. Hosea Stout, *On the Mormon Frontier: The Diary of Hosea Stout,* ed. Juanita Brooks (Salt Lake City: University of Utah Press, 1964), 1:242.

78. Bennett, "Line upon Line, Precept upon Precept," 66–67.

focused on the needs of the living—spiritual, emotional, and physical. Endowments for the dead would have to wait for another twenty years. Baptisms for the dead were virtually nonexistent as were intergenerational sealings. The exigencies of the time and place, and the promises of later revelations and prophecies of a future millennium, all pushed their temple efforts toward the living and not yet to the dead. It was a bridge too far.

Still, we have seen that one of Brigham Young's central contributions to Latter-day Saint history, in addition to being a remarkable pioneer, colonizer, and frontiersman, was to retain within his thousands of followers a consciousness of the abiding place for temple ordinances. They were applied and developed as need demanded and remained a bold fixture in the Mormon Zion in their western wilderness.

FIVE

BLACK SAVIORS ON MOUNT ZION
PROXY BAPTISMS AND LATTER-DAY SAINTS
OF AFRICAN DESCENT

TONYA S. REITER

On September 3, 1875, eight black Latter-day Saints entered the Endowment House in Salt Lake City and, acting as proxies, were baptized
and confirmed for deceased friends and family.[1] Baptisms and confirmations for the dead were the only LDS temple ordinances these
Saints were allowed to do in 1875. Because of the racial priesthood
ban in place during this period, black Mormon men of African descent
were not ordained to the priesthood. A corollary temple restriction
prohibited black men and women from receiving temple endowments
and marriage sealings. Neither black nor white proxies were allowed to
receive higher temple ordinances for black candidates.[2] By performing
vicarious baptisms, these men and women, who were commonly viewed
by many of their contemporaries, in and out of the LDS Church, as
inheritors of the curse of Cain, proved their devotion and commitment
to their faith despite the restrictions it imposed on them.[3] This unique
baptismal event was the only occasion in the nineteenth century when
a group of black Mormons came together to serve as proxies. However,

---

1. "Colored Brethren and Sisters, Endowment House, Salt Lake City, Utah," Sep. 3,
1875, microfilm no. 255498, Family History Library, Salt Lake City, Utah (hereafter FHL).

2. Devery S. Anderson, ed., *The Development of LDS Temple Worship, 1846–2000* (Salt
Lake City: Signature Books, 2011), 82, 101–102.

3. The idea that black Africans and their descendants carried in their dark skins the
mark of the curse God pronounced upon Cain for murdering his brother, Abel, was widely
believed in nineteenth-century America and was used as a justification of the LDS priesthood ban. The curse, supposedly, had been passed down through the great flood by Noah's
son Ham or his wife, Egyptus. "Race and the Priesthood," Gospel Topics Essays, The
Church of Jesus Christ of Latter-day Saints, churchofjesuschrist.org.

it is not the only time black Latter-day Saints either performed or requested vicarious baptisms and confirmations before the repeal of the priesthood ban in June 1978. As black Mormons sought opportunities to participate in work for the dead, LDS leadership responded with pronouncements that shaped and limited temple rituals and practices allowed to them.

When Joseph Smith introduced the concept of vicarious baptism in 1840, Mormons in Nauvoo, Illinois, enthusiastically accepted the new teaching, eager to be baptized for deceased family members and friends who had not been able to join the church during their lifetimes. They soon began to perform the ordinance in the streams and rivers near the city. The boat landing on the Mississippi River at the end of Main Street was a popular place for the rite. In those early days, men were baptized for either men or women and vice versa.[4]

There is no indication that there was any restriction on black Mormons of African descent doing proxy baptisms during Joseph Smith's lifetime. Elijah Abel, early black priesthood holder who was ordained to the office of Seventy, did vicarious baptisms in Nauvoo.[5] Abel had received a washing and anointing in Kirtland, Ohio, which became the initial part of the temple ritual in Nauvoo.[6] He helped to build the Nauvoo temple and probably hoped to take part in the full endowment ritual when the temple was completed.[7] The record of the proxy work

---

4. H. David Burton, "Baptism for the Dead: LDS Practice," in *Encyclopedia of Mormonism*, ed. Daniel H. Ludlow (New York: Macmillan, 1992), 1:95–96.

5. Along with Abel, Joseph T. Ball is often listed as a black priesthood holder and participant in the ordinance of proxy baptisms. See Connell O'Donovan, "Early Boston Mormons, A–C 1831–1860," at http://www.connellodonovan.com/boston_mormonsA-C. pdf. While nineteenth-century sources recognize Abel as a man of color, no contemporaneous sources list Ball as a black man. There was a "Joseph Ball" who was a founding member of the Boston African Society and therefore could have had African ancestry. If this man were Joseph T. Ball's father and if he were biracial, Joseph T. would also have had African ancestry. The senior Ball, if biracial, was apparently light enough to pass into white society and marry a white wife. See Jeffrey D. Mahas, "Biography of Joseph T. Ball," Century of Black Mormons, at https://exhibits.lib.utah.edu/s/century-of-black-mormons/page/welcome.

6. L. John Nuttall, diary, vol. 1 (Dec. 1876–Mar. 1884), typescript, 290–93, L. Tom Perry Special Collections, Harold B. Lee Library, Brigham Young University. Historian W. Kesler Jackson notes Abel's participation in the precursor of the endowment ritual, *Elijah Abel: The Life and Times of a Black Priesthood Holder* (Springville, Utah: Cedar Fort, Inc., 2013), 62–63.

7. By the time the Nauvoo temple was dedicated, Abel had left Nauvoo but would join the followers of Brigham Young later in Utah. For more about Abel and how LDS policies impacted

he did in 1840 and 1841 is listed in the register of Nauvoo Baptisms for the Dead alongside work done by white proxies for white beneficiaries.[8] There is no notation to indicate his race. Abel acted for his mother, Delila, and a friend, John F. Lancaster.[9]

After the death of Joseph Smith in mid-1844, in preparation for their relocation to a new settlement, the Latter-day Saints performed as many endowments and sealings as possible in the Nauvoo temple before abandoning the city. After arriving in the Great Salt Lake Valley, one of the first things Brigham Young did was to designate the place for a new temple to be built. It would be over forty years before the Salt Lake temple was completed and dedicated. To provide a place for limited temple ordinances to be performed, the Endowment House was built on the northwest corner of Temple Square and completed in 1855. In 1856 a font was added for baptisms.[10]

Beginning with the vanguard pioneer company of 1847, Utah became home to men and women of African descent. Three enslaved black men were among the first pioneers to enter the Great Salt Lake Valley. They were soon followed by a handful of Southern converts who brought their slaves with them into the Rocky Mountains. In some Southern households, slaves had been baptized along with their masters, so black Mormons entered Zion as the property of white Mormons. A few free black converts were also part of the small African American community in Utah. Although blacks comprised only a small percentage of the total population, slaves represented a great deal of wealth for their LDS masters, and, in 1852, Brigham Young led the territorial legislature in passing an act to codify the use of unfree

his life, see Newell Bringhurst, "Elijah Abel and the Changing Status of Blacks Within Mormonism," *Dialogue: A Journal of Mormon Thought* 12, no. 2 (Summer 1979): 22–36.

8. "Baptisms for the Dead, 1840–1841," Register Vol. A, microfilm no. 183376, FHL.

9. Abel was baptized for his mother in 1840, and then again for a Delila in 1841. His relationship to the second Delila is listed as "daughter," leading Russell Stevenson and some other historians to believe he had a daughter who had died. This would mean Abel had a daughter and possibly a wife before he married the Mary Ann Adams who came to Utah with him. Abel's name is sometimes spelled "Ables." See Russell Stevenson, *Black Mormon: The Story of Elijah Ables* (Afton, Wyoming: By the author, 2013), 1–2.

10. Lisle G. Brown, "'Temple Pro Tempore': The Salt Lake City Endowment House," *Journal of Mormon History* 34, no. 2 (Fall 2008): 1–68.

labor in Utah.[11] At the same time, in his speeches to the legislature, now-church president and territorial governor Young made it clear that priesthood ordination of black men of African descent would not be done under his administration and that the rightful place of the black man was as a servant to the white man.[12] Slavery legally ended in Utah territory ten years later in 1862.

Between 1847 and 1875, the black community in Salt Lake City and along the Wasatch Front grew. No longer held as slaves, black pioneers and their descendants worked to establish homes and farms and to provide for their families. Their number was added to by newly arrived settlers who were able to join the Saints after emancipation at the end of the Civil War. Former slave and free families intermarried, and some retained their connection to the LDS faith.

Pioneers and frontier settlers, both black and white, were well acquainted with death as the harsh conditions of life in that era took their toll. Travel was arduous, and communication across long distances was slow and difficult. Enslavement often brought with it the breakup of families. Advertisements published in Southern newspapers after the end of the war witness the desire former slaves felt to reunite with family members who had been lost during slavery days:

$200 REWARD

During the year 1849, Thomas Sayle carried away from this city, as his slaves, our daughter, Polly and son, Geo. Washington to the State of Mississippi, and subsequently… when last heard from they were in Lagrange, Texas. We will give $100 each for them, to any person who will assist them, or either of them, to get to Nashville, or get word to us of their whereabouts if they are alive.[13]

It is impossible to know how many of these poignant requests were answered. The longing to reunite with family members was not always

---

11. "Act in Relation to Service," box 1, fd. 55, Territorial Legislative Records, Series 30=150, Utah State Archives and Records Administration, Salt Lake City.

12. W. Paul Reeve, *Religion of a Different Color: Race and the Mormon Struggle for Whiteness* (New York: Oxford University Press, 2015), 137–39, 145–47. There is some evidence to support an earlier date for a race-based priesthood restriction, but Brigham Young presented a public articulation of it in his speeches to the Utah territorial legislature in January and February 1852.

13. "W. B. Scott & Son," *The Colored Tennessean* (Nashville), Oct. 7, 1865.

possible to fulfill in this life, but there was a way for Latter-day Saints to validate familial bonds and offer the message of the gospel to those who had passed on. The performance of proxy baptisms and confirmations for the dead and eternal family sealings offered an otherworldly way to link departed friends and relatives to each other and to the living; to knit together families that had been broken apart by death, war, and religious disagreements. If relationships could not be reassembled in this life, there was hope for a complete family structure in the next. The concept of welding unbreakable family ties proved very appealing to believing Latter-day Saints, but this doctrine must have been particularly important to a people who had lost so much to the cruel realities, separations, and adversities of slave life. The eight black Mormons who entered the Endowment House baptismal font in 1875 were no exception. Most of them had been slaves. With the ordinances they performed, they began to lay claim to beloved family and friends.

Three married couples—Jane Elizabeth Manning James (Perkins) and her second husband, Franklin Perkins; Samuel Davidson Chambers and his wife, Amanda Leggroan Chambers; and Amanda's brother Edward (Ned) Leggroan and his wife, Susan Gray Read Leggroan—were participants in the "temple pro tempore" baptismal service.[14] Annis Bell Lucas Evans and Franklin Perkins's daughter Mary Ann Perkins James, accompanied them.[15] The group performed forty-six baptisms and confirmations with the help of white officiators. Samuel H. B. Smith baptized the proxies, and John Cottam performed the confirmations. Abinadi Pratt and Oluf F. Due acted as witnesses. These four white men were regular participants and officiators in the Endowment House in this period.[16] John D. T. McAllister recorded the proceedings. He later became president of the St. George, Utah, and Manti, Utah, tem-

---

14. For a detailed description of the purpose and layout of the temporary structure used for some proxy ordinances, see Brown, "Temple Pro Tempore."

15. Although the LDS Church does not currently keep racial statistics of members, all the black members of the Salt Lake Eighth Ward listed in the early Record of Members did have a notation written to the side of their names indicating they were "colored." For example, see Record of Members Collection, Eighth Ward, Part 1, CR 375 8, box 1862, fd. 1, images 87–88, Church History Library, Salt Lake City, Utah (hereafter cited as CHL).

16. By consulting the microfilmed records of baptisms for the dead performed both before and after September 3, 1875, one finds the names of these men over and over taking part in the ordinances in different capacities.

ples and worked closely with LDS Church presidents to standardize the endowment and set policy.[17] It seems unlikely this group of African American Mormons could have attended the Endowment House together without the patronage of a church leader, and McAllister may have been that leader. He and some of the other officiators were closely associated with President Young and may have received specific instruction on how to record the baptismal data that day.

Jane Manning James (Perkins) is the best known of the early African American Saints who participated. At the time, she was married to Franklin Perkins.[18] She had divorced her first husband, Isaac James, in 1870 and married Perkins around 1874.[19] Jane used his surname during the approximately two years they remained husband and wife. Jane had come to Utah as a free black woman, but Frank had lived his first years on the Wasatch Front as a slave belonging to LDS converts Reuben and Elizabeth Petillo Perkins. They brought Frank, his former wife, Esther, and their children with them to work a farm in the Sessions Settlement, later renamed Bountiful, Utah. Like their owners, the black Perkins family members were LDS.[20] Frank and Esther were the parents of eleven children, born over a span of twenty-two years. Only five of the eleven lived beyond age twenty-one and married. In 1865, Esther died, leaving Frank with young children to raise. That same year, Frank's daughter Mary Ann married Jane James's oldest son, Sylvester. The early black community of Salt Lake City was very small, and as children grew up and married, family connections became complicated. Nine years later, Frank Perkins and Jane James's marriage made for an especially intertwined relationship between the

---

17. Lucile McAllister Weenig and John Daniel Thompson McAllister, *Biography of John Daniel Thompson McAllister: Utah Pioneer, Second President of the St. George Temple and of the Manti Temple of the Church of Jesus Christ of Latter-day Saints: Also Family Stories and Genealogy of Ancestors and Descendants* (Orem, Utah: L. M. Weenig, 1980); John D. T. McAllister Journals, Vol. 9, Jan.–Dec. 1875, CHL.

18. Record of Members Collection, Eighth Ward, Part 1, images 87–88, CHL.

19. Isaac emigrated from Nauvoo with Jane and was the father of all her children, except Sylvester. He came back to Jane at the end of his life, and she took care of him in his final illness.

20. As is the case for some of the other black Mormons living in the Salt Lake Eighth Ward, there is only a rebaptism date available for Frank Perkins.

two families since the Jameses' mother and son were married to the Perkinses' father and daughter.

Jane James had joined the LDS Church as a single young woman. She helped to convert her immediate family and convinced them to make an arduous trek from their home in Connecticut to Nauvoo. She lived there with Joseph and Emma Smith and later with Brigham Young. Her story has been told in detail in other places, but there is an episode in her later years that is worth re-examining in light of the 1875 baptismal event.[21] Beginning in December 1884, Jane began asking church presidents and leaders to allow her to be adopted into Joseph and Emma Smith's family, something she said Emma had offered to her in Nauvoo.[22] First, she wrote to church president John Taylor. He did not allow the adoption, but six months later, the president of the Salt Lake Stake, Angus Cannon, mailed a recommend to Jane allowing her to do baptisms and confirmations for her "dead kindred."[23]

In 1890, Jane asked Joseph F. Smith, a counselor in the First Presidency, to be sealed to Q. Walker Lewis, a black priesthood holder, and to obtain endowments for her dead. She repeated her request to be adopted into the Joseph and Emma Smith family. In response, in 1894, Smith, acting as proxy for his uncle Joseph Smith Jr., performed a specially written ceremony that "attached" Jane to Joseph Smith Jr. as an eternal "Servitor" (a euphemism for servant). Jane may not have been informed about this unique rite until after it took place, because a white proxy acted for her and Jane was, reportedly, not satisfied with the ceremony. It was soon after this episode that Jane began asking for her own endowment. She continued to make this request until 1903

21. Henry J. Wolfinger, "A Test of Faith: Jane Elizabeth James and the Origins of the Utah Black Community," in *Social Accommodation in Utah*, ed. Clark S. Knowlton (Salt Lake City: American West Center Occasional Papers, University of Utah, 1975), 126–72.

22. The doctrine of adoption was separate from that of sealing a man to a woman in marriage. It was a doctrine Jane could have heard about but not fully understood until later in her life. She says she did not know exactly what Emma Smith was offering her at the time. Elizabeth J. D. Roundy, "Life Sketch of Jane Elizabeth Manning James," qtd. in Wolfinger, "A Test of Faith," 154. On adoption, see Gordon Irving, "The Law of Adoption: One Phase of the Development of the Mormon Concept of Salvation, 1830–1900," *BYU Studies* 14, no. 3 (Spring 1974): 291–314.

23. Angus M. Cannon to Jane E. James, June 16, 1888, Document 2, in Wolfinger, "A Test of Faith," 148.

(she died five years later). Most accounts of her life confuse her asking for a sealing or adoption with her later requests for an endowment. They also assume she was given the opportunity to be baptized for her dead in 1888 as a way to satisfy her and to keep her from continuing to ask for her endowment. In fact, she was asking only for an adoption or sealing in 1884, not an endowment. Knowing that she and other black members of the church did proxy baptisms as early as 1875 suggests that she was not granted the right to participate in vicarious baptisms simply or directly in response to her repeated requests for other temple ordinances. Almost thirteen years before she received a limited temple recommend from Stake President Cannon, she had already been allowed to enter the Endowment House to do proxy baptismal work.

The letters Jane wrote to church authorities shed light on what she saw as her white leaders' obligations toward those of her race and reveal her anxiety to insure her own and her loved ones' exaltations. In her letter of December 27, 1884, to John Taylor, she invoked his membership in the covenant race, and hoped that "as this is the fullness of all dispensations," he would be able to extend a blessing to her, despite the fact that she, being of African descent, was considered, at that time, to be outside of the Abrahamic Covenant.[24] She did not ask for an endowment at that time because of her "race & color," but she did hope that salvation could be extended to her through adoption into the Smith family. This was something that her white friends, who were members of the House of Israel, would have to do on her behalf. Ironically, as someone who considered herself outside the covenant race in 1875, Jane extended a blessing to another black woman by being baptized for her at the Endowment House. She and her husband, Frank, stood as proxies for an elderly couple, Morris and Susan Brown, who had lived in Jane's hometown.[25]

24. In Jane's patriarchal blessing, Hyrum Smith (Joseph Smith's older brother) declared her to be a descendant of "Cainaan," indicating her lineage was not through one of the sons of Abraham. Her blessing did not declare that she, like most white Mormons, was of the House of Israel. LDS Church President Spencer W. Kimball later asserted, "In regard to the matter of becoming members of the House of Israel by adoption when we are baptized, this is not the doctrine of the Church." See Spencer W. Kimball, N. Eldon Tanner, and M. G. Romney to J. Duane Dudley, May 17, 1974, David J. Buerger Papers, 1841–1988, MS 662, box 32, Special Collections, J. Willard Marriott Library, University of Utah.

25. When Jane and Frank went to the Endowment House, she was baptized for one woman, Susan Brown, and Frank was baptized for Morris Brown, who presumably was

Despite her unsuccessful attempts to be granted the temple-related ordinances, Jane remained a committed Mormon until her death, but her son Sylvester did not share her devotion. He did not participate in the Endowment House baptisms with his wife, Mary Ann Perkins James.[26]

Sylvester and Mary Ann were married in 1865 and had eight children together, despite their rumored difficult marriage.[27] Only three of their children lived until adulthood. Their youngest child, named after his father, had died at the age of five months in June 1874. Mary Ann was pregnant with their fourth child at the time she performed the proxy baptisms in September. That little boy, Albert Sherman, who was born the following January, lived only a few days.

The other unaccompanied female member of the group was Annis Bell Lucas Evans.[28] She and her husband, William Evans, and their

<hr>

Susan's husband. It seems reasonable to think that Jane and Frank were acting for an older couple whom Jane had known in New England. United States, 1840 Census, Connecticut, Fairfield, Wilton, digital image, s.v. "Morris Brown," at *Ancestry.com.* The Browns are listed as a "free colored male" and a "free colored female" both in the 55 to 99-year-old category.

26. Mary Ann, Frank Perkins's oldest daughter, was baptized for her grandmother Dawney or Downey, possibly the slave girl, "Rondowney," who was given to Reuben and Elizabeth Perkins by Elizabeth's father. See Anne Williams McAllister and Kathy Gunter Sullivan, eds., *Civil Action Papers, 1771–1806, of the Court of Pleas and Quarter Sessions, Lincoln County, North Carolina: Edited Extant Tryon Civil Action Papers 1771–1779; CRX 298 Lincoln Civil 1812–1813 and Criminal 1779–1788; Selected Lincoln Criminal Action Papers from 1786–1808; Not Extant: 1779–1881 Lincoln Civil Action Papers* (Lenoir, North Carolina: McAllister–Sullivan, 1989), cited in Eugene H. Perkins, *The First Mormon Perkins Families: Progenitors and Utah Pioneers of 1847–1852: A Contemporary History of the Ute Perkins Line* (N.p.: E. H. Perkins, n.d., ca. 2008). She was also proxy for four of her aunts. These aunts may have been Grandmother Downey's daughters. Sylvester, Jane James's oldest son, was biracial. She declined to talk about how she became pregnant with him. Her mother took care of him so Jane could work immediately after he was born, but after Jane's marriage to Isaac, she raised Sylvester with her younger children. Sometime after arrival in Utah, according to his granddaughter, Henrietta, he developed a grudge against the LDS Church and Brigham Young. See Henrietta [Leggroan] Bankhead, Oral interview by Florence Lawrence, Salt Lake City, Utah, 1977, transcript, 16, Helen Zeese Papanikolas Papers, 1954–2001, MS 0471, Special Collections, Marriott Library.

27. Mary Lucile Perkins Bankhead, Oral interview by Alan Cherry, Salt Lake City, Utah, 1985, transcript, 9, Charles Redd Center for Western Studies, LDS Afro-American Oral History Project, 1985–1987, MS 10176, CHL.

28. She is called "Annie" or "Anna" in some records. Annis gave Tennessee as her birthplace in the 1870 US Census. She came to the Endowment House to serve as proxy for three of her sisters, Mary, Sarah, and Ellen, who were born in Purdy, Tennessee, between 1836 and 1849. Two of them had died by 1869. She was also baptized for two other female friends, one as young as eighteen at her death. There are several other men with the surname

daughter came to Salt Lake from Denver, Colorado, where William worked as a waiter in a hotel.[29] The family is listed as "mulatto," or biracial, in census data. LDS ward records do not list William and Annis as members, but they do record the blessings of two of their children who were born in Salt Lake City.[30]

The other two married couples who participated in the 1875 baptisms, the Chamberses and Leggroans, were closely related like the Perkins and James families. Amanda Leggroan Chambers, Samuel's wife, was the younger sister of Ned Leggroan. Amanda and Ned had been born into slavery on a plantation owned by David Lagrone.[31] They grew up in a slave family group with their father, Green, and mother, Hattie.[32] Amanda married Samuel Chambers in 1858. Samuel had converted to the LDS faith as a young enslaved teenager living in Noxubee County, Mississippi. After emancipation, Samuel and Amanda worked as sharecroppers, and, by 1870, they had saved enough money to leave the South and join with other Latter-day Saints in Utah.[33] When they left Mississippi, they brought along Ned, his second wife, Susan, and the Leggroans' three young sons. While many LDS converts migrated to Utah territory in large organized wagon trains or handcart companies put together by leaders and missionaries, the Chambers and Leggroan families funded their trip and arrived in Utah on their own. Remarkably, Samuel was the only member of the LDS Church among the group. By all accounts he was

---

of Lucas or Evans whose baptisms were done by Samuel Chambers. Since Annis Evans's husband was not in attendance, Samuel must have done the work for her male relatives.

29. United States, 1870 Census, Colorado Territory, Arapahoe, digital image, s.v. "William Evans," at *Ancestry.com*. He apparently continued to work in food service in Utah. In 1880, William is listed as a cook for a mining operation in Granite. See United States, 1880 Census, Utah, Salt Lake, Granite, digital image, s.v. "William Evans," at *Ancestry.com*. There are also listings of a William Evans in the Salt Lake City Directory in the late 1880s and into the 1890s who is a cook. He worked at the Cullen and Templeton Hotels and is probably the same William Evans. Found via *Ancestry.com*, US City Directories, 1822–1995.

30. Record of Members Collection, Eighth Ward, Part 1, image 73, CHL.

31. LaGrone farmed in Perry County, Alabama, before relocating his plantation to Noxubee, Mississippi. Ned could have been born in either state, but Amanda was born after the move to Mississippi. United States, 1830 Census, Alabama, Perry, digital image s.v. "David LaGrone," at *Ancestry.com*.

32. Her name is listed various ways: Hattie, Hettie, Hedie.

33. William G. Hartley, "Samuel D. Chambers," *New Era,* June 1974.

a formidable man, and must have convinced his wife, brother, and sister-in-law that life would be good in the latter-day Zion. Amanda, Ned, and Susan may have left the South knowing only what Samuel told them about the religion that they would join and belong to for the rest of their lives.[34]

After settling in Utah, Samuel and Amanda Chambers stayed in close contact with relatives in the South. Samuel brought his teen-aged son, Peter, with the family when they immigrated, but several other children stayed in Texas and Mississippi. Soon after the Endowment House baptisms, the Chambers family purchased land in Millcreek, southeast of downtown Salt Lake City. They did well financially and were able to gather some members of their far-flung family to their home.[35]

During the years the Salt Lake City Endowment House was used for the performance of select temple rituals, records were kept of the ordinances in special register books. There is no record of the African American proxy baptisms that were done on September 3, 1875, with the other listings in the temple register kept for that period.[36] Instead, Brigham Young had the ordinances performed by the black members listed in a separate document. When the Genealogical Society of Utah filmed the two leaves of paper on which these baptisms were listed in 1961, the document was titled "Record of Baptisms for the Dead for the Seed of Cain."[37] On both of the two lined pages, someone wrote these instructions,

---

34. No first baptism dates have been located in LDS sources for Ned, Susan, or Amanda, but Frances Grice, as the Salt Lake correspondent for a black San Francisco newspaper, reported the Leggroans' baptisms. They would have occurred on June 5, 1873, if Grice's information is correct. "Correspondence," *The Elevator* (San Francisco), June 14, 1873. Eighth Ward membership records list rebaptisms for Ned and Susan Leggroan on January 13, 1876, and for Samuel and Amanda Chambers on November 27, 1875. Record of Members Collection, Eighth Ward, Part 1, images 87–90, CHL.

35. Tonya Reiter, "Life on the Hill: The Black Farming Families of Mill Creek," *Journal of Mormon History*, Vol. 44, no. 4 (Oct. 2018): 68–89.

36. Church of Jesus Christ of Latter-day Saints, microfilm no. 1149518 and microfilm no. 1149523, FHL. These two microfilms are photographs of the original Endowment House registers for recording baptisms for the dead. They do not list any rites performed on September 3, 1875.

37. "Colored Brethren and Sisters." Today, the film is listed in the FHL catalog under this title, using the designation "colored" rather than the more provocative "Seed of Cain."

These are to be entered in a Book by themselves;
the book to be headed
"Record of Baptisms for the Dead
of the
(Seed of Cain")
or
(of the People of African Descent)
From Pres. Young.)

It seems clear from the notation "From Pres. Young" that Brigham Young was aware of the baptism event and allowed it to take place but also indicated how the record should be kept. The orders about how to title the document and to keep it as a separate record are underlined two and three times. In addition, the black Saints' baptisms were the only ones performed on that Friday in the Endowment House font. The unwritten policy that allowed black members of the church to do proxy baptisms for their dead had not changed since Nauvoo, but in Salt Lake City, under Young's presidency, the participants seem to have been segregated in the performance of the rite. Even the record of their ordinance work was not to be mingled with the other Endowment House records. The pages that recorded black baptisms were set apart as if they, as well as the participants, were tainted with the curse of Cain.

The record listing the baptisms done by the eight participants in 1875 is a valuable document for genealogical and historical information about these early black Latter-day Saints. They did not leave many written records, and so the relationships that are noted in it give insight into connections that would otherwise not be known. In addition, it offers a glimpse into the lives and minds of these early Saints, showing they remembered and valued family members they had been forced to leave behind.

Slaveholders often offered marriage ceremonies to their slaves, but did not always allow them to make a commitment until death. Owners reserved the right to separate "married" partners. The proxy work of Samuel and Amanda Chambers suggests that Samuel considered his prior marriages to be legitimate. He wanted to bring former wives and in-laws into the church he loved.[38] This record includes the name of

---

38. Amanda was baptized for two of Samuel's former wives and his former mother-in-law.

one of Samuel's wives who is not listed anywhere else. She was probably the wife who was sold to Texas along with their two children.[39] The record of these baptisms also clarifies the marriage histories of Ned and Susan Leggroan and fills in blanks on their family tree.[40]

In 1888, thirteen years after the group of black Saints performed proxy baptism in the Endowment House, Jane Manning James traveled to the Logan, Utah, temple to do more vicarious work. She was one of many who entered the temple baptismal font on April 3, but the only black participant. The record of her work is listed alongside all the other baptisms done that day by white proxies.[41] The same is true of the proxy baptism she performed on November 22, 1894, in the Salt Lake temple.[42] Despite the rulings made against her requests for higher temple ordinances, and Elijah Abel's second denial of an LDS temple endowment by church president John Taylor, black members were still permitted to perform vicarious baptisms.

Throughout the late 1800s and into the administration of church president Joseph F. Smith, as questions were submitted by regional leaders wishing to clarify the church's policy regarding the allowing of persons with various degrees (amounts) of "negro blood" to obtain their endowments and participate in vicarious baptisms, repeatedly the answer was "no" to temple endowments and sealings but "yes" to baptisms. Questions about the priesthood restriction seemed to be answered primarily by referring to precedent reportedly set by the founding prophet, Joseph Smith, while questions regarding black proxy baptisms were not. Instead, leaders reasoned that since people

---

39. "Worthy Couple Married 66 Years," *Deseret News*, May 10, 1924. Diana Ann McNees is only named in the baptismal record, but she is likely the wife to whom he referred in the article.

40. Susan stood proxy for Ned's first wife, Florida or Florinda. Ned was baptized for Susan's first husband, Samuel Read or Reid, and Susan for her former mother-in-law.

41. "Baptisms for the Dead, 1884–1943," Vol. H, Apr. 3, 1888, includes heir index, Logan Temple, microfilm no. 177847, FHL. It was not until this second baptismal experience that Jane served as proxy to her mother, grandmother, sister, and other family members. Her mother and sister had been Latter-day Saints, but may have joined the Reorganized Church of Jesus Christ of Latter Day Saints later in life, necessitating the posthumous rebaptism.

42. "Baptisms for the Dead, Book D, 1894–1895," Salt Lake Temple, microfilm no. 183413, FHL.

of African descent could be baptized in life, vicarious rites could be extended to deceased black men and women. In 1889, Wilford Woodruff responded to David H. Cannon: "Concerning the giving of endowments to persons of negro descent ... we feel you should not administer the ordinance of endowments to any in their behalf. Their relatives can be baptized for them and also confirmed; but beyond this we think nothing more should be done." In 1895, George Reynolds, a secretary to the First Presidency, wrote to Levi Savage: "The same rule holds good with regard to both living and dead. For those who have associated with any upon whom rest the curse of Cain[,] baptisms can be performed, but endowments cannot be received. The fact of them being dead does not make any difference in regard to this law."[43]

The question of allowing black members to enter the sacred space of a temple never seemed to be at issue. On November 10, 1910, the church's Quorum of the Twelve discussed South African Mission president B. A. Hendricks's question, "Is it possible for a promiscuously bred white and negro to be baptized for the dead?" President Joseph F. Smith remarked, "He saw no reason why a negro should not be permitted to have access to the baptismal font in the temple to be baptized for the dead, inasmuch as negroes are entitled to become members of the Church by baptism."[44] He also told Hendricks that he should not "encourage the Negro saints of South Africa to emigrate to Zion in order ... to do temple work in behalf of their dead."[45] In the absence of written policy or a scriptural mandate, when a question was posed about the propriety of black proxies doing baptisms for their kin, the topic was freshly debated or answered from inference from what was allowed for live black converts. From the Nauvoo period until at least 1910, when Smith answered Hendricks, it appears there were no restrictions barring black Latter-day Saints from participating in the rite, but the records of their ordinance work were kept separately from the general temple register, at least for work done in the Salt Lake temple.

---

43. As quoted in Anderson, *Development of Temple Worship*, 82, 101–02.

44. George A. Smith Family Papers, 1731–1969, MS 0038, box 78, fd. 7, Special Collections, Marriott Library.

45. Newell G. Bringhurst, "Mormonism in Black Africa: Changing Attitudes and Practices 1830–1981," *Sunstone*, May/June 1981, 15–21.

On February 6, 1912, one of the black Mormons who had participated in the 1875 visit to the Endowment House requested more baptisms to be done on his behalf. At "the instance of" or by request of Samuel Chambers, sixteen men and thirteen women received vicarious baptisms and confirmations. On this occasion, Samuel and his wife, Amanda, did not act as proxies. Instead, a Norwegian temple worker and his wife performed the ordinances in the Salt Lake temple.[46] The beneficiaries of these baptisms were more of Samuel's relatives and friends whom he knew in the South. There is a "Mr. Green" and a "Hedie Green" listed in the register, probably referring to Amanda's parents who had died by this time. Remarkably, Samuel wanted his white biological father and half-brother to receive baptismal rites, so a proxy acted for James Davidson and his son, David Patton Davidson. In a reversal of what has become a controversial LDS practice, Samuel also asked that members of his white slaveholding family receive vicarious baptisms. He had stayed in contact with his white owner's daughter after he had gained his freedom and left Mississippi.[47] He considered her to be his half-sister, and in 1912 requested that she and her deceased husband receive baptisms and confirmations. Her father, Maxfield Chambers, was also one of the beneficiaries Samuel named. He had been Samuel's owner since he was a young boy. James Davidson, Samuel's father and first owner, had sold or given him to Maxfield Chambers sometime in the late 1830s or early 1840s.

There are no records available to ascertain the reason Samuel and Amanda did not act as proxies in the Salt Lake temple in 1912, but beginning on October 14, 1924, and continuing until June 15, 1942, a register was made for "All Negro Blood Baptisms and Confirmations for the Dead" that were performed in the Salt Lake temple.[48] This ten-page record appears to be another separate document used specifically

---

46. "Baptisms for the Dead, 1893–1943, heir indexes, 1893–1960," Register Vol. 20, Oct. 24, 1911, microfilm no. 183450, FHL.

47. Minnie Lee Prince Haynes, Oral History, interviewed by William G. Hartley, Salt Lake City, Utah, Aug. 22 and Dec. 1, 1972, OH 5, CHL.

48. "All Negro Blood: Baptisms and Confirmations for the Dead," Salt Lake Temple F 183511, photocopied register of ordinance work done from Oct. 14, 1924–June 15, 1942, John D. Fretwell Collection, held by his son, John L. Fretwell in Smithfield, Utah; copy in my possession.

for listing vicarious work done for people of color. In it, the names of proxies, officiators, those for whom the baptisms were performed, and the person who requested the work to be done are all recorded. The register lists 163 baptismal recipients for the eighteen years it was kept. It is similar to the 1875 "Seed of Cain" record, except white proxies served for deceased black men and women, even when the person requesting the baptism was a black Latter-day Saint.

One of the baptisms recorded in this document is for a young boy, Paul Howell. His father, Abner Howell, was a prominent African American LDS convert who joined the church on February 26, 1921, just nine days after the death of his eight-year-old son, Paul. Paul's vicarious baptism was done in 1938 in the Salt Lake temple, but Abner did not serve as the proxy for his son, even though he was living in Salt Lake City at that time. He and his wife were sent to the South as unofficial LDS ambassadors in the 1950s, and he enjoyed presenting firesides as one of very few active LDS black men in Utah and later in California.[49] He is known as a devout Mormon who would have done the work for his son if he had been allowed to do it.[50] There may have been reasons unrelated to race that prevented Abner from serving as proxy for his son, but he is not the only black member whose family was represented in the temple by white proxies.

In 1875, black Mormons had acted for their relatives and friends. Fifty years later, white members were evidently substituted for black members and the record of the ordinances was still segregated from the general register. The listing of Jane James's proxy baptism in the regular Logan temple register is the exception to the rule for Utah temple records.

The apparent policy change to substitute white proxies for black relatives corresponds to the tenure of Apostle George F. Richards as Salt Lake temple president, but that could be coincidental. His view on the status of African Americans is in line with other early LDS leaders: "The Negro is an unfortunate man. He has been given a black skin. But that is as nothing compared with that greater handicap that he is not

49. Margaret Blair Young, "Abner Leonard Howell: Honorary High Priest," unpublished paper, copy in my possession.
50. Kate B. Carter, *The Story of the Negro Pioneer* (Salt Lake City: Daughters of Utah Pioneers, 1965), 55–60.

permitted to receive the Priesthood and the ordinances of the temple, necessary to prepare men and women to enter into and enjoy a fullness of glory in the celestial kingdom."[51] Richards is almost certainly referring to the LDS temple endowment, not baptisms, when he speaks of temple ordinances, but his message is clear: black members were not entitled to the same blessings as white Latter-day Saints.

What may only be hinted at by the "All Negro Blood" register became written policy in 1964. President David O. McKay's diary recorded for February 14, "Temples—Book of Decisions for Presidents ... Presidents [Hugh B.] Brown and [N. Eldon] Tanner [McKay's counselors in the First Presidency] reported to me [David O. McKay] that they had gone through the manuscript of the proposed book of decisions ... and had marked those items which they felt needed decision by me. ... I approved as follows: (6) It was suggested that the ordinance of baptism for members of the negro race be performed by others than negroes if this can be accomplished without offense."[52] McKay may have simply acquiesced to a de facto policy that was in place during the first half of the twentieth century.

Throughout the 1960s, McKay made rulings on allowing or disallowing temple ordinances for a variety of situations where race came into play. Although none of these involved baptisms for the dead, they show that race policy was not always clear, especially when it involved mixed-race individuals or mixed-race families. These had posed the thornier issues for McKay's predecessors' decisions as well. In 1965, McKay did not permit a white mother to have her biracial children sealed to her and her new white husband. In 1966, McKay reaffirmed older rulings, and in a First Presidency letter forbade members from doing temple ordinances for deceased persons with any known "Negro blood." A month later, he authorized the sealing of two children with "Negroid blood" to white adoptive parents. He encouraged local leaders to discourage white couples from adopting black children in 1967,

---

51. George F. Richards, sermon in *One Hundred Ninth Annual Conference of the Church of Jesus Christ of Latter-day Saints, April 1939* (Salt Lake City: Church of Jesus Christ of Latter-day Saints), 58. This was an object lesson offered to show the penalty for being lukewarm towards church service and commitment.

52. As quoted in Anderson, *Development of Temple Worship*, 341–42.

but the next year allowed a white widower to be sealed to a white wife and his biracial children from his first marriage. By so doing, McKay contradicted the decision he had made in 1965 and gave his approval to a sealing requested by a white father even though he had withheld the same from a white mother.[53]

Even as late as 1972 and 1974, LDS First Presidencies were being asked to clarify policy in regard to black Mormons participating in vicarious baptisms. The Provo, Utah, temple president asked President Joseph Fielding Smith if he should permit a black couple to join a group from a Brigham Young University stake to do proxy baptisms. The First Presidency answered by stating, "Provided that this couple can meet every requirement for admission to the temple, there would be no reason why they should not be given temple recommends for the limited purpose of serving as proxies in temple baptisms."[54]

In 1974, a BYU stake president asked if there was any reason a young black woman could not receive a patriarchal blessing. He went on to question if she could do proxy baptisms. President Spencer W. Kimball and his counselors wrote she was entitled to a blessing and that the patriarch should state her lineage, but did not address the question of proxy baptisms.[55]

Of the inquiries that are available to researchers, the majority of the questions that were addressed to First Presidencies concerning the advisability of sending black Latter-day Saints to temples to perform baptisms and confirmations came from local leaders in Utah. During the twentieth century, there were very few black Mormons in the state. Most of the descendants of the original African American pioneers had moved into black churches or had not been able to reconcile with the church's racial prohibitions. There were probably very few black Latter-day Saints in the Intermountain West who requested the "limited-use" temple recommends needed for baptisms for the dead. By 1974, temples were open in Los Angeles, Oakland, and Washington, DC, where the population of black members might have been higher than in Salt Lake City. Since no racial statistics are kept by the LDS Church, it is difficult,

---

53. Anderson, 361, 364, 367, 371.
54. Anderson, 407.
55. Kimball, Tanner, and Romney to Dudley.

if not impossible, to know accurately how many black Mormons did baptisms in temples outside of Utah before 1978. Local leaders outside of Utah may not have questioned the church's general authorities about the practice—or the records are not available to researchers.

In light of the inconsistencies and vagaries of LDS racial policy throughout the history of the church until 1978, it seems remarkable that the Salt Lake Eighth Ward members and friends managed to come together as a group of black Latter-day Saints and act as proxies in vicarious baptisms more than one hundred years before men and women of African descent were able to have access to higher temple worship and ordinances. The separate registers of 1875 and 1924–42 that list vicarious work done by and for people of color stand as a testament to the secondary status assigned to African Americans by former LDS practices and beliefs. In the early days of Mormonism, when black men were ordained to the priesthood, it looked as if the same opportunities for temple ordinances would be available for members of all races. It was during this time of expanding theology that Elijah Abel engaged in the newly introduced practice of baptism for the dead. The fulfillment of what seemed to be promised at that time was not to be. By the beginning of the 1850s, the idea of an inherited race-based curse began to proscribe privileges for black Latter-day Saints. Priesthood ordinations, temple endowments, and temple sealings were withheld. It is within this period of limited access to temple worship that the little group of members and friends of the Salt Lake Eighth Ward performed the only vicarious work for their dead that black members were allowed to do. Despite the demonstrated faithfulness exhibited by Elijah Abel and Jane James through their long lives in the LDS Church, both were denied much-desired temple ordinances. Well into the first half of the twentieth century, questions were raised and debated as to whether black Mormons should even be allowed to do proxy baptisms. Presidents of the church, with their counselors, consistently gave permission for this level of temple service to be extended to members of African descent, while also forbidding their participation in the endowment ritual. By the mid-1960s, it appears that some policy makers thought it would be best if black members could be deflected from entering temple baptismal fonts and acting as proxies in baptisms for the dead.

President David O. McKay seems to have agreed that vicarious ordinances should only be done by white proxies, a practice that seems to have been instigated earlier. By the early 1970s, records indicate that black members, once again, had free access to temple fonts in Utah.

The history of the policy governing the practice of allowing or disallowing black Latter-day Saints of African descent to participate in vicarious baptism affirms the endurance and strength demonstrated by so many who lived their lives under the burden of a supposed curse. They continued to practice their religion without knowing what their place would be in the next life. No matter how faithful they were in this life, they believed they were barred from the ordinances necessary for exaltation in the next one. The leap of faith they took to offer the blessing of baptism to deceased loved ones exhibits the courage and spunk these early black Saints retained in the face of prejudice, opposition, and, at times, almost insurmountable obstacles. Many of them had worked and sacrificed to join with other members of their faith in Utah. They raised their families without the support of a large black social community and with limited economic opportunities. Throughout the years in which black Saints endured intolerance and opposition, including from white members of their congregations, they began to redeem their dead. In so doing, they looked forward to the promised day when those family members and friends could enjoy, with them, the blessings of eternal life and family relationships in an unbroken circle.

SIX

"COME, LET US GO UP
TO THE MOUNTAIN OF THE LORD"
THE SALT LAKE TEMPLE DEDICATION, 1893

BRIAN H. STUY

The Salt Lake temple, under construction since 1853, represented to the Saints in 1893 a literal fulfillment of Isaiah's prophesy (Isa. 2:2–3) regarding the temple in the mountains,[1] and many believed its dedication signaled the imminent commencement of the millennial era, when the church would go back to Jackson County, Missouri, and the Savior would return. Thus, for the members present, the dedication of the Salt Lake temple constituted one of the most important events in the history of the world.

Due to the sacred nature of temple dedications, the church typically does not grant access to the official records of these events; however, by reading the diaries of Saints who participated in the temple dedication, one can almost attend the ceremonies vicariously. As viewed through the pages of the contemporary diarist, the dedication emerges as a spiritual event unparalleled since the dedication of the Kirtland, Ohio, House of the Lord in 1836.

For Wilford Woodruff, president of the church, the dedication of the Salt Lake temple was one of the most important experiences of his life, an event for which he believed the Lord had protected and preserved

---

1. For examples of LDS Church leaders teaching that the Salt Lake temple fulfilled Isaiah's prophecy, see Orson Pratt, Mar. 10, 1872, *Journal of Discourses*, 26 vols. (London: Latter-day Saints' Book Depot, 1854–86), 14:349; June 15, 1873, *Journal of Discourses,* 16:80; Erastus Snow, Sep. 14, 1873, *Journal of Discourses,* 16:202–203; George A. Smith, Mar. 18, 1855, *Journal of Discourses,* 2:212–13; George Q. Cannon, Nov. 2, 1879, *Journal of Discourses,* 21:264–65; also Aug. 3, 1890, *Collected Discourses*, 5 vols., ed. Brian H. Stuy (Burbank: B.H.S. Publishing, 1986–98), 2:93; and Charles W. Penrose, May 15, 1892, *Collected Discourses*, 3:57.

him, and over which he had been foreordained to officiate. Woodruff's experiences regarding the temple began with a vision he said he received while the Saints were still in Nauvoo, Illinois, following the martyrdom of Joseph Smith in 1844. During dedication services in Salt Lake City, Woodruff "related his vision he had in Boston some 50 years ago. How the Lord showed him the Saints would move to the Rocky Mountains and build this Temple, and [that] he would be called upon to open it to the people and dedicate it to the Lord."[2] "I anticipated the dedication of that Temple for fifty years," he proclaimed shortly after, "for I attended the dedication of that Temple fifty years ago in a vision, and when I got through that work, I felt that I had arrived at the end of my work in the flesh."[3] Another time he recounted that "I was ordained to dedicate this Salt Lake Temple fifty years before it was dedicated. I knew I should live to dedicate that Temple. I did live to do it."[4]

Woodruff's experiences with the temple increased as construction progressed. In August 1862 President Brigham Young toured the temple lot with Woodruff and Isaac Morley. While inspecting the temple foundation,[5] Young said, "I expect this Temple will stand through the Millennium & the Brethren will go in and give the Endowments to the people." Turning to the two men, Young then declared, "I do not want to quite finish this Temple for there will not be any Temple finished until the one is finished in Jackson County, Missouri pointed out by Joseph Smith. *Keep this a secret* to *yourselves* lest some may be discouraged."[6]

---

2. Francis Asbury Hammond, Journal, Apr. 10, 1893, Church History Library, Church of Jesus Christ of Latter-day Saints, Salt Lake City, Utah, spelling and punctuation modernized, hereafter CHL.

3. Discourse delivered Dec. 13, 1893, *Collected Discourses*, 3:421.

4. Wilford Woodruff, Apr. 7, 1898, *Sixty-Eighth Annual Conference of the Church of Jesus Christ of Latter-day Saints* (Salt Lake City: Deseret News, 1898), 29.

5. The temple foundation had been buried in preparation for the arrival of Johnston's Army in 1858. In 1860, after the army had settled thirty miles outside of Salt Lake City, Brigham Young began making preparations to resume construction of the temple. As the foundation was uncovered, large cracks were found running from the walls into the foundation. Young was informed by the mason foreman that "the work on one side was defective and such a foundation is dangerous" (Wallace Alan Raynor, *The Everlasting Spires: A Story of the Salt Lake Temple* [Salt Lake City: Deseret Book Co., 1965], 102). After consultation with other specialists, Young decided to have the foundation excavated and relaid. It was the newly completed foundation that Young, Woodruff, and Morley inspected.

6. Wilford Woodruff, *Wilford Woodruff's Journal, 1833–1898*, 9 vols., ed. Scott G. Kenney (Midvale, Utah: Signature Books, 1983–85), 6:71–72, emphasis original (spelling and

The impact of this statement on Woodruff is evident by the fact that he recorded Young's words in both his personal diary and the Church Historian's office journals.[7] Young's statement no doubt impressed Woodruff with the millennial nature and significance of the temple and further heightened in his mind its prophetic destiny.

---

punctuation modernized). As church leaders publicly proclaimed their desire to finish the temple, Young declared, "I want to see the Temple finished as soon as it is reasonable and practicable. Whether we go in there to work or not makes no difference; I am perfectly willing to finish it to the last leaf of gold that shall be laid upon it, and to the last lock that should be put on the doors, *and then lock every door, and there let it stand* until the earth can rest before the Saints commence their labors there" (Brigham Young, Apr. 8, 1867, *Journal of Discourses*, 11:372, emphasis mine). Although an in-depth study of Young's views concerning the return to Jackson County is beyond the scope of this essay, a brief study of Young's sermons indicates a millennialistic cycle that peaked with the commencement of the Civil War in 1861. In response to the question of when the Saints would return to Jackson County, Young proclaimed in 1852, "Not until the Lord commands it" (Aug. 28, 1852, *Journal of Discourses*, 6:269). Earlier he had indicated his belief that if the Saints then listening did not return themselves, their children would (Aug. 15, 1852, *Journal of Discourses*, 6:296; also June 6, 1858, *Journal of Discourses*, 7:66; Oct. 21, 1860, *Journal of Discourses*, 8:225; on Young's expectation to see Jackson County "in the flesh," see Sep. 9, 1860, *Journal of Discourses*, 8:175). Prior to the commencement of the Civil War, Young's teachings indicated an uncertainty regarding when the Saints would return to Jackson County but a conviction that the time was near and that the Saints should be ready to go at any moment.

The beginning of the war increased Young's expectation that the time was nearing for the Saints to return to redeem Zion. "One great blessing the Lord wishes to pour upon this people is that they may return to Jackson county," he declared. "If our enemies do not cease their oppression upon this people, as sure as the Lord lives it will not be many days before we will occupy that land and there build up a Temple to the Lord" (Apr. 6, 1862, *Journal of Discourses*, 9:270). While the Civil War raged in the East, Young boldly declared, "We are determined to build up the kingdom of God on the earth; to bring forth Zion, to promote the cause of righteousness on the earth. ... The time has now come when this work will be consummated" (Aug. 31, 1862, *Journal of Discourses*, 9:368). This declaration was made one week after Young uttered his instructions to Woodruff on the temple grounds to delay completion of the temple until after the return to Jackson County. Two years later the president prepared the Saints for his departure to return to Jackson County by warning them, "I expect to be absent, some time from now, for quite a while" (May 15, 1864, *Journal of Discourses*, 10:290). With the US government still intact following the Civil War, Young's attitudes regarding the imminent return of the church to Jackson County cooled. It became clear that the time frame for the Saints' return was unknown; no longer was the return to Zion as immediate. It is not possible to determine if Young intended to complete the Salt Lake temple irrespective of the return to Jackson County or if the ending of the Civil War altered his views. If Young did change his intent, he did not communicate this change to Woodruff, who clearly held to the original teachings of the president in 1862. (For an in-depth discussion of the millennial fervor brought on by the Civil War among Young and the Saints, see Louis G. Reinwand, "An Interpretive Study of Mormon Millennialism during the Nineteenth Century with Emphasis on Millennial Developments in Utah," [Master's thesis, Brigham Young University, 1971.]

7. Woodruff, *Wilford Woodruff's Journal*, 6:71–72, spelling and punctuation retained; also Church Historian's Office Journal, Aug. 22, 1862, CHL.

In 1887 Woodruff recorded a dream in which he received what he felt was an important message from Young:

> I dreamed last night that the LD Saints were holding a great Conference at Salt Lake City at the great Temple and thousands of Mechanics were laboring hard to finish the Temple. I was requested to open the Conference As I was an Exile and they might not have me with them long. The Key of the Temple was given me to open it. As I went to the door A large Company were assembled and I overtook Presid[en]t Brigham Young and He asked what the matter was with the great Company at the Door. Some one Answered the Elders did not want to Let the people into the Temple. He said *Oh, oh, oh* and turned to me & said let all[,] all into the Temple who seek for Salvation. I saw several who were Dead and among the Number my wife Phebe. I Believe there is some meaning to this dream.[8]

Following the dedication of the Salt Lake temple, Woodruff reflected on the message he felt he was intended to receive from these nocturnal visitations. As he contemplated his accomplishments following the dedication in 1893, Woodruff interpreted his dreams from six years earlier in a new context. "Two nights in succession before John Taylor[']s Death President Young gave me the Keys of the Temple and told me to go and dedicate it which I did."[9] These visitations by Young had evidently impressed Woodruff with the need to hasten the temple's dedication and had effectively reversed the policy he understood to have been established by Young twenty-five years earlier of delaying the temple's completion until the Saints began to return to Jackson County.[10] At the capstone ceremonies held during the April 1892 gen-

---

8. Woodruff, *Wilford Woodruff's Journal*, 8:429, spelling and punctuation retained. A few days later Woodruff recorded: "I dream almost Ev[e]ry night of these great Meetings. I do not understand what those Dreams Mean" (8:429).

9. Woodruff, *Wilford Woodruff's Journal*, 9:279.

10. It is difficult to determine what, if any, delay tactics were actually employed by Young in construction of the temple. In his public discourses Young frequently admonished the Saints to donate means to hurry completion of the temple (Young, Mar. 2, 1862, *Journal of Discourses*, 9:241; also Mar. 8, 1862, *Journal of Discourses*, 10:36; Oct. 6, 1863, *Journal of Discourses*, 10:267; Apr. 8, 1867, *Journal of Discourses*, 11:372). As has been shown above, however, Young felt that the return to Jackson County was imminent, and thus it is probable that, if the temple had been completed, Young would have delayed its dedication and use until after the church had returned to Jackson County. Construction and dedication of the St. George (Utah) temple shows that Young had changed his ideas concerning the need

eral conference, Woodruff instructed Apostle Francis M. Lyman to place the Saints under covenant to hasten the temple's completion. This resolution, adopted by the unanimous vote of the gathered Saints, also alludes to the change in policy regarding completion:

RESOLUTION

Believing that the instructions of President Woodruff respecting the *early completion* of the Salt Lake Temple is the word of the Lord unto us, I propose that this assemblage pledge themselves, collectively and individually, to furnish, as fast as it may be needed, all the money that may be required to complete the Temple at the earliest time possible, so that the dedication may take place on April 6, 1893.[11]

The date for the dedication was thus set to commence the following April, forty years after the cornerstones were laid and building begun. "We have been as long building that Temple as Moses was leading the children of Israel through the wilderness to the land of promise," observed Woodruff, "and I would like to see it finished."[12]

The next year was spent finishing the interior of the temple in anticipation of the dedication. Following the laying of the capstone, Woodruff walked through the interior and noted in his journal that "a great Deal of work [is] yet to be done in order to get the work done by next April Conference."[13]

In the various settlements, the diligence of the Saints was exerted in a more spiritual direction. With the dedication now less than one year away, the Saints sought ways to prepare themselves for what many expected to be a Pentecostal event not witnessed since the days of Kirtland. A wave of community cooperation and forgiveness swept over the settlements. In order to foster this spirit further, many church authorities toured the settlements, admonishing the Saints to put aside their differences, especially regarding politics. Great spiritual manifestations

---

to delay completion of any temple until the building of the Jackson County temple. It is possible that the focus had shifted only to the Salt Lake temple, and that other temples, which were not viewed in the same millennialistic light, could be completed before the Saints' return to Jackson County.

11. *Millennial Star*, July 1892, 436 (emphasis mine).
12. Wilford Woodruff, June 12, 1892, *Collected Discourses*, 3:82.
13. Woodruff, *Wilford Woodruff's Journal*, 9:195.

were promised as a reward for the years of suffering and persecution the members had undergone in defending plural marriage. On one occasion Apostle Lorenzo Snow "spoke of the great sacrifice made by the saints in the issuance of the [1890] manifesto relinquishing the practice of plural marriage. He felt that the Lord had accepted it, and would bless the people. It was one of the greatest sacrifices made by any people since the days of Enoch. Upon this and other accounts he was of [the] opinion the Lord would grant some interesting manifestations in the Salt Lake Temple."[14]

Two weeks prior to the dedication, the First Presidency called on all the Saints to set aside Saturday, March 25, 1893, as a day of fasting and prayer. The Saints were instructed "that the Presidencies of Stakes, the High Councils, the Bishops and their Counselors, meet together with the Saints in their several meeting houses, confess their sins one to another, and draw out from the people all feelings of anger, of distrust, or of unfriendliness that may have found a lodgment; so that entire confidence may then and there be restored and love from this time prevail through all the congregations of the Saints."[15] Apostle Marriner W. Merrill records that he "went to meetings at 11 a.m., met with the people of Richmond, confessed my sins, and asked forgiveness of the Saints if I had done anyone any wrong."[16]

As the Saints gathered in attitudes of forgiveness and penitence, Woodruff repeatedly met with his counselors to the temple to view the work being done on the interior. Woodruff records that his heart was heavy as they viewed the work that still remained to be completed. "We are in hopes to get it ready for Dedication," he wrote in his journal three weeks before the dedication, "but it is a load upon us."[17] On the afternoon of April 5, a scant twelve hours before the dedication services

---

14. Rudger Clawson, Journal, Oct. 23, 1892, Box Elder Stake Quarterly Conference, Special Collections, J. Willard Marriott Library, University of Utah.

15. James R. Clark, ed., *Messages of the First Presidency of the Church of Jesus Christ of Latter-day Saints, 1833–1964*, 6 vols. (Salt Lake City: Bookcraft, 1965–75), 3:244, message dated Mar. 18, 1893.

16. Melvin Clarence Merrill, ed., *Utah Pioneer and Apostle Marriner Wood Merrill and His Family* (Salt Lake City: Deseret Book Co., 1937), 163, hereafter Marriner W. Merrill Diary.

17. Woodruff, *Wilford Woodruff's Journal*, 9:244.

were to begin, the temple received the finishing touches and was ready at last to be presented to the Lord.

DEDICATION, APRIL 6–24, 1893

A large crowd gathered around the temple on the morning of April 6, 1893. Admission to the temple was through a narrow gate at the west end of the temple block, permitting only one person at a time to enter the grounds.[18] As the Saints entered the grounds, a gentle breeze blew across the square. Overhead clouds were visible, with an occasional ray of sunlight adding to the beauty of the day. Promptly at 8:30 a.m. the Saints were conducted through the temple's interior, touring each of the various rooms, until they gathered in the fourth floor Assembly Hall. One participant described what may have been experienced by others: "We were surprised and filled with wonder at the beauty and finish of every room as it was more costly and grand till we came to the upper when we were struck dumb as it were with astonishment at the heavenly grandeur of this room of rooms, it defies description by pen of mortal as to the effect it produced in the mind and heart of the true latter day saint it was indeed the Holy of Holies, and we felt the majesty of heaven was there."[19] John M. Whitaker, private secretary and reporter for Church Historian Franklin D. Richards, described his tour as one of "awe, wonderment and glory."[20]

At 10:15 a.m., after the crowd of over 2,200 had been seated, and with many more left standing in the aisles, the services began.[21] Following the singing of "Let Israel Join and Sing" by the Tabernacle Choir, Wilford Woodruff arose to deliver the dedicatory prayer, "kneeling on a plush covered stool provided for the purpose."[22] The prayer, described by many as comprehensive, requested the blessings of the Lord to rest

---

18. Joseph West Smith, Journal, Apr. 6, 1893, L. Tom Perry Special Collections, Harold B. Lee Library, Brigham Young University.

19. Hammond, Journal, Apr. 6, 1893 (spelling modernized).

20. John Mills Whitaker, Journal, Apr. 6, 1893, 53, transcript, Special Collections, Marriott Library.

21. Joseph H. Dean, Journal, Apr. 6, 1893, 64, CHL.

22. Dean.

upon the temple and everything located therein.[23] "The prayer was simply grand," wrote one witness, "and caused all hearts to overflow with praise and thanksgiving to our heavenly Father, and so manifest was the Spirit of God that the vail was almost rent and we indeed felt we were in the presence of our God and Jesus Christ our Redeemer and hosts of heavenly beings."[24]

The peace and tranquility of the dedicatory services being conducted inside the Assembly Room stood in sharp contrast to the terrible wind storm then raging outside the temple. "The worst windstorm, perhaps, which ever visited Salt Lake, prevailed between 10:30 and 12 o'clock noon," declared the church-owned *Deseret News*, "the destruction … was beyond precedent here."[25] "The air was filled with dust, gravel and debris of many kinds and pedestrians sought shelter in the nearest buildings. Outhouses and small barns were blown down and trees uprooted in all parts of the city. Many fences were badly damaged by falling shade trees."[26]

The timing of the storm with the dedication was not without spiritual overtones. To many who witnessed it, the raging storm stood as a manifestation of the anger and fury of Satan and his angels. One member wrote:

> It is claimed that Heber C. Kimball once predicted that when the Salt Lake Temple should be dedicated the power of Satan should be loosed and the strongest wind storm ever witnessed in Utah should be felt on that occasion. In pursuance and fulfillment of this prediction, a strong breeze began blowing upon our entering the grounds at 9 a.m. and increased to a hurricane of great violence at the precise time the dedicatory prayer was being offered by Pres[ident] Wilford Woodruff.[27]

The storm took on added significance when seagulls were sighted hovering over the temple. "The Evil One seemed *mad*," wrote one observer, and "gulls came and hovered over the House; [they] have not been seen

---

23. *The Contributor*, Apr. 1893, 292–300; N. B. Lundwall, *Temples of the Most High* (Salt Lake City: Zion's Printing & Publishing Co., 1941), 122–32. On average, it took over forty minutes to read the dedicatory prayer at each of the sessions.

24. Hammond, Journal, Apr. 6, 1893.

25. *Deseret News*, Apr. 6, 1893, 1; Apr. 7, 1893, 4.

26. *Deseret News*, Apr. 6, 1893, 1.

27. John Franklin Tolton, Autobiography, Apr. 6, 1893, CHL.

here before for many years. They saved the crops in 1847 by devouring the *crickets*."[28] Thus the twin manifestations of the gulls and the gale became a powerful symbol of the ongoing battle between God and Satan, a battle centered on the Lord's Saints gathered at the temple.

There were other manifestations, of a personal character, that accompanied the dedicatory services. Rudger Clawson recorded in his journal that his wife, Lydia, "heard some beautiful singing that seemed to come from the N[orth] E[ast] corner of the room," even though there was no choir in the area.[29] Apostle Francis M. Lyman also heard this music and declared that he saw "a beautiful light cross the building above the chandeliers."[30] Some witnessed the apparent transfiguration of Wilford Woodruff into the likeness of Brigham Young,[31] while others observed a halo of glory surrounding Woodruff.[32] One individual reported seeing on the stand Brigham Young and several members of the Quorum of the Twelve who had passed away, as well as other spirit beings.[33]

Not everyone went away so blessed. Joseph H. Dean, a carpenter on the temple and member of the Quorum of Seventy lamented that

> Outside of a rich outpouring of the Holy Ghost neither I nor anyone that I have yet heard of saw or heard anything. I was a little disappointed. I had fasted and prayed and tried to prepare my body and mind, so that if pleasing to the Lord my eyes might be opened to see heavenly beings, or my ears to hear their voices as many did at Manti. I also cried to the Lord in my soul with all the faith I could muster, but it was not to be. And I have no complaints to make. The Lord knows best what is good for me.[34]

---

28. Hammond, Journal, Apr. 6, 1893 (emphasis original); also John F. Tolton, Autobiography, Apr. 6, 1893; Jean Bickmore White, ed., *Church, State, and Politics: The Diaries of John Henry Smith* (Salt Lake City: Signature Books/Smith Research Associates, 1990), 289. It seems unlikely that the California gulls had been entirely absent from the city during the preceding years.

29. Rudger Clawson, Diary, Apr. 8, 1893.

30. Melvin A. Lyman, *Francis Marion Lyman Biography* (Delta, Utah: N.p., 1958), 135.

31. Joseph West Smith, Journal, Ninth Session, Apr. 9, 1893, 117; *The Contributor*, Dec. 1894, 116.

32. *Jesse Nathaniel Smith Journal* (Salt Lake City: Jesse N. Smith Family Association, Deseret News Publishing Co., 1953), Apr. 6, 1893.

33. Abraham H. Cannon, Journal, May 18, 1893, Perry Special Collections, Lee Library; also Dennis B. Horne, ed., *An Apostle's Record: The Journals of Abraham H. Cannon* (Cleaerfield, Utah; Gnolaum Books, 2004), 268.

34. Joseph H. Dean, Journal, Apr. 6, 1893, 65–66.

Another unusual event that occurred following the second day's services was the delivery of a baby boy in the font room of the temple.[35] The church's *Contributor* magazine described the circumstances of the birth of the child:

An unusual incident occurred in the Temple on Friday, April 7, shortly after the close of the evening session. Benjamin F. Bennett and his wife, Emma, had attended the meeting. The journey from Provo [Utah] had doubtless hastened an event that had not been expected on that particular occasion. Before Mrs. Bennett could leave the building she gave birth to a son. She was attended by Mrs. Julina Smith; and as soon as mother and child could be safely moved they were taken to the residence of Andrew J. Gray and given all necessary care. On the evening of Saturday, April 15, the infant was carried into the Temple, to the room where it first saw light in mortal probation, and was there blessed by President Joseph F. Smith [of the First Presidency], the name conferred being Joseph Temple Bennett.[36]

The circumstances surrounding the boy's birth provided much discussion for the Saints, many speculating "who that boy could be, born in the Temple."[37]

The program of each of the thirty-one dedicatory sessions, held between April 6 and 24, was essentially the same. Woodruff delivered the dedicatory prayer at the first session. He then allowed the prayer to be read by his two counselors, George Q. Cannon and Joseph F. Smith, and by the Quorum of the Twelve at the remaining sessions. Thus each apostle received the opportunity to deliver the prayer.[38]

---

35. John Lee Jones, Biography, 90, Perry Special Collections, Lee Library.

36. *The Contributor*, Apr. 1893, 301.

37. John Mills Whitaker, Journal, 278, Perry Special Collections, Lee Library. See also www.keepapitchinin.org/2018/10/16/to-little-templeton-bennett/.

38. The following table lists the individual who delivered the prayer in each session of the dedication. The prayers were offered by the apostles in descending order, according to their position in the First Presidency and Quorum of the Twelve, with President Woodruff delivering the prayer only at the first session. Although Moses Thatcher was present at most of the dedicatory services of April 6–11, lingering illness prevented his delivering the dedicatory prayer (Edward Leo Lyman, "The Alienation of an Apostle from His Quorum: The Moses Thatcher Case," *Dialogue: A Journal of Mormon Thought* 18, no. 2 [Summer 1985]: 67–92; also Thomas G. Alexander, *Things in Heaven and Earth: The Life and Times of Wilford Woodruff, a Mormon Prophet* (Salt Lake City: Signature Books, 1991), 292–95; *Millennial Star*, May 29, 1893, 363).

Following the dedicatory prayer, Elder Lorenzo Snow arose to lead the Saints in the Hosanna Shout, an act he performed at each of the dedicatory services.

President Lorenzo Snow, at the request of President Woodruff, instructed the congregation as to the manner of crying "Hosannah, hosanna, hosanna to God and the Lamb. Amen, amen, amen," and the hall resounded with the cry of the host that was present in following him in these words. It was a grand sight and one that is not soon to be forgotten to see the people standing on their feet and waving their handkerchiefs in unison at each cry and uttering a volume of sound which might be heard a long distance.[39]

"This was truly the grandest sight my mortal eyes ever beheld," recorded one participant, "it seemed the heavenly hosts had come down to mingle with us."[40] "The Shout was given with such vehemence and force," wrote another, "as to almost shake the building on its foundations."[41]

Following the Hosanna Shout, the choir sang the "Hosanna Hymn,"[42] after which the congregation arose and joined in singing "The Spirit of

	Morning	Afternoon	Evening
April 6	Wilford Woodruff	George Q. Cannon	
April 7	Joseph F. Smith	Lorenzo Snow	Franklin D. Richards
April 8	Brigham Young Jr.	Francis M. Lyman	
April 9	John Henry Smith	George Teasdale	
April 10	Heber J. Grant	John W. Taylor	
April 11	Marriner W. Merrill	Anthon H. Lund	
April 12	Abraham H. Cannon	George Q. Cannon	
April 13	Joseph F. Smith	Lorenzo Snow	
April 14	Franklin D. Richards	Brigham Young Jr.	
April 15	Francis M. Lyman	John Henry Smith	
April 16	George Teasdale	Heber J. Grant	
April 17	John W. Taylor	Marriner W. Merrill	
April 18	Anthon H. Lund	Abraham H. Cannon	
April 19	PRIESTHOOD LEADERSHIP MEETINGS		
April 20	NO SESSIONS		
April 21	Three Children's Sessions; No Dedicatory Prayers		
April 22	Two Children's Sessions; No Dedicatory Prayers		
April 23	George Q. Cannon	Joseph F. Smith	
April 24	Lorenzo Snow	Franklin D. Richards	

39. George Q. Cannon, Journal, Apr. 6, 1893, typescript online only at www.church-historianspress.org/george-q-cannon/.

40. Hammond, Journal, Apr. 6, 1893.

41. Rudger Clawson, Diary, Apr. 6, 1893.

42. L. John Nuttall, Journal, First Session, Apr. 6, 1893, typescript in my possession. Other popular hymns were often substituted for the "Hosanna Hymn," including Eliza

God Like a Fire Is Burning." The rest of the session was then set aside for various members of the First Presidency and Quorum of the Twelve to address the Saints. "The Lord has accepted this House as an offering from the Saints" was the common theme of the discourses, and "he has forgiven his penitent people." President Joseph F. Smith, in the first session of the dedication,

> arose and spoke with great emotion. He wept like a child and all that were present wept with him. In conclusion he called upon all who felt that the Lord had accepted of the House to say Aye! A united shout went up. And for all who felt the House was not accepted of God to say No! but not a single response was made.[43]

This theme of acceptance and forgiveness was consoling to the Saints, many of whom harbored lingering feelings of confusion and anxiety regarding the 1890 Woodruff Manifesto ostensibly banning plural marriage. The dedicatory services thus became a time of recommitment to the laws and covenants of God, and many Saints came prepared to receive divine confirmation that they and the church were accepted of the Lord.

No person sought this confirmation more than President Woodruff. Perceiving the expectations of the Saints regarding the spiritual manifestations they had been promised, Woodruff sought on every occasion to relate visions, revelations, and other manifestations he had received regarding the temple dedication. "I feel at liberty to reveal to this assembly," he announced during the second day of dedication, "what has been revealed to me since we were here yesterday morning." He proceeded to relate a marvelous vision in which he had seen the heavens singing with the Saints:

> Last night I had a vision: I saw President Joseph Smith, Brigham Young, John Taylor and all the heavenly hosts who have died in this dispensation shouting praises to the Lord; and that as the shouting of the Hosannah went up from the temple, the shout was re-echoed to Christ and the saints, up to the throne of God: That they were more interested in

---

R. Snow's "O My Father, which was sung with a solo by R. C. Easton in a "soul-inspiring manner" Joseph West Smith, Journal, Thirteenth Session, Apr. 11, 1893).

43. Joseph H. Dean, Journal, Apr. 6, 1893, 65.

the dedication of this temple than we possibly could be and that the Lord accepted this temple."[44]

Another witness recorded that Woodruff stated that "Our Saviour had appeared unto [me] in the East Room in the Holy of Holies, & told [me] that He had accepted of the Temple & of the dedication services, & that the Lord forgave us His Saints who had assisted in any manner towards the erection and completion of the Temple."[45]

It was also crucial for Woodruff to assert his calling as God's true prophet, which he accomplished by emphasizing his frequent spiritual witnesses. The manifestations recounted emphasized his role in the early church, including his experiences with the prophet Joseph Smith, and divine manifestations he had received throughout his life. One vision, which Woodruff alluded to frequently during the dedication discourses, portrayed to him "thousands of the Lamanites [Native Americans] enter[ing] the temple by the door in the west end of the [temple] previously unknown to him. They took charge of the temple and could do as much ordinance work in an hour as the other brethren could do in a day."[46] Another experience occurred in St. George in 1877, following the dedication of that temple, when "a class of men came to me in the night visions, and argued with me to have the work done for them. They were the Signers of the Declaration of Independence."[47] "Pres. Woodruff said today that he had received more revelation in the last week than during any one year of his life. He also said that the testimony of the Holy Ghost was more to be relied on than the visitation of angels."[48]

---

44. John M. Whitaker, Journal, Third Session, Apr. 7, 1893; also Archibald Bennett, ed., *Saviors on Mount Zion*, Advanced Senior Department Course of Study (Salt Lake City: Deseret Sunday School Union Board, 1950), 142–43; Anthon H. Lund, Journal, Apr. 7, 1893, CHL.

45. John Lee Jones, Biography, 90. The Holy of Holies is the central sealing room (of three) just off the Celestial Room. It is reserved primarily for the administration of second anointings.

46. Jesse Nathaniel Smith, Journal, Apr. 8, 1893, 393; Joseph West Smith, Journal, Apr. 12, 1893.

47. Joseph West Smith, Journal, Apr. 11, 1893; John D. T. McAllister, Journal, Apr. 7, 1893, Perry Special Collections, Lee Library. See also Brian H. Stuy, "Wilford Woodruff's Vision of the Signers of the Declaration of Independence," *Journal of Mormon History* 26, no. 1 (Spring 2000), 64–90.

48. Joseph H. Dean, Journal, Apr. 12, 1893, 71.

Through these experiences, Woodruff sought in nearly every session in which he spoke to reconfirm to the Saints his position as prophet, seer, and revelator of the church. He hoped that the dedication would manifest to the Saints that the church was still under the guidance of the Lord.

During his opening remarks, Woodruff uttered a prophesy in which he said "a better day was dawning, and as the Apostles were now united Satan would not have power to create division among them." "He said the light & power of this Temple would be felt all over the earth, that our enemies should not have power over his Saints. The Lord is going to give His Saints the good things of the earth in greater abundance."[49]

The topics presented to the Saints varied from speaker to speaker and session to session. However, a study of the documentary sources shows that three prominent themes were discussed by Woodruff, by the other members of the First Presidency, and by the Quorum of the Twelve: namely, forgiveness, the millennial reign, and union/unity.

The Woodruff Manifesto, issued three years previously, relinquished what many Saints felt to be a vital and essential commandment of the Lord. Many questioned the Manifesto's divinity,[50] and leaders of the church often taught that a lack of diligence on the part of the church as a whole led to the Lord's removing plural marriage from the church. These points were also broached in the various sessions of the dedication.

Joseph F. Smith, in addressing the congregation, introduced the subject of the Manifesto by testifying, "[There is] not one principle of the Gospel but what is true. No not one! They can never be false." In answer to the rhetorical question "Why did the church abandon plural marriage?" Smith "explained that a number of laws had been given,

---

49. John Lee Jones, Biography, 90.

50. General authorities who tended to view the Woodruff Manifesto as politically expedient included apostles John W. Taylor, John Henry Smith, Marriner W. Merrill, Heber J. Grant, Brigham Young Jr., and George Teasdale (Alexander, *Things in Heaven and Earth,* 269). For additional comments on the views of these men and of the general church membership towards the Manifesto, see Richard S. Van Wagoner, *Mormon Polygamy: A History* (Salt Lake City: Signature Books, 1986), 145–56; B. Carmon Hardy, *Solemn Covenant: The Mormon Polygamous Passage* (Urbana: University of Illinois Press, 1992), 127–53; D. Michael Quinn, "LDS Church Authority and New Plural Marriages, 1890–1904," *Dialogue: A Journal of Mormon Thought* 18, no. 1 (Spring 1985): 46–49.

and withdrawn on account of the people not being prepared for them. Only 2% of the people ever entered the Celestial order of marriage; … some were only too glad of an excuse to forsake and abandon. Now if any man shall forsake and abandon his loved ones, he shall wither away and die. Obey the laws of the land but do not forsake your covenants."[51] Smith also reminded the Saints that "the Prophet Joseph suspended the Law of consecration after the people had rejected it in a conference. Pres[iden]t Woodruff suspended Plural Marriage when the Lord told him to and not till then. We would have been ground to powder by this Government if we had not been led by the Lord to do as we did."[52] Smith admitted, however, that "had the Lord given the Manifesto earlier than He did, he could not have accepted it but he had become convinced it was right."[53]

Smith echoed what was probably felt by many of the authorities and by other church members, namely, that the Lord had withdrawn plural marriage due to the lack of obedience on the part of many Saints. For this reason, the tenor of the talks relating to forgiveness centered on the Lord's pardoning his people as a whole, not necessarily as individuals. "Prest. Woodruff told us the Lord had accepted the House," wrote one observer, "and the people as a Church and our sins were all forgiven and would not be proclaimed on the house tops."[54] Like Joseph F. Smith, Woodruff also sought to explain the reasons for the Manifesto, but rather than focus on the failings of the Saints, he emphasized governmental pressure to relinquish the practice of plural marriage.

> I feel disposed to say something upon the Manifesto. To begin with, I will say that this work was like a mountain upon me. I saw by the inspiration of

---

51. Joseph West Smith, Journal, Eighth Session, Apr. 9, 1893, 116. Studies have shown that a significantly higher percentage of members entered into, participating in, or were involved with polygamy. Stanley S. Ivins estimated that at the time of the Woodruff Manifesto more than 10 percent of church members were in polygamous relationships (Stanley S. Ivins, "Notes on Mormon Polygamy," *Utah Historical Quarterly* 35, no. 4 [Fall 1967]: 311.) Davis Bitton places the percentage at 10–20 percent ("Mormon Polygamy: A Review Article," *Journal of Mormon History* 4 [1977]: 111). The actual percentage varies according to time period/decade and community.

52. Hammond, Journal, Nineteenth Session, Apr. 14, 1893.

53. John Henry Smith, Diary, Eighteenth Session, Apr. 14, 1893 (spelling and punctuation modernized), White, *Church, State, and Politics*, 290.

54. Hammond, Journal, First Session, Apr. 6, 1893.

Almighty God what lay before this people, and I know that something had to be done to ward off the blow that I saw impending. But I should have let come to pass what God showed me by revelation and vision; I should have lived in the flesh and permitted these things to come to pass; I should have let this temple gone into the hands of our enemies; I should have let every temple been confiscated by the hands of the wicked; I should have permitted our personal property to have been confiscated by our enemies; I should have seen these people—prophets, and apostles, driven by the hands of their enemies, and our wives and children scattered to the four winds of heaven—I should have seen all this, had not the Almighty God commanded me to do what I did.[55]

Woodruff sought to console the Saints, repeatedly stressing that the Lord would never have permitted him to do something contrary to his will. He reminded the Saints that he had lived with Joseph Smith, Brigham Young, and John Taylor. "Was there a man on God's footstool that could have moved them to the right or the left from anything that they felt inspired to do?" he asked. Directing the Saints' attention to the assembled First Presidency and Twelve, Woodruff asked the defining question that the Saints needed to answer in order to come to grips with the Manifesto:

Here are George Q. Cannon, Joseph F. Smith, and these Twelve Apostles. I want to ask you if Wilford Woodruff could have done anything that these men would have accepted, in performing the work that was done, that pained the hearts of all Israel, except by the spirit and power of God? No. I would just as soon thought of moving the foundations of this world as to have taken any course to move these men only by the revelations of God. When that Manifesto was given they accepted it. Why? Because they had the Spirit of God for themselves; they knew for themselves it was right. It was passed also before ten thousand Latter-day Saints and there was not a solitary hand lifted against that edict.[56]

Woodruff's sentiments were echoed by his counselor George Q. Cannon, who also reminded the Saints, "A little while ago the U.S. Government had possession of this Temple and ground surrounding it

---

55. "Manifesto of 1890, Extract of sermon by President Wilford Woodruff at the Sixth Session of the Dedication Services of the Salt Lake Temple," Perry Special Collections, Lee Library.
56. "Manifesto of 1890."

and clouds of darkness hung heavy over us[. It] seemed as though the
Lord had hid his face from us, but now behold the peace and joy we
are permitted to see and partake of[.] Should we not praise the Lord
and thank his most Holy name! He it is that has wrought out this great
deliverance and not man."[57]

The Salt Lake temple became, in essence, a symbol and token of
the Saints' penitence to the Lord, and the message of the leaders to
the Saints was that the Lord had accepted their sacrifice. "The Lord
had forgiven the sins of the people," Woodruff assured, "and accepted
our offering of broken hearts and contrite spirits." In addition, Woodruff "promised great blessings to the people[;] if [we] are united Satan
should never have power to cause us to stray away from the Lord."[58]

A second theme prominently discussed during the dedicatory services concerned the imminent return of the Saints to Jackson County
and the approach of the Millennium. The commencement of the
1890s found the Saints anxiously awaiting the expected migration of
the church to Missouri and the return of Jesus Christ. As a result of
several prophecies made by Joseph Smith—prophecies which, in turn,
had been reinterpreted and promulgated by some later church authorities—the millennial expectations of the Saints reached a crescendo
in the early 1890s.[59] No one individual felt this urgency more than
Woodruff. For him, dedication of the temple signified the fulfillment
of ancient and modern prophesy and the approaching millennial era.
"The Savior is here and rejoicing with us and many of the now born
will live to see him in the flesh," Woodruff declared, "the vail [between
this life and the next] is growing thinner."[60] "The Ancient Prophets,
Isaiah and others prophesied and we are fulfilling, Christ is near and
the work must be hastened, we are approaching the time for Jesus to
come and be in our midst. ... [The] Millennium is at hand [and] we
must wake up."[61] "I urge the saints to enter into their secret chambers

---

57. Hammond, Journal, Sixteenth Session, Apr. 13, 1893.
58. Hammond, Twelfth Session, Apr. 11, 1893.
59. See Dan Erickson, "Joseph Smith's 1891 Millennial Prophecy: The Quest for Apoc-
alyptic Deliverance," *Journal of Mormon History* 22, no. 2 (Fall 1996): 1–34.
60. Hammond, Journal, Tenth Session, Apr. 10, 1893.
61. Hammond, Sixteenth Session, Apr. 13, 1893.

and pray for the redemption of Zion—prayers which will assuredly be heard and answered, for Zion's redemption is at hand."[62]

Others also exhibited their feelings regarding the future: "I dare say there are many under the sound of my voice who will be present in Jackson County,"[63] declared Lorenzo Snow, "some of you will give this [Hosanna] shout in the great Temple to be built in Jackson County."[64] George Q. Cannon told the Saints that women have "a right to prophecy when wrought upon by the Holy Spirit, and that we are approaching the time when the Saints will go back to Jackson County and there build up the Center Stake of Zion and redeem the land of Zion."[65] Thus, even though the temple was dedicated prior to the Saints' return to Jackson County, as Brigham Young had wanted, the dedication should not be seen as an indication of the demise of millennial expectations in the church. "We have built this House to have the Savior come to it, which will be soon."[66]

By far, the most emphasized theme of the dedication dealt with unity. After the dissolution of the People's political party in 1892, the issue of partisan politics had become increasingly important to church leaders and members in general. Evidence shows that even within the highest ranks of the church the discussion of politics tended to bring contention and ill will. The dedication thus became a time of reflection and evaluation for those caught in the web of politics. "Many good humble souls have had their feelings sorely tried because of the divisions among the *leaders* in politics," Cannon explained, "but thank the Lord we are now united as never before, and Satan shall never have power [to] divide us again on those lines, we must give heed to the Counsel of the first Presidency in all things for the Lord will [not] suffer us to lead you astray; we are after liberty for this people and we care not whether it comes through Democrats or Republicans, we want Statehood."[67]

---

62. Joseph C. Muren, "When the Dead Shout Hosannas: Remarks made by Wilford Woodruff at the Salt Lake Temple Dedication," part 4 in *The Temple and Its Significance* (Ogden, UT: Temple Publications, 1973).

63. Joseph West Smith, Journal, Fifteenth Session, Apr. 12, 1893.

64. Hammond, Journal, Sixteenth Session, Apr. 13, 1893.

65. John Mills Whitaker, Journal, n.d., 55.

66. William Derby Johnson Jr., Apr. 13, 1893, Perry Special Collections, Lee Library.

67. Hammond Journal, Sixteenth Session, Apr. 3, 1893 (emphasis original).

For several days prior to the dedication, the First Presidency and Twelve had sought unity with each other. One member of the group, Moses Thatcher, had been the source of contention and discord in the quorum dating back to President John Taylor's administration. Ill will had been generated between Thatcher and George Q. Cannon over Cannon's assumption of leadership when Taylor had been in declining health prior to his death in 1887. These problems, and several others, had alienated Thatcher from the majority of his quorum.[68] The most significant source of friction, however, was the extremely partisan position taken by Democrat Thatcher in open opposition to the First Presidency, which sought to obtain political parity in Utah between the Republican and Democratic parties. In a May 1892 speech before the Utah Democratic Territorial Convention in Ogden, Thatcher reportedly implied that "Jesus Christ would have been a Democrat and Lucifer a Republican."[69] This angered several members of the First Presidency and Twelve, especially Joseph F. Smith, and threatened to prevent a unity of leadership at the dedication.

To resolve the disunity within the leadership, the apostles began meeting almost daily beginning on March 21, 1893. Of utmost importance was their desire to establish a genuine spirit of harmony and goodwill before the dedication commenced. However, little progress was made; thus as leaders entered the last week before the dedication, the meetings intensified. Apostle Marriner W. Merrill recorded on April 3: "Went to meeting of Quorum at 2 p.m. when Apostle Moses Thatcher's case was again discussed, F[rancis] M. Lyman and John W. Taylor having visited him since our last meeting. They reported him as being very defiant and justifying himself in his course, and treating them in a very discourteous manner while at his house. President Snow was very pronounced against Brother Thatcher's course."[70]

As the dedication approached, it appeared that leaders would be unable to bring full unity to their ranks. One last meeting was scheduled to convene two days before the dedication. Although Thatcher had been too ill to attend the previous day's meeting, he telegraphed

---

68. Lyman, "Alienation of an Apostle," 68–72.
69. Lyman, 73.
70. Marriner W. Merrill, Diary, Apr. 3, 1893, 163.

his intention to attend this last meeting. For over two hours members of the quorum pleaded with Thatcher to acknowledge his being out of harmony with the First Presidency. Finally, as the meeting neared midnight, Thatcher "confessed he had done wrong in the position he had taken in regard to political matters and that he desired the fellowship of the presidency and his quorum."[71] "All voted to forgive him freely."[72] With union ostensibly restored to their ranks, all looked forward to the spiritual blessings expected at the dedication services.

Given the intense focus church leaders had placed on establishing unity in their ranks over the previous weeks, it is no surprise that the topic should be given such emphasis during the dedicatory services. In announcing his intention to avoid political controversy, Woodruff "prophesied that the Presidency and Twelve would never again be disunited, but if any one of them got wrong the Lord would remove them."[73] Before leading the congregation in the Hosanna Shout, Lorenzo Snow stated, "Pres. Woodruff would not allow the Hosanna Shout to be given unless he believed there was union in our midst."[74] George Q. Cannon stated that "he had almost dreaded to see the Dedication day come on account of the division among the people."[75] Alluding to the political troubles within the quorum, Cannon also "spoke of the great division among the people caused by deviding on national politics, how many humble and meek souls had been grieved and sorely tried, but now through the great mercy of the Lord all these ill feelings have been healed up and we are united as never before since he orga[n]ization of the Church." Seeking to obtain the last word on the subject, Canon continued, "[This union] has been brought about by obeying the counsel of the first Presidency[.] Some had thought the Presidency had no right to counsel in political matters, but the Lord understands all things and we must be led by him to seek liberty in any way he may mark out."[76] Also alluding to the political troubles within the quorum,

71. Franklin D. Richards, Journal, Apr. 3 [4], 1893, as quoted in Lyman, Alienation of an Apostle, 77.
72. Marriner W. Merrill, Diary, Apr. 3, 1893, 163.
73. Jesse Nathaniel Smith, Journal, Apr. 8, 1893, 393.
74. Joseph West Smith, Journal, Eighth Session, Apr. 9, 1893.
75. Smith.
76. Hammond, Journal, Tenth Session, Apr. 10, 1893.

Francis M. Lyman stated matter-of-factly that "there is not a man in the chief councils of the Church but what sees eye-to-eye; we are united."[77]

PRIESTHOOD LEADERSHIP MEETINGS, APRIL 19–20, 1893

In an effort to increase the unity experienced by local leaders who attended the dedication, Woodruff decided to call as many stake leaders as could attend to a series of leadership meetings with the First Presidency and Twelve in the Assembly Room of the newly dedicated temple. Following the afternoon session of April 18, stake leaders were called forward and invited to attend two special leadership meetings to be held on April 19 and 20.

The first meeting commenced on April 19 at 10:00 a.m., with the assembled leaders meeting in the President's Room in the temple. In attendance were all members of the First Presidency. The entire Quorum of Twelve Apostles also attended, except Moses Thatcher, who had returned home on April 11 due to illness. The Seven Presidents of Seventies, the Presiding Bishopric, and the presidents of stakes and their counselors were also in attendance.[78] In all, the group numbered 115 men. Following the opening song, "Now Let Us Rejoice," Apostle Brigham Young Jr. offered the opening prayer. The assembled body then sang "Come All Ye Sons of God."[79] Woodruff began the testimony meeting "by saying that he would like to hear the brethren express themselves in relation to the dedicatory services of the Temple, as to whether they endorsed what been said and done, and also desired them to state how they felt towards the First Presidency and Apostles."[80] This approval was important to Woodruff. He wanted to know if the Saints harbored any lingering doubts as to his leadership and the direction he was taking the church. To manifest this unity among the Saints, he had Joseph F. Smith request at each session a vote of acceptance by attending members. This

---

77. Joseph West Smith, Journal, Apr. 15, 1893, 126–27.

78. B. H. Roberts notes that each stake was represented by a member of the presidency "except one—St. Joseph—and a bishop represented that [stake]" (Brigham H. Roberts, Journal, Apr. 19, 1893, Special Collections, Marriott Library); also John Sillito, ed., *History's Apprentice: The Diaries of B. H. Roberts, 1880–1898* (Salt Lake City: Signature Books, 2004), 282.

79. Nuttall, Journal, Apr. 19, 1893.

80. Rudger Clawson, Journal, Apr. 19, 1893.

vote was always unanimous.[81] Each leader stood and bore testimony to his happiness and satisfaction with the dedication proceedings and with Woodruff's leadership. Following these emotional and heart-felt testimonies, Woodruff rose to address the assembled group:

> We have been here about 4 hours and it is time of course for us to dismiss this meeting: but before dismissing I feel that it is a duty resting upon me and my counsellors to say a few words to this assembly, and it is our right and privilege to speak to you by the revelations of the Lord and by the power of truth, and I will promise this assembly that the Holy Ghost will bear witness to them of the truth of what I say, and it is this: The God of heaven and the Lord Jesus Christ and the heavenly hosts—I say this to you in the name of Jesus Christ the Son of God—have accepted the dedication of this Temple at our hands. The God of heaven has accepted His people, has accepted the people who have assembled here. The God of heaven has forgiven the sins of those Latter-day Saints in those that bear the Priesthood in this house, and those who have been humble before the Lord and have attended this Conference. Their sins are remitted, and will be remitted by the power of God, and will not be remembered anymore against his people, unless we sin further.

Shifting the emphasis from the Lord's acceptance of their offering to the leadership's willingness to make that offering, Woodruff continued:

> And again I say to you that the God of heaven and the heavenly hosts accept of your offering. You recollect now, you have been making an offering; and I, as the President of the Church, accept the offering you have made before God and the heavenly host. It is this: you acknowledge the Presidency of this Church, that they bear the Priesthood, and that they are set to govern and control the affairs of the Church and Kingdom of God. This offering you have made before the heavens, and the heavens accept of it. I accept of it as the President of the Church; and I hope that while you live, from this time henceforth, wherever you see that spirit manifest that there is no power on the earth—that the Presidency of the Church have no power to govern or teach anybody—you will remember that you have all testified to the truth that upon their shoulders rests the responsibility of teaching, governing, controlling and counseling the church and Kingdom of God in *all* things on the earth.[82]

---

81. John D. T. McAllister, Journal, Apr. 11, 13, 1893.
82. Rudger Clawson, Journal, Apr. 19, 1893 (emphasis original).

Following Woodruff, counselor Joseph F. Smith stood, as he had in each of the dedicatory services, and called on the assembled brethren to support Woodruff and the First Presidency. Not surprisingly, "all answered with a hearty amen, signifying that they bore witness to the truth of the remarks of Pres. Woodruff."[83] The meeting concluded with Smith offering the benediction, and participants were requested to reconvene the following morning.[84]

As leaders gathered again the next morning, the absence of Woodruff was immediately apparent. The assembled leaders were informed that Woodruff had overexerted himself in addressing them the previous day and was unable to attend this day's meeting. Woodruff later commented on just how sick he had become: "I marvel that I am here. I know that the Lord has preserved my life. ... The Lord gave me power and strength of lungs to fulfil my mission there, until we nearly got through [with the Salt Lake temple dedication]. But one day I staid [sic] there some six hours and I heard all the speeches of the presidents of Stakes. I staid too long and that prostrated me, and I went down apparently to the gates of death."[85]

As the same 115 participants of the previous day regrouped in the President's Room, they once more had the opportunity to listen to the remarks of the president's counselors and several of the Twelve. Beginning the testimony meeting was Joseph F. Smith, who remarked that "we lose nothing in remaining here waiting on the Lord. We must learn to wait upon the people, the Spirit of the Lord has reclaimed us from the cares of the world. The love of God casts out all bitterness, I am the brother of Christ. I love you because the Lord can speak through you and save the people. God is love, we must love God and our neighbour." In closing, Smith instructed the brethren in the ancient method of partaking of the sacrament, "read[ing] from 3rd Nephi how Jesus administered the sacrament, how we are to eat and drink in the presence of God."[86] The leaders were promised the opportunity to receive the sacrament in this method following the remarks by the general authorities.

---

83. John Franklin Tolton, Diary, Apr. 19, 1893.
84. Nuttall, Journal, Apr. 19, 1893.
85. Wilford Woodruff, Dec. 13, 1893, *Collected Discourses*, 3:421.
86. Hammond, Journal, Apr. 20, 1893.

Following Smith's testimony, George Q. Cannon bore testimony of his personal experiences with the Savior. "My joy is full, my desires are granted to see union again prevail in our midst. I have been greatly favored of the Lord. My mind has been rapt in vision and have saw the bea[u]ties and Glory of God. I have saw and conversed with the Savior face to face. God will bestow this upon you."[87]

As noon approached, participants adjourned and clothed themselves in their temple robes. Meeting in the Celestial Room, all 115 men formed a prayer circle, "the largest ever formed in this generation."[88] Following introductory instructions by Joseph F. Smith, George Q. Cannon offered the prayer. During the prayer, one member of the group, Charles Kelly, stake president of Brigham City, fainted, "either for having the arm raised so long or on account of our fast, for we went to this meeting fasting."[89] After the prayer circle, the leaders returned to the President's Room where bishops William B. Preston, Robert T. Burton, and John R. Winder of the Presiding Bishopric had prepared three long tables for the sacrament. Each participant was given a large tumbler with the Salt Lake temple etched into it and a napkin. Presiding Bishop Preston blessed the bread and "Dixie" wine (from southern Utah), "and the brethren were invited to 'eat till they were filled,' but to use caution and not indulge in wine to excess."[90] "The Sacrament as we partook of it was after the ancient pattern as taught to the Saints by the prophet Joseph."[91] As the men broke bread and drank the wine, each shared his thoughts on the temple dedication or bore testimony of any experiences he had had with the prophet Joseph Smith. For many, the leadership meetings, especially the sacrament, constituted the high point of their dedication experience. After nearly six hours of intense camaraderie and companionship, the group adjourned at 6:00 p.m.[92]

Previous to the leadership meetings, it was decided to set aside two days during which Sunday school children throughout the church would be allowed to participate in the dedication. On the days chosen,

87. Hammond.
88. Hammond.
89. B. H. Roberts, Journal, Apr. 20, 1893; Sillito, *History's Apprentice*, 283.
90. John Franklin Tolton, Diary, Apr. 20, 1893.
91. B. H. Roberts, Journal, Apr. 20, 1893; Sillito, *History's Apprentice*, 283.
92. Hammond, Journal, Apr. 20, 1893.

April 21 and 22, over 12,000 children attended one of five sessions. Although the dedicatory prayer was not read at these sessions, the children were able to participate in the hosanna shout and to hear from each of the attending apostles. One participant described the events of the children's session:

> President Lorenzo Snow showed the children a lock of the Prophet [Joseph]'s auburn hair at each session. Apostle Franklin D. Richards testified he had seen the Prophet Joseph Smith, and heard him speak at many a meeting and on one occasion when his face shown bright as the sun, and how great was this manifestation, and so on at all the sessions. Most of the First Presidency arose and spoke briefly so all the children had a personal introduction to all of the General Authorities of the church and heard their voices in the temple, all bore fervent testimony of the greatness and majesty and power possessed by the Prophet Joseph Smith as the Prophet who restored, or was the medium through whom was restored, all the Keys of Power, also the Priesthood of all former holders thereof, and of the place he will occupy in the future of this great work.[93]

Following the children's sessions, regular dedicatory services were held for two more days. The final session concluded on the afternoon of April 24, a full twenty days after they had begun.

As the Saints returned to their homes, many no doubt reflected on the events they had witnessed. The dedication became a time of rebirth, both for the church as a whole and for the individuals who constituted its membership. Throughout the dedicatory services, Woodruff sought to convey to the Saints the Lord's forgiveness of the church as a people. The Salt Lake temple became, in fact, a sacrifice presented to the Lord to obtain corporate forgiveness of sins. The emphasis on the 1890 Woodruff Manifesto and justification for its issuance show that many felt the Saints had brought the Manifesto upon themselves through a lack of obedience to the law of plural marriage. The donations and efforts of each member, and of the church collectively, resulted in Woodruff's promise that God had accepted their offering and forgiven their sins. But each member also reflected personally upon his or her own standing before God. Having been promised forgiveness as a people for the

---

93. John Mills Whitaker, Journal, Apr. 21, 1893, 279.

lack of diligence in obeying God's commandments, many looked inward to assess their personal standing before God. Elder B. H. Roberts wrote: "It has been a Pentecostal time with me, the Lord has shown to me my inner parts, myself; and there I have found such grained and gnarled spots that I have been humbled into sincere repentance. At times I have wondered even how the Lord could tolerate me at all as His servant. Truly it is a manifestation of long suffering & mercy. I am deeply moved with gratitude toward Him for his mercy to me; and now Oh My Father if thou wilt give me grace, how hard will I try to reform, and cease from all my wrong doing."[94]

Along with confirmation of the Saints' forgiveness, Woodruff and the other leaders sought to convey to the Saints that the Lord was still with his church. The issuing of the Manifesto had not caused the Lord to desert them. Woodruff's often recounted vision of the Savior, along with Joseph Smith, Brigham Young, and other prominent leaders on the other side of the veil, was seen as evidence that the church was being guided by continual revelation. The Saints could now focus their attention on the quality and dedication of their own lives. The spirit of unity and love seemed palpable. "I never saw a time when everyone felt so humble and forgiving," wrote one participant following her dedication experience, "a good feeling prevails."[95] Even those not privy to visions or other manifestations returned to their homes uplifted and strengthened. "The dedication of this temple, has not been attended with many great visions of the appearance of angels," wrote B. H. Roberts, "but the spirit of the Lord has been there—the Holy Ghost and that is greater than the angels!"[96] "Pen cannot describe," wrote another participant, "the feeling I had in that most glorious place. ... I cannot express myself in words how we were all in heaven the time we were in the Temple."[97]

94. B. H. Roberts, Journal, Apr. 24, 1893; Sillito, *History's Apprentice,* 284.

95. Jane Wilkie Hooper Blood, "Autobiography and Abridged Diary," Ivy Hooper Blood Hill, ed., 103, Perry Special Collections, Lee Library.

96. B. H. Roberts, Journal, Apr. 24, 1893; Sillito, *History's Apprentice,* 284.

97. William Derby Johnson Jr., Diary, Apr. 6, 1893.

SEVEN

A CONTEST FOR "SACRED SPACE"
THE INDEPENDENCE, MISSOURI, TEMPLE

R. JEAN ADDAMS

"There is not one who calls himself a Latter Day Saint that does not believe a temple is to be reared at Independence [Missouri] on the site of ground owned by the Church of Christ."
—*The Evening and Morning Star*, July 1907[1]

In response to a revelation received in September 1830, the Mormon prophet Joseph Smith Jr. sent missionaries to Missouri in an attempt to convert Native Americans to his new church.[2] Smith himself visited Jackson County, Missouri, in the summer of 1831. Shortly after his arrival, he announced a revelation that designated the town of Independence as "the center place of Zion," and added that "a spot for the temple is lying westward, upon a lot which is not far from the courthouse."[3] In December 1831, following Smith's trip, church bishop

---

1. In the late 1890s and early 1900s, *The Evening and Morning Star* was the official newspaper of the Church of Christ (Temple Lot). The name was derived from the name of the first newspaper of the original church published in the early 1830s in Independence, Missouri. *The Evening and Morning Star* replaced the *Searchlight* in May 1900 as the official organ of the Church of Christ (Temple Lot). *The Evening and Morning Star* ceased publication in late 1916, perhaps due to the reduced membership of the church. *Zion's Advocate* began publishing in May 1922 as the official newspaper and has been continually published from its inception to the present time.

2. LDS D&C 28:8–9; RLDS D&C 27:3a–d. For the purposes of this article, The Church of Jesus Christ of Latter-day Saints will hereafter be cited as the LDS Church and the Reorganized Church of Jesus Christ of Latter Day Saints will hereafter be cited as the RLDS Church. The name of the RLDS Church was changed to Community of Christ in 2001; however, in this essay, the church will be referred to as the RLDS Church because that was the name of the organization as discussed in this essay. Both the LDS Church and the RLDS Church use the book of scripture called the Doctrine and Covenants (D&C), although sections and verses are arranged and numbered differently.

3. LDS D&C 57:1–4; RLDS D&C 57:1–2.

Edward Partridge purchased a 63.27 acre tract of land in Independence which encompassed the location where Smith and others had dedicated the "spot" for the millennial temple.[4]

The dedication and subsequent purchase of this property, known as the Temple Lot,[5] became "sacred space" to the various "Expressions of the Restoration"—a variety of churches claiming their original basis on the revelations of Smith as the prophet of the Restoration. The construction of a House of the Lord (or temple) on the Temple Lot became a fundamental tenet of the church.[6] Moreover, the Temple Lot and its proposed temple or temples continue to be seen as crucial elements in preparing for the return of the church to Independence, for the "Redemption of Zion, and for the eventual return of Jesus Christ, Himself, to commence His millennial reign."[7]

Contributing to the sacred significance of the Temple Lot was the expulsion of early church members from Jackson County in late 1833 by agitated local non-Mormon residents. In December of that year, the Lord responded to Smith's concern for his displaced followers and the unfulfilled promise of building the temple in Independence with a revelation containing the following words: "that you may know my will concerning the redemption of Zion."[8] This statement has been expressly interpreted as meaning an eventual return to Jackson County

---

4. Jones H. Flourney and Clara Flourney to Edward Partridge, Dec. 19, 1831, B:1 (Jackson County, Missouri, property records, Independence, Missouri). The legal description of the parcel is: "63 and 43/160th acres in Section 3, Township 9, Range 32."

5. The Temple Lot or Temple Block is generally understood by the various "Expressions of the Restoration" to be the 2.75 acres owned by the Church of Christ (Temple Lot). Other names including Temple Property, Temple Tract, Temple Site, and Temple Land are often applied to the larger 63.27-acre parcel.

6. LDS D&C 42:35–36; RLDS D&C 42:10c.

7. On June 24, 1833, Smith released his building plat for the City of Zion, showing there would be twenty-four temples at its center. He also gave explanations for their use. See Joseph Smith Jr., *History of the Church of Jesus Christ of Latter-day Saints*, ed., B. H. Roberts, 7 vols. (Salt Lake City: Deseret Book Co., 1971), 1:357–60; hereafter cited as *History of the LDS Church*. Also Richard H. Jackson, "The City of Zion Plat," in S. Kent Brown, Donald Q. Cannon, and Richard H. Jackson, eds., *Historical Atlas of Mormonism* (New York: Simon and Schuster, 1994), 44–45; Arnold K. Garr, Donald Q. Cannon and Richard O. Cowan, eds., *Encyclopedia of Latter-day Saint History* (Salt Lake City: Deseret Book Co., 2000), 211.

8. LDS D&C 101:43; RLDS D&C 98:6a.

by the Saints, and the reclaiming of property—in particular, that "sacred space" known as the Temple Lot.

BACKGROUND

Two churches sharing geographical proximity, a common origin as expressions of Smith's religious thought, and numerous doctrinal overlaps have produced a fascinating story. The intertwined, but separate histories of the Church of Christ (Temple Lot) and the Reogranized Church of Jesus Christ of Latter Day Saints (RLDS, later Community of Christ) reveal a stimulating, but ultimately failed, effort over the course of 128 years (1856–1984) to accommodate each others' beliefs and doctrines.[9] The story of their ongoing relationship can be best understood as they contested control over the Temple Lot.

In the years following Smith's murder in Carthage, Illinois, on June 27, 1844, several men claimed Smith's prophetic mantle. But as the claims of Sidney Rigdon, James Strang, William Smith, Lyman Wight, Gladden Bishop, and others faded in the late 1840s and early 1850s, two significant new groups of faithful Saints developed in the Midwest.

GRANVILLE HEDRICK AND THE CHURCH OF CHRIST

One group of these scattered Saints consisted of three Illinois congregations or branches of the original Mormon church: Half Moon Prairie (Woodford County), Bloomington (McLean County), and Eagle Creek (Livingston County).[10] Due to their distance from church headquarters in Nauvoo, approximately 135 miles to the west, these

---

9. Historically, members of the Church of Christ (Temple Lot) have been called Hedrickites. The organization is but one of several schisms of the original church founded by Smith on April 6, 1830. For an in-depth study of the numerous schisms of Mormonism, see Steven L. Shields, *Divergent Paths of the Restoration*, 4th ed. (Independence, MO: Herald Publishing House, 2001); hereafter Shields, *Divergent Paths of the Restoration*.

10. *Crow Creek Record: From Winter of 1852 to April 24, 1864* (Independence, Missouri: Church of Christ [Temple Lot], n.d.), preface; hereafter *Crow Creek Record*. The original document is presumably in the possession of the Church of Christ (Temple Lot), which allowed the Church of Jesus Christ of Latter-day Saints to microfilm it on October 4, 1977, in Independence, Missouri. Microfilm copies are available at the LDS Church History Library (hereafter CHL) and the LDS Family History Library in Salt Lake City, Utah (microfilm no. 1,019,781), and Community of Christ Library-Archives (hereafter CCLA), in Independence, Missouri (MO 1-48A, Reel 294).

Saints escaped the violence that followed the death of Smith and the subsequent expulsion of Mormons from the area.

Beginning in the winter of 1852,[11] members from these three branches met together periodically in north-central Illinois. The first recorded meeting took place in the home of Granville Hedrick near Washburn, Woodford County, originally known as Half Moon Prairie.[12] Hedrick, a farmer and teacher, was an elder in the original Mormon church.[13] By 1857, this new assemblage came to be known as the Crow Creek branch of the Church of Jesus Christ (of Latter day Saints),[14] but members no longer affiliated with the LDS group that followed Brigham Young to the Great Salt Lake Valley. A conference in December 1860 discussed the church's name. Some members argued for the Church of Christ, the name under which the Mormon church was first organized in April 1830.[15] By 1900, this name was unofficially standardized. The name (Temple Lot) in parenthesis distinguishes this specific Church of Christ from other denominations using the same name.[16]

---

11. *Crow Creek Record*, 1.

12. Hedrick's farm was located approximately 1.5 miles directly west of Washburn in Cazenovia Township, Woodford County. See Jane Hedrick to Granville Hedrick, Jan. 14, 1851, E:278–79 (Woodford County, Illinois, property records, Eureka, Illinois). Washburn was originally named Half Moon Prairie by early settlers who thought the prairie had that particular shape (*Woodford County History* [Woodford County, Illinois: Woodford County Sesquicentennial History Committee, 1968]), 20.

13. Hedrick was born in Clark City, Indiana, in 1814, and converted to Mormonism sometime between 1839 and 1843. He was ordained an elder between 1841 and 1843 ("More Testimony If Called For," *Truth Teller*, Aug. 1864, 31). Hedrick purchased property in Johnson County, Kansas, about thirty-five miles southwest of Independence in 1874 when he was sixty. He made his home there until his death in 1881. Membership Record, Church of Christ at Independence, Missouri, 1.

14. *Crow Creek Record*, preface, 1, 14.

15. *Crow Creek Record*, 10.

16. From 1860 to approximately 1900, the Church of Christ used a variety of names. The *Truth Teller*, published monthly by the Church of Christ between 1864 and 1865, and followed by two issues in 1868, used the name "Church of Jesus Christ of Latter-Day Saints" or "Church of Jesus Christ (of Latter Day Saints)" in the masthead. When John H. Hedrick conveyed his three individual parcels of the Temple Lot to his brother Granville by quit-claim deed, he used the term "President of the Church of Christ (of Latter day Saints)." The *Searchlight*, the official organ of the church between February 1896 and March 1900, used the name "Church of Christ in Zion" in the masthead. Church of Christ (Temple Lot) Apostle William A. Sheldon, in an email, August 23, 2006, stated: "There has never been church action to attach 'Temple Lot' to the church name of Church of Christ. It has been done parenthetically according to whim. ... We have local congregations which do not use

JOSEPH SMITH III AND THE EMERGENCE OF THE RLDS CHURCH

A second group of scattered Saints emerged in June 1852, under the early leadership of Jason W. Briggs and Zenas H. Gurley Sr.[17] These two men, ordained elders in Smith's original church, had sought divine guidance after they rejected the claims of Brigham Young and others in the years that followed 1844. Briggs and Gurley continued to preside over church branches in Wisconsin after Smith's death.[18]

Beginning in late 1851, both men independently said they received visions or revelations directing them to reject all claimants to Smith's prophetic mantle. Briggs claimed the revelation he received told him: "In my own due time will I call upon the seed of Joseph Smith."[19] Briggs and Gurley both proclaimed that Joseph Smith's successor would be Smith's eldest son, Joseph Smith III. After some correspondence, the two agreed to hold a conference in Beloit, Wisconsin, in June 1852.[20] The Briggs and Gurley group initially called itself the New Organization.[21]

---

the appellation at all" (original in my possession). A particular motivation in using the title Temple Lot in parenthesis seems to be to clarify that there was no direct relationship to the Church of Christ founded by Alexander Campbell. I use the name Church of Christ in this essay unless further differentiation is necessary. See R. Jean Addams, "Reclaiming the Temple Lot in the Center Place of Zion," *Mormon Historical Studies* 7 (Spring/Fall 2006): 7–20.

17. Joseph Smith III and Heman C. Smith, *The History of the Reorganized Church of Jesus Christ of Latter Day Saints*, 8 vols. (Lamoni, Iowa: Herald Publishing House and Bookbindery, 1896; Independence, Missouri: Herald Publishing House, n.d.), 3:209; hereafter cited as the *History of the RLDS Church*. Briggs was baptized and ordained an elder in 1841. After Smith's assassination, Briggs followed James Strang and William Smith (Joseph Smith's younger brother), but became disillusioned with their leadership. He then presided over the New Organization's first conference in 1852. He was ordained an apostle in 1853 and became president of the quorum of apostles. Members at the RLDS conference in 1885, however, did not sustain him in that position, and he formally withdrew from the church in 1886. He died in 1899. Gurley was baptized and ordained an elder in 1838. He followed Strang and William Smith after Joseph Smith's death and was ordained an apostle in the New Organization in 1853. He functioned in this capacity until his death in 1871. See Scott M. Norwood, *Who Was Who in RLDS History* (Warrensburg, Missouri: All Good Books, 2007), 13, 43; hereafter cited as Norwood, *Who Was Who in RLDS History*.

18. *History of the RLDS Church*, 3:196–204.

19. *History of the RLDS Church*, 3:201. Briggs received this revelation in October 1851 and published the text in the *Messenger*, Nov. 1875, 1. This periodical, published 1874–77, in Salt Lake City, Utah, was reprinted in 1996 by Price Publishing in Independence, Missouri.

20. *History of the RLDS Church*, 3:201.

21. Shields, *Divergent Paths of the Restoration*, 65. The unofficial full name of the group was the New Organization of the Church of Jesus Christ of Latter Day Saints. Shields used the name "New Organization" in the first edition of his book. Ronald E. Romig, Community

In March 1860, Joseph Smith III, after receiving divine confirmation of his own calling, wrote to William Marks, former church leader under Joseph Smith in Nauvoo, advising him, "I am soon going to take my father's place as the head of the Mormon Church."[22]

EFFORTS AT EARLY UNITY

As early as 1856, leaders in both the Church of Christ (Temple Lot) and the RLDS Church made efforts to create "a working basis of harmony"—and even a union—between the two groups.[23] In June 1857, W. W. Blair of the New Organization traveled to the home of David Judy in Mackinaw, Tazewell County, Illinois, to attend a meeting of the not yet "officially organized" Church of Christ.[24]

Between the fall of 1857 and early 1858, representatives of the New Organization also attended at least one conference of the Crow Creek branch, and Hedrick attended at least an additional New Organization conference in Amboy, Illinois, probably in 1858.[25] One of the reasons these early attempts to unite failed was the issue of lineal descent, a major point of disagreement for the next 130 years.[26] A second major doctrine on which the two groups disagreed was the prophetic role of Joseph Smith Jr. The Church of Christ contended then (as they do now) that

---

of Christ archivist, in an email on February 7, 2008, clarified: "The term New Organization was never an official name of the church. The name was: Church of Jesus Christ of Latter Day Saints. However, the term was and still is often used to describe the early Reorganization" (original in my possession). See also Charles Millard Turner, "Joseph Smith III and the Mormons of Utah," PhD diss. (University of California–Berkeley, Graduate Theological Union, 1985) chap. 4; Bert C. Flint, *An Outline History of the Church of Christ (Temple Lot)* (Independence, Missouri: Board of Publications, Church of Christ, 1953), 92–96; hereafter Flint, *Outline History*.

22. *History of the RLDS Church*, 3:264; Frederick B. Blair, comp., *Memoirs of President W. W. Blair* (Lamoni, Iowa: Herald Publishing House, 1908; Independence, Missouri: Price Publishing, 1994); Mary Audentia Smith Anderson, ed., *Memoirs of Joseph Smith III (1832–1914)*, (Independence, Missouri: Herald Publishing House, 1979), 72; first serialized in the *Saints' Herald*, Nov. 6, 1934–July 31, 1937; hereafter cited as Anderson, *Memoirs of Joseph Smith III*.

23. W. P. Buckley, *A Brief History of the Church of Christ (Temple Lot)* (Independence, Missouri: Church of Christ, 1929), 25.

24. Flint, *Outline History*, 103; *Crow Creek Record*, 4.

25. *History of the RLDS Church*, 3:637.

26. Arthur M. Smith, *A Brief History of the Church of Christ [Temple Lot]: Origins of the Church and Some Differences between It and Factions of the Restoration* (Independence, Missouri: Board of Publications, Church of Christ, 1971), 12; *History of the RLDS Church*, 3:209.

Smith became a fallen prophet in 1834. This reportedly occurred after the Saints were expelled from Jackson County and Smith announced a revelation for the Saints to return to Jackson County for "the redemption of Zion" and that such redemption might come "by power," if necessary.[27] This revelation, the Church of Christ maintained, was contrary to earlier revelations that Zion should be purchased with money.

THE CONTEST BEGINS: THE RETURN TO THE CENTER PLACE OF ZION

In 1864, Hedrick published a revelation that instructed him and his followers to "gather together upon the consecrated land which I have appointed and dedicated by My servant Joseph Smith," in other words, Independence, Missouri. The year of gathering to Jackson County was identified in the revelation as 1867.[28] Between 1867 and 1874, John Hedrick and William Eaton bought the eight lots (2.5 acres)[29] that comprised the immediate area on or near the spot where Joseph Smith Jr. dedicated the temple site on August 3, 1831.[30] John Hedrick and

---

27. LDS D&C 103:15, 29; RLDS D&C 100:3d–e, 6b. For excellent readings on this subject, see Roger D. Launius, *Zion's Camp* (Independence, Missouri: Herald Publishing House, 1984; James L. Bradley, *Zion's Camp 1834: Prelude to the Civil War* (Salt Lake City: Publishers Press, 1990); and James L. Bradley, *The Eternal Perspective of Zion's Camp* (Logan, Utah: n.p., 2004).

28. Granville Hedrick, "Revelation," *Truth Teller*, July 1864, 4. A narration of the personal delivery of the revelation by an angel does not appear in the 1864 article nor, to my knowledge, anywhere else in print. Nicolas F. Denham, in an emotional reminiscence, related that, when he was a teenager, the Hedrick family showed him the bed Hedrick was sleeping on when "an angel appeared to him and gave him the revelation to return to Jackson County" (Nicholas F. Denham, interview with the author, Sep. 2005).

29. Jacob Tindall to John Hedrick, Aug. 22, 1867, 50:331–32 (lot 21); John Montgomery to John H. Hedrick, Sep. 24, 1867, 50:332 (lot 20); and George W. Buchanan to John H. Hedrick, Dec. 12, 1867, 53:526–27 (lot 16). Also, Joseph C. and Mary Irwin to William Eaton, July 9, 1873, 104:311 (lots 17, 18, 19, 22), and Maria McClanahan and Susan Nelson to William Eaton, Mar. 7, 1874, 104:517 (lot 15), Jackson County, Missouri, property records, Independence, Missouri.

30. There is some controversy over who dedicated the "spot" for the temple. *History of the LDS Church*, 1:199, states: "On the third day of August, I [Joseph Smith Jr.] proceeded to dedicate the spot for the Temple, a little west of Independence." On August 2, 1831, the day previous, as noted in B. H. Roberts, *A Comprehensive History of the Church of Jesus Christ of Latter-day Saints: Century I*, 6 vols. (Salt Lake City: Deseret News Press, 1930) 1:255, "Sidney Rigdon by prayer consecrated the land to the gathering of the saints." See also Bruce N. Westergren, ed., *From Historian to Dissident: The Book of John Whitmer* (Salt Lake City: Signature Books, 1995), 86–87. John Whitmer stated: "Sidney Rigdon dedicated the ground where the city is to Stand: and Joseph Smith Jr. laid a stone at the North east corner of the

Eaton quit-claimed these lots to Granville Hedrick as "trustee in trust" for the Church of Christ on November 8, 1869, and on November 5, 1877, respectively. [31] The *Kansas City Times* on November 17, 1877, announced, though without attribution, "It is definitely asserted that the erection of the Temple will shortly be commenced" as envisioned by Joseph Smith in 1831. [32]

In reaction to the Hedrick revelation, Joseph Smith III initially instructed his followers: "We would caution all our readers against going to that land before God commands His Saints to go there by His prophet Joseph. If any go there before that time, they may expect that the judgments of God will come upon them." [33] Smith and the RLDS Church held to this position over the next decade. However, by 1877, the RLDS Church had developed its own gathering strategy. In January 1877, Joseph Smith III announced: "We now state that we are decidedly of the opinion that those who may so desire, can move into that state [meaning Missouri] in safety." [34]

THE CONTEST CONTINUES: PRELUDE TO LITIGATION

After seven years both the Church of Christ and the RLDS Church, during their respective October 1885 conferences, appointed represen-tatives to a committee assigned "to confer in a friendly discussion over the differences, real or supposed, existing between the two bodies." [35] From an examination of the extant correspondence between officials

contemplated *Temple* in the name of the Lord Jesus of Nazareth … Sidney Rigdon pro-nounced the Spot of ground wholey [sic] dedicated unto the Lord forever, Amen." See, also, Donald Q. Cannon and Lyndon W. Cook, eds., *Far West Record: Minutes of the Church of Jesus Christ of Latter-day Saints, 1830–1844* (Salt Lake City: Deseret Book Co., 1983), 9–10.

31. John Hedrick quit-claimed three lots to Granville Hedrick, Nov. 8, 1869, 73:1–2 (lots 16, 20, 21); William Eaton quit-claimed five lots to Granville Hedrick, Nov. 5, 1877, 115:452–54 (lots 15, 17, 18, 19, 22) (Jackson County, Missouri, property records).

32. "A Mormon Temple for Missouri," *Kansas City Times*, Nov. 18, 1877, 2.

33. Joseph Smith [III], "The Truth Vindicated–No. 1," *Saints' Herald*, Aug. 15, 1864, 49. Immediately after Hedrick's April revelation, Joseph Smith III counseled the Saints at a special conference: "You are forbidden to receive his [Hedrick's] teachings" (Minutes of a special conference held at Amboy, [Illinois], June 25–26, 1864, Material provided to the author by Ronald E. Romig, archivist, CCLA).

34. *History of the RLDS Church*, 4:166–67; Joseph Smith III and Henry Stebbins, "Notes on Travel," *Saints' Herald*, Jan. 15, 1877, 25.

35. Anderson, *Memoirs of President Joseph Smith III*, 314; see also Flint, *Outline History*, 117; *History of the RLDS Church*, 4:480–81.

within the RLDS Church, the meeting was likely the result of their interest in acquiring the Temple Lot.[36] In May of the preceding year (1884), Alexander H. Smith[37] (brother of Joseph Smith III) wrote to Edmund L. Kelley[38] (counselor to the presiding bishop of the RLDS Church) and asked him, "What think you of buying the Temple lot here? We can now buy it for just the cost of purchase, back taxes, and cost of improvements. $1800.00. The Hedricites [sic] wants [sic] us to buy it."[39] Continuing, Alexander Smith stated: "I favor buying it. Think of it and talk to William and Blakeslee. Dont [sic] talk to any one [sic] else. Write me soon and let me know what you think of the project."[40] One can only speculate as to why someone from the Church of Christ would ever suggest such a transaction. Obviously nothing developed regarding this potential ownership change.

---

36. Alexander H. Smith to Edmund L. Kelley, May 22, 1884; G. A. Blakeslee to Edmund L. Kelley, June 21, 1884, letters, P16, f6, CCLA.

37. Alexander Hale Smith was born on June 2, 1838, at Far West, Missouri, the son of Joseph and Emma Hale Smith. In 1873, he was ordained an apostle in the RLDS Church, and in 1897 he was ordained a counselor in the first presidency of his brother, Joseph Smith III, president of the RLDS Church. Alexander was simultaneously ordained as the patriarch/evangelist to the church. In 1902, Alexander was released from the First Presidency but continued in his responsibilities as the patriarch/evangelist. He died August 12, 1909 (Ronald E. Romig, ed., *Alexander: Joseph & Emma's Far West Son* [Independence, Missouri: John Whitmer Books, 2010]).

38. Edmund L. Kelley was born on November 17, 1844, at Vienna, Illinois. He was baptized a member of the RLDS Church at age nineteen in 1864. He graduated from the University of Iowa, School of Law, in 1872. In 1882, he was ordained an elder and counselor to the presiding bishop of the church in 1882. Kelley was designated to represent the RLDS Church in the Temple Lot Case. He was ordained as the presiding bishop in 1891, and in 1897, he also assumed the position of counselor to President Joseph Smith III. Kelley was released as presiding bishop in 1916 and died May 23, 1930. See Norwood, *Who Was Who in RLDS History*, 55.

39. Alexander H. Smith to Edward L. Kelley, May 22, 1884, Alexander H. Smith letters, P16, f6, CCLA.

40. Smith to Kelly. Assumption here is that Smith is referring to William W. Blair based on additional correspondence in the years that followed. However, it could be William H. Kelley. Blair was born on October 11, 1828, in Orleans, New York. He was baptized on October 8, 1851; ordained an apostle on October 7, 1858, and a counselor in the First Presidency on April 10, 1873. He died on April 18, 1896. William H. Kelley was born on April 1, 1841, in Johnson County, Illinois. He was baptized on March 1, 1860; ordained an apostle on April 10, 1873; and died on August 14, 1915. Either William, both ranking members of the RLDS Church, could have been aware of what Smith was interested in and may have been a confidant in this matter. Blakeslee is undoubtedly George A. He was born on August 22, 1826, in Ellisburg, New York. He was baptized in 1836 and in April 1882 was ordained the presiding bishop. He died on September 20, 1890. Certainly he, too, would have been aware of what Smith was pursuing. See Norwood, *Who Was Who in RLDS History*, 8, 9, 56.

NOTICE TO QUIT POSSESSION

When the meeting did not produce meaningful results, the RLDS Church filed a "Notice to Quit Possession" in the local court on June 11, 1887.[41] It claimed that the 2.5 acres in possession of the Church of Christ should be relinquished to the RLDS Church as the rightful owner/successor of the original trust created when Edward Partridge purchased 63.27 acres for the church in 1831.

Certainly, the Temple Lot had thus become a major point of self-identification and competition between these two expressions of Joseph Smith's theology.[42] To no one's surprise, the Church of Christ moved quickly to solidify their ownership—in fact, even before the RLDS Church filed its notice. For twenty years, the Church of Christ had planned to build a chapel on the property, but the plans had never advanced beyond discussion. Perhaps having heard of the action planned by the RLDS Church, or sensing a change in attitude, the Church of Christ's April 1887 conference appointed "a committee of three ... to superintend the building of a house of worship and to locate the same on the temple grounds."[43] Construction began sometime thereafter and was completed before October 5, 1889, at a cost of $377.41.[44] From the point of view of RLDS Church leaders, this was an act of overt defiance of their "Notice to Quit Possession."

The question arises: Why had the RLDS Church waited two and a half years after the "Notice," regardless of the construction of the small meeting house of the Church of Christ? The answer may be more in

---

41. Notice to Quit Possession, Served by G. A. Blakeslee, by Attorney, Bishop and Trustee for the Reorganized Church of Jesus Christ of Latter Day Saints, June 11, 1887, Independence, Exhibit 24, in *The Temple Lot Case* (Lamoni, Iowa: Herald Publishing House, 1893; Independence, Missouri: Price Publishing Co., 2003), 247–48. The 1893 printing did not include the "Decision of John F. Philips, Judge in Temple Lot Case" since his decision was not announced until March 3, 1894. The "Decision" was printed separately, together with selected interrogatories, by Herald Publishing House. Price Publishing Company printed Philips's ruling and briefly summarized the decision of the US Court of Appeals, which reversed Philips.

42. R. Jean Addams, "The Church of Christ (Temple Lot) and the Reorganized Church of Jesus Christ of Latter Day Saints: 130 Years of Crossroads and Controversies," *Journal of Mormon History* 36, no. 1 (Spring 2010): 73.

43. Church Record (Independence, Missouri: Church of Christ), 65, quoted in Flint, *Outline History*, 114–15.

44. Flint, 115.

the motive than in the means. Joseph Smith III was very determined to prove to one and all that the church over which he presided was the legitimate successor to the organization founded by his father in 1830. Acquisition of the "sacred space" known as the Temple Lot was a way of solidifying that perspective.[45]

THE RLDS CHURCH PLANS ITS NEXT MOVE

Meanwhile, the RLDS Church acquired, on June 9, 1887, the Partridge–Cowdery–Johnson deed by which the church hoped to prove its ownership of the contested Temple Lot. However, Joseph Smith III was specifically counseled against using the recently acquired deed as a means of validity. A month prior to the actual purchase of the problematic deed, William W. Blair wrote to Edmund L. Kelley that "the deed by E[dward] Partridge to the children of O[liver] Cowdery ... is doubtless a fraud."[46] Joseph Smith III was undoubtedly informed by Kelley of Blair's thoughts or by Blair himself.

Nevertheless, Smith next sought legal advice from RLDS Church counsel George Edmunds. On June 22, 1887, Edmunds wrote to Smith, after questioning the deed itself, noting: "It seems that organization [Church of Christ] has title ... I think you are too late to enforce a resulting trust in Partridge. The rights of Auditors have intervened."[47] Regardless, Joseph Smith III was personally dedicated to the proposition that the RLDS Church was the rightful successor to the original church. He intended to prove it in the court of law and was determined to do so, notwithstanding internal and external advice.[48]

THE CIVIL SUIT IS FILED: THE TEMPLE LOT CASE

On August 6, 1891, the RLDS Church filed a Bill of Equity in the US District Court in Kansas City, Missouri, against the Church of Christ.[49]

---

45. Addams, "The Church of Christ (Temple Lot) and the Reorganized Church of Jesus Christ of Latter Day Saints," 73.

46. William W. Blair to Edmund L. Kelley, May 12, 1887, E. L. Kelley Papers, P16, f15, CCLA.

47. George Edmunds to Joseph Smith III, June 22, 1887, Miscellaneous Letters and Papers, P13, f341, CCLA.

48. Anderson, *Memoirs of President Joseph Smith III*, 310.

49. The Reorganized Church of Jesus Christ of Latter Day Saints, Complainant, vs. The Church of Christ at Independence, Missouri: Richard Hill, Trustee; [et. al.], Bill of Equity,

This action initiated a tangle of litigation known historically as the Temple Lot Case. The litigation consumed the attention of both organizations for the next four and a half years. At the time of the filing, the Church of Christ had fewer than a hundred members, while the RLDS Church had approximately 25,300.[50]

Counsel for the RLDS Church developed a two-fold strategy to secure the Temple Lot. First, they intended to prove that it was the legitimate successor to the original church founded by Joseph Smith Jr. on April 6, 1830. By so doing, the RLDS Church was the rightful possessor of the Temple Lot, since the property had been purchased with church funds in December 1831 by the bishop of the church, Edward Partridge, acting in a trustee-in-trust relationship for the church. The second point of argument was that the RLDS Church now held the rightful deed, notwithstanding internal communication to the contrary, to the property recently acquired from the heirs of Oliver Cowdery, one of Joseph Smith's earliest confidantes.

Escalating the controversy was Charles A. Hall, a member of the RLDS Church since 1878.[51] Unexpectedly, Hall left the RLDS Church in the spring of 1885 and became a member of the Church of Christ. He was ordained an elder in that organization on April 12, 1885, and was formally expelled from the RLDS Church on May 17, 1885.[52] The talented Hall was chosen "presiding High Priest over the High Priesthood of the Church," on April 7, 1889. In essence, this made him the president of the Church of Christ.[53] Hall threw all his

United States Circuit Court, Western Missouri District, Kansas City, Aug. 6, 1891; hereafter cited as RLDS, Complainant, vs. The Church of Christ. Typescript copies of the Temple Lot Case can be researched at various locations including the following: CCLA, CHL, and Kansas City, Missouri, Public Library. See, also, Ronald E. Romig, "The Temple Lot Suit after 100 Years," *John Whitmer Historical Association Journal* 12 (1992): 3–15; and Paul E. Reimann, *The Reorganized Church and the Civil Courts* (Salt Lake City: Utah Printing, 1961), 149–64.

50. John R. Haldeman, "Secretary's Report," *Searchlight*, Aug. 1896, 56; *History of the RLDS Church*, 5:643.

51. Membership Record, Reorganized Church of Jesus Christ of Latter Day Saints, Book B, 272 (Henderson Grove, Illinois), and Book B, 296 (Burlington, Iowa), CCLA.

52. Membership Record, Reorganized Church of Jesus Christ of Latter Day Saints, Book B, 272 (Henderson Grove, Illinois): "Expelled. 17 May 1885."

53. Church of Christ, Minutes, Apr. 7, 1889. Typescript provided by officials of the Church of Christ (Temple Lot); original record in possession of the Church of Christ (Temple Lot).

energy and skill into resolving the Temple Lot Case for the benefit of the Church of Christ.[54]

During the early years of his leadership, Hall made at least one trip to Salt Lake City, Utah. Perhaps he had anticipated the legal move initiated by the RLDS Church in 1891. In any case, he developed several important relationships within the LDS Church, including John M. Cannon, an attorney in Salt Lake City. Cannon was counsel for the LDS Church and a nephew of George Q. Cannon, influential first counselor in the First Presidency of the LDS Church. Through Cannon, Hall arranged for loans in his own name,[55] so as not to encumber the Church of Christ, in order to pay the legal fees required to defend the church's title to the Temple Lot.[56]

Depositions were taken in Kansas City and Salt Lake City. These depositions provide rich historical detail and insight regarding the early history of the Mormon church. In total, the transcribed official record of the Temple Lot Case measures over 1,000 pages. Events and personalities, travels and revelations of Joseph Smith Jr. and other early leaders, missionaries, and ordinary members are remembered and discussed. The subsequent actions and interpretations of doctrine following Joseph Smith's death, and direction taken by Brigham Young, Joseph Smith III, Granville Hedrick, and others are examined by the attorneys of plaintiff and defendant. Of note, there is considerable

---

54. *The Temple Lot Case*, 4–5. Hall is cited frequently through the record. As noted elsewhere in this essay, the first building constructed on the Temple Lot was completed in October 1889, during Hall's presidency.

55. Charles A. Hall to John M. Cannon, Mar. 26 and May 27, 1893, J. M. Cannon Papers, MS 2625, CHL.

56. Over time, these loans were repaid by church members to Hall, who, in turn, repaid Cannon. However, after Hall left the Church of Christ, there was a small amount of unpaid obligation, which, in Hall's absence, fell to the Church of Christ. On June 24, 1896, John M. Cannon "called on the Presidency [of the LDS Church] in behalf of the Hedrickites of Independence, Missouri, in relation to assistance rendered that body in defending their title to the Temple lot at that place. Part payment of the amount was made and it was understood that the balance, about $1,000, would still be held against them as a debt of honor, as the Church (LDS) rendered assistance without desire to engage in or be responsible for the law suit of the Hedrickites against the Josephites, and with no intention on the part of the Church [LDS] to claim or gain possession of the Temple lot" (Journal History of the Church of Jesus Christ of Latter-day Saints [chronological scrapbook of typed entries and newspaper clippings, 1830–present], June 24, 1896, 2, CHL; hereafter cited as Journal History of the LDS Church).

discussion regarding the controversial topic of Nauvoo plural marriage. The legal maneuverings, depositions, and travel to Salt Lake City dragged out the litigation for four and one-half years.

Despite his departure from the Church of Christ in 1894—and much to the dismay of the RLDS Church—Hall did not abandon his efforts to see the Temple Lot Case through to its conclusion.[57] When Hall resigned his position in the Church of Christ on February 19, 1894, the local press speculated that the Utah LDS Church was the "power behind the throne in the Temple lot controversy," that Hall was now drawn to that movement, and that the LDS Church would eventually build a temple at Independence.[58] Hall was indeed baptized a member of the LDS Church four months later.[59]

Finally, on March 4, 1894, the RLDS Church obtained a favorable ruling at the US District Court level from Judge John F. Philips, who ordered that the Temple Lot be relinquished to the RLDS Church.[60] The Church of Christ appealed, and in 1895 the US Court of Appeals reversed the earlier decision, ruling: "The members of the Reorganized church have acquiesced too long in assertion of adverse right to the property in controversy to be now heard to complain. ... Under these circumstances, we think that laches is a good and sufficient defense to the action."[61]

---

57. Following the close of the Temple Lot Case in 1896 but sometime before 1900, Hall relocated his family to Pueblo, Colorado. He died in California in 1946. See family history provided to the author by Tracey Long of Las Vegas, Nevada, great-granddaughter-in-law of Charles A. Hall. See also the 1900 Federal Census, Pueblo County, Colorado.

58. "News at Independence: President C. A. Hall Renounces the Hedrickite Belief," *Kansas City Times*, Feb. 20, 1894.

59. "On this day, my wife Helen, Mary, Martha and G. A. Cole and myself was [*sic*] baptized and confirmed members of the Church of Jesus Christ of Latter Day Saints by Elder D. F. Stout" (Charles A. Hall, Diary, June 24, 1894, MS 596, f2, CHL); see also, John Pratt, "Homesick Missionary," johnpratt.com. This personal essay quotes excerpts from David F. Stout's missionary journal and confirms the date and place of Hall's baptism.

60. RLDS, Complainant, vs. The Church of Christ; "Temple Lot Case Decided: Josephites Rout the Hedrickites and Certain Possession," *Kansas City Times*, Mar. 4, 1894, 5.

61. The Church of Christ [et. al.], vs. The Reorganized Church of Jesus Christ of Latter Day Saints, United States Circuit Court of Appeals, Eighth Circuit, St. Louis, Mo., Sep. 30, 1894 (70 Fed 179.), 188–89, and "rehearing," (71 Fed 250); "Judge Philips's Decision Reversed in the U.S. Court of Appeals," *Deseret Evening News*, Sep. 30, 1895. The second circuit court citing is a request for a "rehearing" which was dismissed and thus set the stage for an appeal to the US Supreme Court. "Laches" means "negligence in the observance of a duty or opportunity." See Addams, "The Church of Christ (Temple Lot), Its Emergence, Struggles,

In January 1896, the US Supreme Court refused to hear an RLDS Church appeal and remanded the case to the US Court of Appeals for compliance.[62] The Church of Christ therefore retained the property they had lawfully acquired between 1867 and 1877. This clash between the two churches colored their personal relationships for at least the next eighty years. The financial cost of the litigation was significant for both organizations, but was particularly crippling for the small Church of Christ, which had laid out more than $7,600.[63] At the time of the US Supreme Court decision, the membership of the Church of Christ had dropped below 100 members, while the RLDS Church had grown to 34,814.[64]

RENEWED EFFORTS AT UNITY

Four months earlier, in April 1896, John R. Haldeman, editor of the Church of Christ newspaper, *Searchlight*, expressed bitterness over the situation as his people interpreted it: Joseph Smith III "allowed his people to do wrong to drag us into the courts of the land and force many of our people to spend the earnings of a life time in defense of a God given trust."[65] For their part, the RLDS Church interpreted Judge Philips's ruling (the initial federal court decision) as the correct one—in the mistaken belief that the US Court of Appeals ruling only applied to the possession of the Temple Lot.[66] In particular, Philips's identification of the RLDS Church as "but a reproduction of that

---

and Early Schisms," in *Scattering of the Saints: Schism within Mormonism*, ed. Newell G. Bringhurst and John C. Hamer (Independence, Missouri: John Whitmer Books, 2007), 215.

62. The Reorganized Church of Jesus Christ of Latter Day Saints, Complainant, vs. The Church of Christ At Independence, Missouri [et. al.], U.S. Supreme Court, Washington, DC, June 27, 1896 (163 U.S. 681); "Temple Lot Suit," *Saints' Herald*, Jan. 29, 1896, 69; "By Way of Explanation," *Searchlight*, Feb. 1, 1896, 1. Legal terminology used for this appeal to the US Supreme Court was "writ of certiorari." James H. McKenney (clerk of the Supreme Court), Telegram to E. L. Kelley, Jan. 27, 1896: "Petition for certiorari in the church case denied." Also "Temple Lot Suit," *Saints' Herald*, Jan. 29, 1896, 69.

63. The US Court of Appeals required the RLDS Church to pay the Church of Christ approximately $2,200 for costs of litigation (George P. Frisbey et al., *Searchlight*, Aug. 1896, 55).

64. *History of the RLDS Church*, 5:643.

65. John Haldeman, "Editorial," *Searchlight*, Apr. 1896, 19.

66. Romig, "Temple Lot Suit After 100 Years," 3–15; Reimann, *Reorganized Church and the Civil Courts*, 149–64.

of the church as it existed from 1830 to 1834,"[67] and by interpretation, the rightful successor to the original church, was heralded by the RLDS Church and its members. Despite Haldeman's printed complaint, he initiated correspondence with his counterpart at the *Saints' Herald*, hoping for an adjustment of the difficulties which existed between these two neighbors of the Restoration.[68]

Indeed, meetings between the two groups took place on January 16–20, 1897, and involved RLDS participants: Joseph Smith III, Alexander Hale Smith, Rhoderic May, William H. Garrett, and George E. Harrington; and Church of Christ participants: Richard Hill, John R. Haldeman, George P. Frisbey, George D. Cole, and James A. Hedrick.[69] Although these meetings did not result in unity, they laid the groundwork for future conversations between the two bodies and produced a statement of concurrence or an "Epitome" on several points of belief and doctrine.[70] Of note, however, no mention was made of the ownership of the Temple Lot.

In January 1900, another joint meeting was held in Lamoni, Iowa, between representatives of the Church of Christ and the RLDS Church.[71] Again, the call for the meeting came from members of the Church of Christ.[72] It is recorded that the elders of the Church of Christ "were being moved upon by the Spirit" to see what could be done to "bring together the different factions of the original church."

---

67. RLDS, Complaint, Mar. 1894 (60 Fed 954.)

68. "A Noteworthy Incident," *Searchlight*, Feb. 1, 1897, 1–2.

69. As previously noted, Alexander Smith was Joseph III's brother and counselor. Frisbey was born in Marietta, Ohio, in 1834, and was baptized a member of the Church of Christ in Tazewell County, Illinois, in 1865. Frisbey left Illinois with other members of the Church of Christ and traveled to Independence in 1867, where he became a successful merchant. A few years before his death in 1919, Frisbey served as the Church of Christ's presiding elder. Hill baptized Cole into the Church of Christ in April 1870 in Independence. Cole became a very successful missionary. He died in 1918. James Hedrick was the eighth child of Granville Hedrick. He was born on August 19, 1865. James served the church in a variety of capacities, including presiding elder in the early 1900s. He died in 1926.

70. *History of the RLDS Church*, 5:382; Flint, *Outline History*, 118; Richard Hill and William H. Garrett, "Minutes of a Conference," *Searchlight*, Feb. 1897, 98–99; "*The Searchlight* on the Doctrine and Covenants," *Saints' Herald*, Aug. 18, 1897, 517–18. Several versions of the "Epitome" exist with slight but unimportant differences in detail.

71. *History of the RLDS Church*, 5:488–89.

72. *History of the RLDS Church*.

Their specific concern was "building a temple on the ground they had in their possession and which was recognized by all the various factions of Mormonism to be 'the place' and where a temple 'was to be reared in this generation.'"[73] At the Lamoni meeting, Haldeman proposed that two representatives from the Church of Christ travel to Utah to meet with the LDS First Presidency to ask that the church participate in a proposed joint meeting in Independence.

Soon thereafter, George P. Frisbey and George D. Cole, representatives of the Church of Christ, traveled to Salt Lake City in hopes of meeting with the LDS First Presidency. On the afternoon of February 8, 1900, Frisbey and Cole were able to arrange a meeting with President Lorenzo Snow and counselor Joseph F. Smith. (George Q. Cannon was forty miles south in Provo, Utah.) After brief introductions and an explanation of the Church of Christ elder's agenda, Snow suggested that they meet again on Saturday, February 10, when Cannon could be present. On the 10th, Frisbey and Cole were asked by Snow to restate their objective in traveling to Salt Lake City for Cannon's benefit. They responded that it was for "the purpose of ascertaining if it is not possible for a delegation of our church, a delegation of the 'Reorganite' church and a delegation of [our] own organization could not meet together for the purpose of trying to harmonize their views on doctrine with a view to our coming together and uniting into one body" and that we "ought to take some steps towards placing this ground [the Temple Lot] so it can be used for the purpose indicated in the revelations." Cannon commented that "while I favored the proposition ... I had no faith in the result, because I was of the opinion that there were insuperable obstacles in the way of the recognition of authority."[74] Snow asked his visitors if they were willing to remain in Salt Lake City until such time that he could assemble a quorum of the

<hr />

73. *History of the RLDS Church.*

74. Journal History of the LDS Church, Feb. 8 and 10, 1900. For several years before and after the turn of the twentieth century, the Journal History of the LDS Church included summaries of the minutes of the First Presidency and Quorum of Twelve Apostles. The official minutes of these meetings are otherwise usually restricted. Also cited George Q. Cannon, Journal, under date(s), at www.churchhistorianspress.org/george-q-cannon. See also "Probable Amalgamation," *Independence Sentinel,* Mar. 1, 1900.

apostles and relate their proposition directly to them. The Hedrickite elders readily agreed.

As promised, the anticipated meeting took place on the morning of February 21, 1900, with Cole and Frisbey and the LDS First Presidency, Quorum of the Twelve, and Presiding Bishopric in attendance. Cannon reported that there was "a full conversation on the object of their mission. They laid before the brethren ... that which they had laid before the First Presidency. After doing so, they withdrew, in order that we might come to some decision." The LDS leadership adjourned and met again in the afternoon to further consider the proposal. Cannon remarked in his journal that "after all had expressed themselves, President Snow said that his feelings were clear that we should not accept the proposition of these men." Later that afternoon, Snow met privately with "Elders Frisby [sic] and Cole, having been called for ... and advised them that their proposal would not be accepted."[75]

While the trip to Salt Lake City did not bring about the results hoped for by the Church of Christ elders, representatives of the RLDS Church and the Church of Christ did meet together in Independence the following month, March 1900. The previous "Epitome" of 1897 was again agreed to and other points of doctrine were added.[76] However, on March 8, Alexander Smith, who had been chosen chair of the joint committee, after retiring for the evening "was awakened by an Angel and told to get up and write as he [the angel] gave the message."[77] Smith announced the revelation at the committee meeting held the following day. He stated the Lord had told him that, "My children of the Church of Christ are not sufficiently humble or willing to submit to my will," and instructed, "Let my children of the church of Christ cease to contend ... against the revelations I have given through my servant." The revelation concluded, "Behold it is my will that you become reconciled to thy brethren of the Reorganization of my Church, and join

---

75. Journal History of the LDS Church, Feb. 21, 1900; George Q. Cannon, Journal, under date.

76. *History of the RLDS Church*, 5:490–91; Flint, *Outline History*, 118; "Denies Rumor of Union: Joseph Smith Says LDS Will Not Join the Mormons," *Independence Sentinel*, Mar. 16, 1900.

77. Frederick Alexander Smith, "Details of Revelation to Hedrickites," n.d., Miscellany Collection, P19, f54, CCLA.

with them in the work of building up Zion ... and the building of my Temple, which I will command in my own time to be built."[78] This revelation obviously put the burden of change and accommodation upon the Church of Christ[79] and postponed action on a possible union.[80]

Although occasional efforts to re-commence dialog were made by both churches between 1900 and 1917, nothing noteworthy transpired; each party held tightly to its previous position. By 1917, however, a new era of possibilities and potential cooperation developed—the two central personalities of this interim period, Richard E. Hill, presiding elder of the Church of Christ, and Joseph Smith III, president of the RLDS Church, having passed away. Hill was replaced by George P. Frisbey, Smith by son Frederick M. Smith.[81] At the April 1917 conference of the RLDS Church, the Committee on the Church of Christ was revived.[82] During the summer of 1917, the two churches jointly sponsored "tent" or "union" meetings on the Temple Lot. The result was a better understanding and increased fellowship between the members of both churches, along with a renewed interest in building the temple.[83] However, scheduled meetings were canceled in September when some members of the Church of Christ began to suspect the RLDS Church's participation was motivated by a desire to gain access to the Temple Lot.[84]

Despite the end of the union meetings, both churches named representatives to participate in a joint committee that first met on December 30, 1917. These meetings continued through January 27, 1918, and culminated in a document titled "Agreements of Working Harmony," which significantly surpassed former efforts.[85] The committee used the 1900 "Epitome" as its beginning point, with minor adjustments, and

---

78. *History of the RLDS Church,* 5:492.

79. *History of the RLDS Church,* 5:492–93.

80. *History of the RLDS Church,* 5:493.

81. "Elder Richard Hill," *Evening and Morning Star,* Feb. 11, 1911, 1; "Richard Hill Is Dead," *Jackson Examiner,* Feb. 17, 1911; *History of the RLDS Church,* 6:577.

82. *History of the RLDS Church,* 7:192.

83. Large Record, Church of Christ, n.d., 241, quoted in Flint, *Outline History,* 134; *History of the RLDS Church,* 7:204.

84. Flint, *Outline History,* 134.

85. "Next Conference, Iowa—Building of An Assembly Hall Being Considered—Hedrickites and Reorganized in Agreement," *Independence Examiner,* Apr. 9, 1918, 1.

greatly expanded the document.[86] While the Church of Christ legally maintained control of the Temple Lot, monumental changes occurred in relationships between the two bodies. The document provided for the transfer of membership between the two churches with no requirement for rebaptism, since both "recognize the standing of the other." This point would have major and critical implications in the years ahead.

THE CONTEST CONTINUES

This period of "almost unity" ended in 1924 due to an administrative position put forth by RLDS President Frederick M. Smith, successor to Joseph Smith III,[87] that became known as Supreme Directional Control (SDC).[88] As a result, many disgruntled RLDS Church members transferred their memberships to the Church of Christ as provided for in the "Agreements of Working Harmony."[89] The departure of talented and prominent members caused great consternation to Smith,

---

86. *History of the RLDS Church*, 7:280–82. The document is also referred to as "Articles of Working Harmony" in later reports and is cited by that title in *History of the RLDS Church*. The Church of Christ generally referred to this same document as the "Agreement of Working Harmony" or "Working Agreement." See Stebbins, Papers, P24, f34, CCLA; Flint, *Outline History*, 119–21, 134. The authors of the document were the joint committee participants, namely: George D. Cole, Clarence L. Wheaton, and James M. Hartley for the Church of Christ; and Francis M. Sheehy, Walter W. Smith, and Mark H. Siegfried for the RLDS Church. Others who participated by invitation were Estie Stafford, Thomas J. Sheldon, and Israel A. Smith.

87. *History of the RLDS Church*, 6:586–87.

88. *History of the RLDS Church*, 7:600, 626–38. As early as 1919, differences in opinion had arisen between the RLDS Quorum of Twelve, Presiding Bishopric, and the First Presidency over the role of the First Presidency—and in particular the church president—in directing the affairs of the church. By 1924 the position that President Frederick M. Smith had continually advocated since 1919 became the focal point of the 1924 April conference when he set forth what became known as Supreme Direction Control.

89. Flint, *Outline History*, 138–39; "Plans Are from God Three Churchmen Say," *Independence Examiner*, Apr. 3, 1929. In this article, Apostle Clarence L. Wheaton stated: "Three years ago [1926] we had only one hundred members. We now have one thousand." The official membership totals for the Church of Christ in 1928 and 1929 were 889 and 1,232, respectively. Wheaton's underestimate of one hundred members "three years ago" (1926) was incorrect. Allowing for continued growth, i.e., transferees from the RLDS Church after the 1925/1926 period, an estimate of 500 members by the year 1925 seems more reasonable. Flint, in *Outline History*, stated: "During this period the Church of Christ grew rapidly, and from a membership of a couple of hundred in 1915, by 1926 it had grown to several thousand, and continued to grow" (139). Based on the above cited information, Flint's estimates are significantly overestimated.

his counselors, and others in RLDS Church leadership.[90] At the 1926 RLDS Church conference, Smith finally dealt with the deteriorating relationship with the Church of Christ. Using as a point of argument the time-trodden debate of acceptance of the Book of Commandments versus the 1835 edition of the Doctrine and Covenants, a designated committee reported to the conference "that the 'Church of Christ' had greatly modified if not abrogated article four of the Articles of Working Harmony." The conference voted to rescind the "Articles of Working Harmony" and declared them "null and void."[91]

THE CONTEST ESCALATES:
CHURCH OF CHRIST ANNOUNCES REVELATION TO BUILD A TEMPLE

The perpetual contest between the RLDS Church and the Church of Christ over the Temple Lot took on new meaning when former RLDS Church local leader Otto Fetting—now an apostle in the Church of Christ—announced that he had received a visitation and a "message" from an angelic being at his home in Port Huron, Michigan, on February 4, 1927. Among other instructions, this messenger stated, "The revelation that was given for the building of the temple (Malachi 3:1) was true and the temple soon will be started."[92]

A second message followed on March 4, 1927, also in Fetting's home. This time, the messenger identified himself as John the Baptist.[93] On March 22, 1928, Fetting announced the receipt of his "Fifth Message," which informed church members that they were to begin construction of a temple on the Temple Lot in 1929 and complete it within seven years.[94]

Accordingly, the Church of Christ held an impressive groundbreaking ceremony on Saturday, April 6, 1929, in conjunction with the church's annual conference. "After appropriate songs, sermons, prayers, and scripture reading, Bishop Alma O. Frisbey 'took the spade and cut

---

90. Flint, *Outline History*, 138–39.

91. *History of the RLDS Church*, 8:67–68.

92. *The Word of the Lord* (1971; repr., Independence, Missouri: Church of Christ with the Elijah Message, 1943), 7. Fetting numbered his messages sequentially as he received them.

93. *Word of the Lord*, 8–10.

94. *Word of the Lord*, 13–16.

out and laid upon the ground a small square of sod.'"[95] Excavation commenced in late April 1929.[96]

RLDS church apostle J. Franklin Curtis followed up this event quickly by writing a sixty-three-page pamphlet, published in June 1929: *The Temple of the Lord; Who Shall Build It?* The pamphlet was published by Herald Publishing House, which was owned by the RLDS Church.[97] It examined the claims of the Church of Christ, and rehashed topics that had been argued over for many years. The resulting rhetoric escalated with an editorial, "The Enemy Shows His Hand," in the September 1929 issue of *Zion's Advocate*. A direct response to the Curtis pamphlet, it scathingly denounced him and his writings:

> At last, the enemy who has been beating about the bush and hurling missiles at the workmen on the walls of Zion sallies forth to launch an open attack on the Church of Christ. ... Space in the Advocate is too limited for a comprehensive reply. But let Mr. Curtis and his fellows know that a reply is forthcoming. We will meet him with his chosen method of expression, and lay bare his glaring misrepresentations. ... Nor is that all ... WE HAVE THE TEMPLE LOT.[98]

FRACTURE IN THE CHURCH OF CHRIST

The temple project never moved beyond the foundation, in spite of the efforts of faithful Church of Christ members. The first reason was the Great Depression, which began in late 1929 and lasted through the

95. Flint, *Outline History*, 141; Church of Christ, Program for the Breaking of the Ground for the Temple, Independence, Apr. 6, 1929, photocopy courtesy of Geri Adams, a great-great-granddaughter of Granville Hedrick, Blue Springs, Missouri; R. Jean Addams, *Upon the Temple Lot: The Church of Christ's Quest to Build the House of the Lord* (Independence, Missouri: John Whitmer Books, 2010), 78–80. Alma O. Frisbey was a son of George P. Frisbey, one of the original 1867 pioneers of the Church of Christ.

96. "Clearing Temple Lot: Trees Being Removed from Temple Site," *Independence Examiner*, Apr. 26, 1929.

97. J. Franklin Curtis, *The Temple of the Lord; Who Shall Build It?* (Independence, Missouri: Herald Publishing House, 1929). Curtis was baptized RLDS in 1883 at age eight, was ordained an apostle in 1909, and became an evangelist in 1938. In addition to *The Temple of the Lord: Who Shall Build It?*, Curtis authored *Our Beliefs Defended* (1928) and was a star participant in the much heralded Curtis–Wheaton debates of this period. Curtis died in 1966. See J. F. Curtis Papers, P57, Box 2, CCLA. Curtis died in December 1966. See Norwood, *Who Was Who in RLDS History*, 26.

98. Elmer E. Long, "Editorial: The Enemy Shows His Hand," *Zion's Advocate*, Sep. 1929, 119.

1930s. This economic event shrank disposable funds to a bare minimum, especially since few members of the Church of Christ were affluent.

The second reason for the collapse of the temple project was an internal schism, which began on July 18, 1929, when Apostle Otto Fetting interpreted his "Twelfth Message" as requiring all new members from other Mormon groups, including the RLDS Church, to be rebaptized for membership in the Church of Christ. The Council of Apostles ruled that the "Agreements of Working Harmony," still accepted by the Church of Christ, specifically allowed membership based on a person's original baptism. However, Fetting and those associated with him continued the practice and were silenced at a special October 1929 conference called to deal with the issue.[99] Fetting was defiant and rejected the silencing. He continued to preach publicly and was finally disfellowshipped at the April 1930 conference along with several others.[100]

RENEWED CONTROVERSY

The lingering Great Depression, World War II, and other issues minimized dissension and controversy between the two churches for many years. However, after nearly a quarter of a century, at the RLDS Church conference of 1952, the RLDS Church chose to resurrect the controversy over Judge Philips's 1894 decision and old wounds were reopened.

---

99. The "Twelfth Message" to Otto Fetting, July 18, 1929, *The Word of the Lord*, 28–32, does not use the term rebaptism, but the crucial passage reads: "Behold, the Lord has rejected all creeds and factions of men, who have gone away from the word of the Lord and have become an abomination in his sight, therefore, let those that come to the Church of Christ be baptized, that they may rid themselves of the traditions and sins of men" (v. 4).

100. Flint, *Outline History*, 142; Arthur M. Smith, "Recorder's Report," *Zion's Advocate*, Apr. 1932, 54. Flint stated that the church's membership at the time of the October special conference was approximately 4,000, and that "nearly one-third of the membership" left the church and followed Fetting. I consider this figure to be significantly overstated. Likewise, the percentage of those who left the church at this time seems to be too high. A more realistic percentage of departing members is probably nearer to 20–25 percent. Allowing for a continued influx of transfers from the RLDS Church between April and October 1929, the revised total membership before the Fetting departure was probably closer to 1,500. Finally, the 1932 membership reported number of 1,607 seems reasonable. Ronald E. Romig, Community of Christ archivist, after reviewing RLDS membership data for this period, concluded that the maximum number of transfers to the Church of Christ in the 1920s and 1930s was approximately 1,500 (Romig, email, Mar. 5, 2009, in my possession). This number matches my estimate of 1,250 to 1,600 RLDS transfers in the period 1916–36.

Elder Leonard J. Lea brought up the Temple Lot Case in his front page article (printed beside the transcript of church president Israel A. Smith's opening conference address) in the March 31, 1952, conference edition of the *Saints' Herald*: "A great victory for the Reorganization was the winning of the Temple Lot Suit in March, 1894, in the U.S. Circuit Court under Judge John F. Philips." Lea added: "The decision cleared Joseph Smith of the charge of polygamy and recognized the Reorganized Church as the true successor of the original church—a decision that has never been controverted successfully, nor reversed."[101]

A three-man committee from the Church of Christ immediately penned "An Open Letter" of rebuttal, rebuke, and disappointment, and hand delivered it to the RLDS Church.[102] The letter quoted Lea's comments, then chastised the misrepresentation: "Surely you brethren are not so ignorant of the facts of this case that you will acquiesce in such misleading statements, for you know that after this 'great victory' decision was handed down by Judge Philips as of March 16, 1894, that the same was appealed to the U.S. Circuit Court of Appeals in 1895, and the Church of Christ in this action not only 'controverted successfully' the decision of the Circuit Court but succeeded also in getting the Appellant Court to *reverse* the decision of Judge Philips."[103] Charges and counter-charges followed.

Heated correspondence between the two bodies continued on this issue and others for the rest of the year. As a result of this unresolved situation, relationships were strained for another eighteen years.

---

101. Leonard J. Lea, "Centennial of the Reorganization, 1852–1952," *Saints' Herald*, Mar. 31, 1952, 34, 39. In the same issue, under "The Return: Conference Address of the President," Israel Smith made similar remarks about Judge Philips's comments, 37. In fact, the judge had not yet ruled on the organization's claims to be the true successor to Joseph Smith's church, but merely confirmed its long-standing possession of the building. See also Kim Loving, "Ownership of the Kirtland Temple: Legends, Lies, and Misunderstandings," *Journal of Mormon History* 30, no. 2 (Fall 2004): 1–80. In 1952, Leonard J. Lea was book-and-tract editor at the RLDS-owned Herald Publishing House and was also on the RLDS Church's standing high council. He resigned in 1954 and died in 1960.

102. Clarence L. Wheaton, Arthur M. Smith, and Robert R. Robertson to "The First Presidency and Council of Twelve of the Church of Jesus Christ of Latter Day Saints in Conference Assembled," Apr. 5, 1952, original and typescript, Miscellaneous Letters and Papers, P13, f1914, CCLA.

103. "An Open Letter." In the hand-delivered original, "reverse" is underlined; in the printed *Independence Examiner* version, it is all capital letters.

Finally, in 1970, the Joint Relations Committee was re-established at the request of W. Wallace Smith, who became president of the RLDS Church in October 1958.[104]

CURRENT PERSPECTIVES ON THE RLDS CHURCH

While continuing to discourse on the "what ifs'" of the Temple Lot Case and the RLDS Church's arguments about the other points of the Philips's decision, President Frederick M. Smith, as early as 1942, asked Samuel Burgess, RLDS Church Historian, to "look into" whether the temple "might be shifted considerable from that spot [the Church of Christ's 2.75 acres[105]] and still be in the confines of the sixty-three acres."[106] Burgess's answer is unknown; but RLDS members rejoiced in 1968 at the church's world conference when President Wallace Smith announced a revelation: "The time has come for a start to be made toward building my temple in the Center Place. It shall stand on a portion of the plot of ground set apart for the purpose many years ago by my servant Joseph Smith, Jr."[107] Ground breaking was held April 6, 1990, and the edifice was dedicated April 17, 1994.[108]

CURRENT PERSPECTIVES ON THE CHURCH OF CHRIST (TEMPLE LOT)

The Church of Christ continues to be headquartered in Independence, Missouri. A lovely church building, including general and local church offices and a visitors' reception area, is located on the northeast corner of the Temple Lot. Currently, the Church of Christ has no plans for the physical construction of a temple, even though the church does

---

104. Minutes of the Relations Committee Meeting, Internal Memorandum, Church of Christ, Nov. 14, 1970, signed by Robert H. Jensen, E. Leon Yates, and Archie F. Bell, Acc 8155, f38, CCLA.

105. On July 17, 1906, the City of Independence sold Richard Hill, acting as trustee in trust for the Church of Christ, a small, triangular strip of land (approximately .25 acres) lying just north of the 2.5 acres the church already owned. He paid $75. The small triangle had originally been platted as part of a street but had been abandoned by the city. City of Independence to Richard Hill, July 17, 1906, 264:621–22 (Jackson County property records).

106. Frederick M. Smith to Samuel A. Burgess, Aug. 21, 1942, Temple Lot, Subject Collection, P22, f111, CCLA.

107. RLDS D&C 149:6a.

108. H. Michael Marquardt, "The Independence Temple of Zion," *Restoration,* Oct. 1986, 13. photocopy courtesy of Marquardt.

continue to maintain a temple fund. The temple project is not considered a "primary focus" of the church. Regarding the specific future construction of a temple on this sacred ground, Apostle William Sheldon stated in April 2006: "The Church of Christ considers it their sacred duty to be … the physical custodian of the property … and, as custodians, we will patiently wait for the time when we will be told by divine commandment to build the holy temple."[109]

CONCLUSION

While the majority of the many "Expressions of the Restoration" continue to hold to the 1831 revelation of Joseph Smith—that the millennial temple will be built on the "sacred space" known as the Temple Lot—the original temple tract of 63.27 acres is now entirely owned by Community of Christ, the LDS Church, and the Church of Christ (Temple Lot). Other branches of the Restoration have established a presence near the Temple Property or within the Independence area. Although fundamental doctrinal differences remain between the Community of Christ and the Church of Christ (Temple Lot), these two early neighbors of the Restoration now exhibit much greater understanding, accommodation, and respect toward each other.

---

109. Apostle William A. Sheldon, Interview with author, Apr. 2006, Independence, Missouri, original in my possession; Sheldon, in an email message dated December 2006, confirmed: "The Temple project is not a primary focus of the church … the primary focus today is missionary work and building up the Kingdom of God." As for the temple, "We will simply await the Lord's further direction."

EIGHT

A TIME OF TRANSITION
THE KIRTLAND TEMPLE, 1838–80

CHRISTIN CRAFT MACKAY AND LACHLAN MACKAY

The Mormons of Kirtland, Geauga County, Ohio, having broken up, and nearly all removed to the State of Missouri, it has been thought expedient to establish an institution of learning in the place, and thus occupy buildings which would otherwise remain comparatively useless. For this purpose, the use of their large and commodious Temple, has been secured for five years from the 1st [of] Sept. 1838.[1]

The preceding advertisement for the Western Reserve Teacher's Seminary and Kirtland Institute marked the beginning of a period in the history of the Kirtland temple that has generally been overlooked and misunderstood. Forty-plus years in length, this "time of transition" covers the period between the departure from Kirtland, Ohio, of the majority of the faithful Latter Day Saints in 1838 and the 1880 decision in the Kirtland Temple Suit that resulted in a clear title to the temple for the Reorganized Church of Jesus Christ of Latter Day Saints (RLDS, later Community of Christ).[2] Contrary to popular belief, the temple was not forgotten by the various Latter Day Saint churches during this period. However, immediately following the exodus to Missouri, there seems to have been little worship activity there.

The emphasis was instead on education, with the Teacher's Seminary meeting on the second floor of the temple and a "model school" being held on the third floor so that the teachers-to-be could practice on the local children. The first floor was not used by the seminary and was

---

1. Broadside by Nelson Slater, dated July 25, 1838, copy in possession of the authors. Published by Steel's Press of Painesville, Ohio.

2. The RLDS Church typically rendered its name as Latter Day Saints. The Utah-based LDS Church has preferred Latter-day Saints.

perhaps not initially in use by the Latter Day Saints either.[3] The seminary had a five-year lease on the temple, but moved out after one year because there were too many steps in the building and it was too hard to heat.[4]

Even before the seminary made the decision to vacate the temple, a May 1839 church conference at Quincy, Illinois, passed a resolution encouraging the Saints living in the eastern states to "move to Kirtland and the vicinity thereof, and again settle that place as a Stake of Zion." The same resolution appointed Oliver Granger to preside over the Kirtland church (branch) and to take charge of the House of the Lord.[5] As a result, the church in Kirtland began to once again grow, and by November 10, 1839, a small congregation was again meeting in the House of the Lord. On November 17, apostles Heber C. Kimball, George A. Smith, Brigham Young, and John Taylor met in the temple so that Taylor and Theodore Turley could be endowed or empowered before continuing their missionary efforts.[6]

By December 1839 word spread that "some at least, and probably many" members were preparing to move back to Kirtland, including the families of Brigham Young and Heber C. Kimball.[7] Those relo-

---

3. Mrs. H. Ferry Tayer to the editor of the *Herald,* Dec. 14 [no year], Newspaper Clippings File, Kirtland History Room, Kirtland Public Library, Kirtland, Ohio. The Kirtland elders quorum met in the temple throughout the summer of 1838 with their last meeting on August 26, 1838, just five days before the school's lease took effect. The elders quorum was not to meet in the House of the Lord again for over two years. Record of the First Quorum of Elders, Aug. 26, 1838, and Oct. 22, 1840, Library–Archives, Community of Christ, Independence, Missouri.

4. *Pioneer and Personal Reminiscences,* 35, cited in Elwin C. Robison, *The First Mormon Temple* (Provo, Utah: Brigham Young University Press, 1997), 162.

5. Joseph Smith Jr. et al., *The History of the Church of Jesus Christ of Latter-day Saints,* ed. B. H. Roberts, 7 vols. (Salt Lake City: Deseret Book Co, 1976), 3:345; hereinafter cited as *History of the Church.*

6. Elden Jay Watson, ed., *Manuscript History of Brigham Young, 1801–1844* (Salt Lake City: Smith Secretarial Service, 1968), Nov. 10 and 17, 1839. See also Jeni Broberg Holzapfel and Richard Neitzel Holzapfel, eds., *A Woman's View: Helen Mar Whitney's Reminiscences of Early Church History* (Provo, Utah: Religious Studies Center, Brigham Young University, 1997), 162. Note that the use of the term "endowment" during the Kirtland period differed from its use during the Nauvoo period.

7. *Times and Seasons,* Nov. 1839, 29. "Sister Young, we heard, had received a letter from Uncle Brigham, telling her to come to Kirtland; and my brother William ... returned with the news that they were packing up. Sister Orson Pratt ... met Bro. Hyrum Smith that day and spoke of Sister Young's going east; he said he should advise her, by all means, to stay where she was" (Holzapfel and Holzapfel, *Woman's View,* 170); "Bro. Bond and wife are true and

cating to Commerce/Nauvoo, Illinois, were perhaps motivated by the unhealthy conditions there, the availability of inexpensive housing in Kirtland, and the relative proximity of Kirtland to family members farther east. However, the church had already purchased hundreds of acres of land in Nauvoo on credit. It became crucial that members gather not to Kirtland, but to Nauvoo, to buy the land and to help relieve the church of that debt. A December 8, 1839, epistle from the First Presidency and High Council at Nauvoo to "the Saints scattered abroad, in the region westward from Kirtland, Ohio," warned the brethren "in the name of the Lord, not to remove back there [Kirtland]."[8] Although slowing the return of those who lived west of Kirtland, the epistle contained nothing to counteract the earlier conference resolution encouraging members in the eastern states to gather there.

Joseph Smith Jr. again encouraged those living in the east to gather to Kirtland at the October 1840 conference. In an effort to ensure that Kirtland "might be built up," and believing that Oliver Granger was returning to Nauvoo, Smith suggested that someone be appointed to preside over the Kirtland Stake. The conference selected Almon W. Babbitt to be president of the church in Kirtland.[9] If the primary role of the stake president was to build up Kirtland, then Babbitt had the credentials. He had been disfellowshiped just a few months earlier for encouraging those "who have lately come into the church" to move to Kirtland rather than to Nauvoo.[10] Under Babbitt, the church in Kirtland experienced explosive growth, similar to the growth of the church in the area a decade earlier. Membership grew from about 100 in 1839 to between 300 and 400 by

---

steadfast; are much pleased that you are coming here" (Heber C. Kimball to Vilate Kimball, Nov. 16, 1839, from Kirtland, in Holzapfel and Holzapfel, *A Woman's View,* 163).

8. *History of the Church,* 4:45. Concern about the unhealthy conditions in Nauvoo continued to hinder Joseph's attempts to convince members to gather there rather than Kirtland. See *History of the Church,* 4:281.

9. *History of the Church,* 4:204; Dean C. Jessee, ed., *The Personal Writings of Joseph Smith* (Salt Lake City: Deseret Book Co., 1984), 490.

10. Jessee, *Personal Writings,* 476–77. Babbitt was not the only Kirtlander encouraging people to gather to Kirtland over Nauvoo. Hiram Kellog came across a group of English Saints in Buffalo, New York, on October 24, 1840, on their way to Commerce (later Nauvoo). They were short on money, and Kellog convinced thirteen families and four individuals to go to Kirtland instead, "as they would winter more comfortable there than in Commerce." See George D. Smith, ed., *An Intimate Chronicle: The Journals of William Clayton* (Salt Lake City: Signature Books/Smith Research Associates, 1995), 74–75.

May 1841. At the May 22, 1841, Kirtland conference, the church was incorporated in Ohio as the "Church of Christ of Latter Day Saints."[11]

Just two days later in an effort to "promote the prosperity" of the church, and stressing the need to concentrate on building the temple, university, and other buildings in Nauvoo, Joseph Smith dissolved all stakes (units) but those in Hancock County, Illinois, (home of Nauvoo) and neighboring Lee County, Iowa. Members were instructed to prepare to gather to Nauvoo without delay.[12] This drastic step was made necessary by the church's earlier purchase of land in Nauvoo. They had initially planned on meeting some of their financial obligations with money obtained as redress for the earlier Missouri persecutions.[13] When it became clear that this was not going to happen, they realized that land speculation was their only hope. By August 1841 the interest alone due on the notes had risen to $6,000 or more.[14] The pressure created by creditors attempting to collect on these notes drove the church leaders to unfortunate extremes as they encouraged members to gather to Nauvoo and build a city on a swamp.[15]

---

11. Milton V. Backman Jr., *The Heavens Resound: A History of the Latter-day Saints in Ohio 1830–1838* (Salt Lake City: Deseret Book Co., 1983), 140. For the incorporation, see *Times and Seasons*, July 1, 1841, 458. See also *Abstract of Title and Incumbrances*, 18, Kirtland Temple Historic Center, "Trustees in Trust for the Church of Jesus Christ of Latter Day Saints [of Nauvoo], and ... Trustees of the Church of Christ of Latter Day Saints of Kirtland vs. Richard Roe."

12. *History of the Church*, 4:362.

13. Robert Bruce Flanders, *Nauvoo: Kingdom on the Mississippi* (Urbana: University of Illinois Press, 1975), 128–29.

14. *History of the Church*, 4:435.

15. "The lower part of the town is the most healthy. In the upper part of the town the Merchants will say I am partial &c., but the lower part of the town is much the most healthy. I tell you in the name of the Lord I have been out in all parts of the city at all times of night to learn these things. ... There are many sloughs on the islands from where Miasma arises in the summer, and is flown over the upper part of the city, but it does not extend over the lower part of the city." Joseph Smith Jr., Journal, Apr. 13, 1843, cited in Scott H. Faulring, ed., *An American Prophet's Record: The Diaries and Journals of Joseph Smith* (Salt Lake City: Signature Books/Smith Research Associates, 1987), 363–64. Compare this with Joseph's earlier statements regarding the lower part of the city: "I presume you are no stranger to the part of the city plot we bought of you being a deathly sickly hole, and that we have not been able in consequence to realize any valuable consideration from it, although we have been keeping up appearances, and holding out inducements to encourage immigration, that we scarcely think justifiable in consequence of the mortality that almost invariably awaits those who come from far distant parts (and that with a view to enable us to meet our engagements) ..." Joseph Smith to Horace Hotchkiss, Aug. 25, 1841, in *History of the Church*, 4:407.

The Saints in Kirtland either did not learn of the decision to pour all available resources into Nauvoo or chose to ignore it. At the fall conference in Nauvoo, Almon Babbitt was disfellowshiped a second time for counteracting the efforts of the presidency to gather the Saints, and in enticing them to stop in places not appointed for the gathering."[16] As the Nauvoo conference was disfellowshiping Babbitt, he was presiding over the Kirtland conference as they made arrangements to re-establish a press and to purchase a horse and wagon for the bishop to use in collecting and distributing aid for the poor.[17] The Kirtlanders were settling in, with no apparent plans to move anywhere soon. When word of the actions of the Kirtland Saints reached the leaders of the Nauvoo church, they were not at all pleased. Not only were the members in Kirtland not preparing to gather, but 100 English converts who were on their way to Nauvoo had instead stopped in Kirtland.[18] The English Saints and their resources, even if limited, were desperately needed in Nauvoo. Hyrum Smith, Joseph Smith's older brother, who had earlier raised the initial complaint that led to Babbitt's being disfellowshiped, stressed again that the building up of Nauvoo now took precedence over any previously planned building up of Kirtland: "All the Saints that dwell in that land [Kirtland] are commanded to come away, for this is 'Thus saith the Lord;' therefore pay out no moneys nor properties for houses, nor lands in that country, for if you do you will lose them, for the time shall come that you shall not possess them in peace, but shall be scourged with a sore scourge."[19]

The leaders of the church in Kirtland responded with a plea that they be allowed to stay. The presidents in Nauvoo replied by letter on December 15, 1841:

---

16. *History of the Church*, 4:424.

17. *Times and Seasons*, Nov. 15, 1841, 588.

18. Davis Bitton, "The Waning of Mormon Kirtland," *BYU Studies* 12, no. 4 (1972): 457.

19. *Times and Seasons*, Nov. 15, 1841, 589. To emphasize the need of the Ohio Saints to gather to Nauvoo, Hyrum Smith echoes an earlier reference from Joseph to a future "scourge" on Kirtland. It is unclear what this scourge was and when it was going to happen. Hyrum claims that the children of the Kirtland residents at that time (1841) would again be able to own property there, indicating that the scourge would be a thing of the past by the end of the life span of the second generation.

It remains for Almon Babbitt to offer satisfaction, if he wishes so to do, according to the minutes of the conference. *You are doubtless all well aware that all the stakes except those in Hancock Co. Illinois & Lee county Iowa, were discontinued some time since by the First Presidency, as published in the Times and Seasons;* but as it appears that there are many in Kirtland who desire to remain there and build up that place, and as you have made great exertions, according to your letter, to establish a printing press, & take care of the poor, &c since that period, you may as well continue operations according to your designs, & go on with your printing, & do what you can in Righteousness to build up Kirtland but do not suffer yourselves to harbor the Idea that Kirtland will rise on the ruins of Nauvoo. It is the privilege of brethren emigrating from any quarter to come to this place [Nauvoo], and it is not right to attempt to persuade those who desire it, to stop short.[20]

The number of members in Kirtland topped out for the decade in 1842 and 1843 at 500.[21] In the fall of 1842, Apostle Lyman Wight had told the Kirtland Saints "not to leave this place [Kirtland] until you were instructed by revelation."[22] In a confusing turn of events, Wight told the members at the April 1843 conference that, although he had not shared it the previous fall, he had with him then the revelation on gathering to Nauvoo. Those in attendance at the conference responded with a unanimous vote in favor of gathering and proceeded to make arrangements to depart.[23] Most members had successfully gathered to Nauvoo by 1844.[24]

Following the death of Joseph Smith Jr. in the summer of 1844, many of the Saints remaining in Kirtland supported the Twelve Apostles as the presiding authorities of the church. These members were able to hold a conference in the temple on April 5, 1845. A motion was passed to assist in building the temple at Nauvoo, and support was expressed for gathering to Nauvoo. According to Hiram Winters, who presided over the conference, "Order and unanimity of feeling characterized the conference, and the Saints in this place appear to be more

---

20. Dean C. Jessee, ed., *The Papers of Joseph Smith*, 2 vols. (Salt Lake City: Deseret Book Co., 1992), 2:339–40.

21. Backman, *Heavens Resound*, 140.

22. *Times and Seasons*, Aug. 1, 1843, 284.

23. *Times and Seasons*.

24. Backman, *Heavens Resound*, 140.

united than they have been for some time past."[25] This does not say much for the unity shown by the Kirtlanders, for a number of members were cut off from the church during the conference for joining with Sidney Rigdon and his Church of Christ.[26]

Preaching in the temple three times to standing room only crowds, Rigdon had won a number of Kirtland followers in February of 1845. By chance, William Law and William E. McLellin, both former leaders in the church, turned up in Kirtland while Rigdon was there and participated in one of his services. Rigdon returned to Kirtland in July, but the audiences were smaller this time and he converted no one.[27]

Although Rigdon's influence was on the decline in Kirtland, other dissenting groups soon posed a more serious threat to Brigham Young for the loyalty of the Kirtland Saints. By the fall, Young was informed "that the apostates were doing every thing they could to injure the Saints. S. B. Stoddard, Jacob Bump, Hiram Kellogg, and Jewell Raney are the leaders of the rioters; That they have broken into the House of the Lord [i.e., the Kirtland temple], and taken possession of it."[28]

The leaders of these "rioters" managed to maintain possession of the temple for the next several years. By 1846, their sympathies were with James J. Strang and his Church of Jesus Christ of Latter Day Saints, which meant that the temple was under Strang's control. According to Strang's *Voree Herald:* "The Saints in Kirtland are in full legal and peaceable possession of the temple of God in that place. They hold it by legal title. The usurpers have brought a suit against them, and after preparing the cause of trial they withdrew the suit and paid up the cost leaving the true church in possession of the temple. Moreover the organization includes nearly every person in [K]irtland who held a standing in any of the parties into which the church has been divided."[29] Strang's hold on the temple might not have been as "peaceable" as is suggested

---

25. *Times and Seasons*, Apr. 15, 1845, 871–72.

26. *Times and Seasons.*

27. Richard S. Van Wagoner, *Sidney Rigdon: A Portrait of Religious Excess* (Salt Lake City: Signature Books, 1994), 375–76, 379.

28. *History of the Church*, 7:484.

29. *Voree [Wisconsin] Herald*, Sep. 1846, 1. Strang held a conference in the temple on August 7, 8, 9, and 10. He had "about 100" followers in Kirtland by the autumn of 1846. See Henry Howe, *Historical Collections of Ohio* (Cincinnati: Bradley & Anthony, 1849), 284.

in the newspaper. Writing from Kirtland, William Smith suggested to Strang at about the same time that a wall be built around the temple to, among other things, "help keep posesion [possession]."[30]

Strang's claim to legal title to the building rested on the argument that the land the temple was built on was conveyed to Joseph Smith Jr. as "sole trustee in trust for the Church" and to his "Successors in the First Presidency." Strang claimed to be the successor in the presidency. The Twelve had not yet reconstituted a presidency, and thus could not make this same claim. According to Strang, "The Brighamites brought a suit" against the Strangites in Kirtland, "but on examination of title deeds they withdrew the suit, paid up the costs, and left the house of God in the possession of his children."[31] Strang, however, would not maintain possession of the building for long.

Some of the more prominent members of the Kirtland Latter Day Saint community wrote to Strang in October 1846 to express their concern over the organization of a "secret society" among Strang's Saints at Voree, Wisconsin.[32] By December, the presiding authorities of Strang's Kirtland church went public with their complaints. They resolved to withdraw fellowship from James J. Strang as the prophet of the Church of Jesus Christ of Latter Day Saints. Among the complaints against Strang was that he had established a "private order" in the church and had placed men around him "of corrupt principles, wicked hearts, and grossly immoral conduct," apparently a reference to John C. Bennett and William Smith.[33]

Strang was now out of the picture in Kirtland, and support began growing for William McLellin and what would become by January

---

30. William Smith to James J. Strang, Aug. 20, 1846, James Jesse Strang Collection, Special Collections, Beinecke Library, Yale University, New Haven, Connecticut. Appreciation to H. Michael Marquardt for sharing this source.

31. *Voree Herald*, Sep. 1846, 2.

32. Jacob Bump, Leonard Rich, Amos Babcock, and S. B. Stoddard to J. J. Strang, postmarked Oct. 16 [1846], Strang Papers, Library–Archives, Community of Christ.

33. *The New Era and Zion's Watchmen* (Voree), Jan. 1847, 4. The communication is signed by Jacob Bump, Amos Ranney, Horace Bentley, Leonard Rich, Amos Babcock, S. B. Stoddard, and W. E. McLellin. Appreciation to William Shepard for sharing this source.

1847 "The Church of Christ."[34] McLellin's group would soon be involved in a series of confrontations, some violent, as those loyal to Brigham Young attempted once again to gain control of the temple.

By the spring of 1846, Young had recognized that the Kirtland temple was of little value to him and his followers as they had few members living in the area. The same would soon be true of the Nauvoo temple. If these properties were sold, the money could be used to move poor members west. Young also recognized that the buildings would be more likely to survive in the hands of another owner. At some future point, members could return to "redeem" the buildings.[35] Almon Babbitt was given the job of selling the temple in Kirtland, a difficult task since the structure was not in his possession. He managed to overcome, at least temporarily, this hurdle. By February 1847, Babbitt was preaching in New York and telling people that he had sold the temple at Kirtland for $10,000. The sale later fell through.[36]

It became clear that the temple could not be sold until it was again in the possession of the seller. An agent for the Twelve secured a writ of ejectment against the McLellinites with interesting results. According to Amos Babcock:

> Judgment obtained against them [the McLellinites] by default and a writ of ouster issued, and the sheriff, in obedience to its mandate, early in the morning of the memorable 19th of June, the day of Mc.'s [McLellin's] Conference, did dispossess the defendants of the Temple, and put the agent in possession of the same, delivering him the key. This deranged the appointment of the Conference ... to be held in the Temple. Some rude boys soon, through a window, got possession. The agent, in trying to dislodge them, opened the door, and some of the Mcites [McLellinites] took forcible possession, and took off one lock; but for some reason replaced it, when the agent again locked it and secured the windows. The Doctor [William McLellin] held his Conference in the A.M. at his own house.

---

34. Richard P. Howard, *William E. McLellin: "Mormonism's Stormy Petrel,"* in Roger D. Launius and Linda Thatcher, eds., *Differing Visions: Dissenters in Mormon History* (Urbana: University of Illinois Press, 1994), 88–89.

35. Juanita Brooks, ed., *On the Mormon Frontier: The Diary of Hosea Stout*, 2 vols. (Salt Lake City: University of Utah Press/Utah State Historical Society, 1982 reprint edition), 158; Robison, *First Mormon Temple*, 103.

36. J. Tyler to W. E. McLellin, Feb. 1847, in the *Ensign of Liberty*, Jan. 1848, 60.

But to fulfill all righteousness, or which the doctor thinks the same, the prophecy that his Conference should be held in the Temple, one of his most valiant men with an axe made a way, *a* HIGH *way*, through a window; and … got into the house, … the door was opened and a jack McLellinite made the keeper, who committed assault and battery on the agent, who held the keys of the house, on his attempting to enter it. The Conference ended that afternoon, and adjourned to next May.

Since Conference the agent has procured locks and put them on the doors outside. But the power of the Doctor's arm is too mighty for them, with a missile he broke them … and still holds possession by violence.[37]

Although McLellin managed to hold on to the temple for a time, he was not able to hold on to his followers. He had pinned his hopes on David Whitmer, one of the Three Witnesses of the Book of Mormon, whom McLellin wanted to assume the role of prophet for the Church of Christ. Whitmer was courted for several years, but by August 1849 it was clear that he would not join McLellin's group.[38] With the passing of time, enthusiasm waned for McLellin's Church of Christ, and soon James Colin Brewster's Church of Christ took its place. Brewster's Kirtland Branch had access to the temple in the late 1840s and early 1850s, and held conferences there, but did not meet in the temple regularly.[39]

James F. Ryder inquired about setting up a daguerreotype photographic studio on the second floor of the temple in the spring of 1850. He was told that the temple was "as free as the common surrounding it. No one pretends to exercise any right or inclination to manage it. The people of the village the strangers who visit it go and come without question. It is free to all." Ryder was also told that although there were still many Mormons in Kirtland, "They gave up holding services,

---

37. Amos Babcock to Pres. Strang, Sep. 8, 1848, in the *Gospel Herald*, Sep. 28, 1848, 134–35.

38. Howard, *William E. McLellin*, 93.

39. Roger D. Launius, *The Kirtland Temple: A Historical Narrative* (Independence, Missouri: Herald Publishing House, 1986), 97. For more information on James Colin Brewster, see Dan Vogel, "James Colin Brewster: The Boy Prophet Who Challenged Mormon Authority," in Launius and Thatcher, eds., *Differing Visions*. The cost of heating the temple in the winter months would be enough to prevent any group with limited resources from worshiping there for six months out of every year.

and the temple has been abandoned as a place of worship for years."[40] This was not an accurate assessment of worship activity in the temple, but the small size of the groups and the lack of regular meetings led to this conclusion.[41] The reference to the people of the village visiting the temple is accurate; they used it as a lecture hall and later advertised a "grand Christmas Ball" to be held in the building.[42]

Francis Gladden Bishop arrived in Kirtland in the fall of 1850 and managed to attract a few followers.[43] James W. Bay passed through Kirtland in 1851 on a mission for the Twelve. Bay and Isaac Bullock put together a small organization, but they encouraged converts to gather to the west and so had no lasting presence.[44] On October 7, 1855, Martin Harris (another of the Three Witnesses of the Book of Mormon), William Smith, Stephen Post, and others convened a conference in the temple. They decided not to organize a church at the first conference, but they did put together a series of resolutions on their basic beliefs. The group met again the following April but were not able to agree on an organization. By October 1857, William Smith was "trying to organize as president in Kirtland."[45]

W. W. Blair and James Blakeslee, two Elders for the infant Reorganized Church of Jesus Christ of Latter Day Saints, visited Kirtland in 1860. They preached in the temple on August 12, with Leonard Rich opposing them in the afternoon session. Rich, along with Zadoc Brooks and Martin Harris, had formed an organization of "7 souls, 4 of them … women," and they had control of the House of the Lord. On August 19, another service was held in the temple. Simeon Atwood, representing the LDS Church was in the stand, with Leonard Rich and Martin Harris representing their "Church of Christ." Blair and Blakeslee were

---

40. James F. Ryder, *Voigtlander and I in Pursuit of Shadow Catching* (Cleveland: Cleveland Printing & Publishing Co., 1902), 68.

41. For example, the Church of Christ held a general assembly in the temple on June 23, 1849. See the *Olive Branch*, Oct. 1849, 50. Appreciation to H. Michael Marquardt for this source.

42. Bitton, "Waning of Mormon Kirtland," 461; *Painesville Telegraph*, Dec. 19, 1855, 1, 3.

43. Richard L. Saunders, "The Fruit of the Branch: Francis Gladden Bishop and His Culture of Dissent," Launius and Thatcher, eds., *Differing Visions*, 112.

44. Bitton, "Waning of Mormon Kirtland," 463.

45. Stephen Post, *Journal*, Oct. 7, 1855, Apr. 5 and 6, 1856, and Oct. 27 1857, Church History Library, Church of Jesus Christ of Latter-day Saints, Salt Lake City.

invited to join them on the stand, setting up one of the more interesting services ever to take place in the building. Atwood spoke first, but soon sat down. He was followed by Rich, who was interrupted by a "tall, long-haired, blue-eyed, ashy-complexioned but well dressed man," later identified as Increase Van Duesen of New York. According to Blair, Van Duesen "sprang upon the partition between the seats, [and] came to the front, facing the stand, stamping, hissing, and making other violent demonstrations." It became clear to Blair that Van Duesen was about to launch himself onto the stand. Convinced that Van Duesen was possessed by the devil and wondering if he should attempt to stop or rebuke him, the voice of the spirit came to Blair, telling him, "This is not your meeting, step out." Blakeslee, Harris, Rich, and Atwood were right behind him. Van Duesen continued to the top of the highest pulpit, took off his coat, ripping it to shreds in the process, and swung it around his head while stamping, hissing, and screaming. Again according to Blair, "The people fled out of the house like sheep, and the men—they generally get the start if they can—went out first and left the ladies to get out as well as they could."[46] Van Duesen preached in the temple several times in the weeks following this service, with the *Painesville [Ohio] Telegraph* noting that he was "edifying a few addle headed people with a Spiritual-mormon exhibition."[47]

A sale was held in 1862 in an attempt to settle the estate of Joseph Smith Jr. Russell Huntley, a member of Zadoc Brooks's "Church of Christ," purchased the temple, and this group continued meeting in the building through at least 1864. Visitors to Kirtland at this time were greeted with a dizzying array of representatives from various Latter Day Saint tradition churches. James Twist represented the RLDS Church, Samuel Parsons belonged to "Mr. Miners organization," and

---

46. We have located four accounts of this event, all from Blair. See W. W. Blair, *The Memoirs of President W. W. Blair* (Lamoni, Iowa: Herald House, 1908), 35–38; W. W. Blair sermon excerpt, *Saints' Herald*, Apr. 22, 1883, 675–76; W. W. Blair, "Simeon Atwood," in *Saints' Herald*, Mar. 9, 1889, 145; and W. W. Blair, Journal, Aug. 19, 1860, Library–Archives, Community of Christ.

47. *Painesville Telegraph*, Sep. 6, 1860, 3. At his death in 1882, Van Deusen was buried in the cemetery adjacent to the temple.

Brooks's church had a number of members.[48] As this group dissolved, Russell Huntley's sympathies turned to the RLDS Church. He gave them access to the temple, and although source material is scarce for this period, a small branch seems to have been organized. It did not survive for long.

RLDS church president Joseph Smith III passed through Kirtland in 1866 and preached in the temple, as did LDS elder Edward Stevenson on April 7, 1870, and again on August 10, 1870, as he came to pick up Martin Harris and take him to Utah.[49] In 1873, Russell Huntley sold the temple to Joseph Smith III and Mark Forscutt. RLDS members continued meeting in the temple when it was not too cold, and the Kirtland community used the temple as well.[50] In 1874, the "Boys of Battery C" held their reunion in the temple with a meeting on the first floor followed by a dinner on the second floor.[51] On October 11, 1874, Joseph F. McDowell again organized an RLDS branch in Kirtland, calling it the "Siona Branch." Under McDowell's leadership, the branch grew from thirteen members to thirty members in less than a year.[52] Despite his missionary successes, two women in the branch soon became upset with McDowell and charged him with some unknown offense. Joseph Smith III advised McDowell in 1877 that if he wanted to relieve himself of the care of the Kirtland Branch, he should simply resign and move away, thus forcing the dissolution of the branch. McDowell did just that, and the branch "dwindled away, until the keys of the temple were left in charge of Sr. [Sister] Dayton, who ... remained a devoted and faithful witness to whoever might call to see the temple."[53]

---

48. On the sale of the temple, see Launius, *Kirtland Temple*, 104. For the church representatives, see Stephen Post, Journal, Mar. 15, 1864.

49. On Smith, see Launius, *Kirtland Temple*, 105; on Stevenson, see Andrew Jenson, *Church Chronology* (Salt Lake City: Deseret News, 1914), Apr. 7, 1870, and Edward Stevenson, "One of the Three Witnesses," *Millennial Star*, Jan. 30, 1882, 78.

50. Launius, *Kirtland Temple*, 106.

51. *Painesville Telegraph*, Oct. 8, 1874, 1.

52. For the date of the branch organization, see the *True Latter Day Saints' Herald*, Nov. 15, 1875, 678; for the name of the branch, see *Saints' Herald*, Dec. 1, 1875, 732 (the name was perhaps chosen in honor of Siona, Tahiti, where the church was experiencing incredible growth at this time); for the branch size, see the *Saints' Herald*, Jan. 1, 1875, 17, 22; Aug. 15, 1875, 498; and Nov. 1, 1875, 664.

53. *Saints' Herald*, May 19, 1883, 305.

One of the callers in 1879 was E. L. Kelley. Sent by Joseph Smith III and the leadership of the RLDS Church, Kelley's mission was to lay the groundwork for the Kirtland Temple Suit. Smith and Mark Forscutt had hoped to sell the temple in 1875, but they were soon convinced that the temple belonged not to any individuals, such as themselves, but to a church, specifically the RLDS Church. The Kirtland Temple Suit was designed to prove this as a matter of law. After a few surprises, the objectives were achieved, and the case resulted in a clear title to the temple for the Reorganized Church of Jesus Christ of Latter Day Saints.[54] A new branch was soon organized, and the temple was restored and again used regularly as a house of worship.

The Kirtland Temple Suit brought to a close a forty-two year period of transition. These years were a time of uncertainty for many, with little or no consistency and even less direction. It was not, however, a time of abandonment for the temple. Saints of some variety were in Kirtland and caring for the temple throughout, although limited resources meant that this care was generally emotional, rather than physical, in nature. The Latter Day Saint community in Kirtland today in some ways mirrors the community during the transition years. Among Kirtland's citizens can be found RLDS, LDS, Restorationist, and Church of Jesus Christ (Bickertonite) members and representatives of these and other Latter Day Saint tradition churches continue to visit and/or worship in the House of the Lord.

---

54. For the details of this complicated case, see Launius, *Kirtland Temple*, 100–16.

NINE

"SO WE BUILT A GOOD LITTLE TEMPLE TO WORSHIP IN"

MORMONISM ON THE PEDERNALES—TEXAS, 1847-51

MELVIN C. JOHNSON

[Author's note: Lyman Wight's colony in Texas had become a scholastic challenge to me after several years of being a research fellow at the Texas Forestry Museum in Lufkin, Texas. We had been constructing a database on the history of the east Texas lumber industry and its accompanying Milltown culture and logging railroad technology. Early in the research references came up to "Mormon Miller's" in central Texas before the Civil War. The reader learned that it was a frontier milling community that first brought water power, then horsepower to the Texas Hill Country, and was led by renegade LDS Church apostle Lyman Wight. Bill Shepard, the wonderful Strangite historian, sent me an attestation, signed by Wight, documenting that baptisms for the dead were being performed in Zodiac, Texas, in 1851. By this time, Wight had been estranged for some years from his former quorum and from LDS church president Brigham Young. That attestation was one of the reasons I paid a visit to the library/archives of the Reorganized Church of Jesus Christ of Latter Days Saints (now Community of Christ), headquartered in Independence, Missouri. Ron Romig, ably assisted by Barbara Bernhauer, was the senior archivist and guru of all documents Mormon. He studied the attestation, then stood up and said, "Follow me." He walked into a small room where a huge iron vault stood, reached up on top of it (not inside), lifted an old register, and handed it to me. It was dated from the 1850s and contained a record of baptisms for the dead in Zodiac in February–March 1851. Ron handed me the original as well as a working typescript of the Autobiography of John P. Hawley, in which I found a little known personal account of Hawley at the tragic events at Mountain Meadows (Utah). I immediately made a copy of the Hawley typescript and sent it to Will Bagley, historian of the Mountain Meadows Massacre. Then, as I read and studied the temple register, I realized that Mormon-oriented Restoration temple history beyond the Mississippi began in Zodiac, not in my beloved St. George, Utah, where I had graduated from Dixie College. Some individuals and groups in the Mormon history world pushed back against the idea of the Zodiac temple being the first in the West. However, noted LDS historian Richard E. Bennett gave a resounding endorsement of the Zodiac temple in his presidential address in San Antonio, Texas, during the Mormon History Association conference in 2014. Some of his remarks included: "Melvin C. Johnson in his fine study *Polygamy on the Pedernales*[1] offers convincing evidence that Lyman Wight's Zodiac Community near San Antonio, Texas, completed a two-story log temple in February 1849. Ordinances performed in the Zodiac temple from 1849 to 1851 included baptisms for the dead, washing of feet, a general endowment, adoption, and the marriage sealing of men and women for time and eternity. Wight believed that all ordinances performed in the Nauvoo Temple after Joseph Smith's death were unauthorized and that he, 'not Brigham Young, was the Lord's appointed messenger' and that his temple at Zodiac was the only 'acceptable' place for such ordinances." I agree with Bennett's assessment "that Wight's involvement and belief in temple work owed everything to Joseph Smith and not to Brigham Young."[2] My updated revision of "'So We Built a Good Little Temple to Worship In'" follows.]

The first functional, active Mormon temple west of the Mississippi River no longer exists. A significant, if little known, fact about the Lyman Wight Colony, a small independent Mormon group of the 1840s and 1850s, is that its members performed their version of the Mormon temple endowment ceremony and baptized their dead from 1849 to 1851 in their own temple. It was built on the banks of the Pedernales River in the small Mormon colony known as Zodiac, located in Gillespie County, Texas. This should not be surprising, for performing

---

1. Melvin C. Johnson, *Polygamy on the Pedernales: Lyman Wight's Mormon Villages in Antebellum Texas, 1845–1858* (Logan: Utah State University Press, 2006).
2. Richard E. Bennett, "The Upper Room": The Nature and Development of Latter-Day Saint Temple Work, 1846–55," *Journal of Mormon History* 41, no. 2 (Apr. 2015): 7.

rites and rituals associated with the temple was not limited to the Utah Latter-day Saint Church. The Wightites (followers of Lyman Wight) and the Strangites (followers of James J. Strang), as well as other sects, either built temples for such rites or participated in temple ritualism outside them. Some contenders to the mantle of Joseph Smith Jr. were aware of the Texas temple and were either spurred by it or desired to partake in its sacred rites.

Those who followed William Smith, youngest brother of and self-professed successor to Joseph Smith, believed that "the pretended endowments in the temple at Nauvoo [Illinois]" were not acceptable to God.[3] Examples abound. For instance, a year after James Strang took his first plural wife (1849) in Michigan, former LDS bishop George Miller and his polygamous family arrived at Beaver Island, Strang's headquarters, from Lyman Wight's Texas colony. Miller brought the news that the Wightites were using the temple. Implementation of earlier Strangite plans for construction of a temple had begun the previous fall; however, the Michigan design with its twelve towers and a great hall was never finished. William Smith wanted to merge his religious organization with that of Wight's, according to the minutes of his church's conference at Covington, Kentucky (1850). The report included a plan for Smith's church group to immigrate to Texas. There they were to unite with the Wightites and receive "endowments and blessings" in the Zodiac temple.[4] Some members did join their co-religionists in the Lone Star state.[5]

---

3. *Aaronic Herald* (Covington, KY), Feb. 1, 1849,1.

4. *Melchisedek & Aaronic Herald* (Covington, KY), Apr. 1850, 1. Some of William Smith's followers were to "depart immediately from this land, to the land that I have appointed for the gathering of my people, in the land of Texas, to the place of my servant Lyman Wight, where my people may rest in peace, where they may plant and not another inherit, and where they may build unto me an house, that shall be called the house of my glory, and prepare themselves for the redemption of Zion, and for the endowments, and for the ordinances, and for the redemption of their dead, and for their priesthood qualifications."

5. "Correspondence of Bishop George Miller," *Northern Islander* (1855), 151, 152, 155; David Rich Lews, "'For Life, the Resurrection, and Life Everlasting': James J. Strang and Strangite Mormon Polygamy," *Wisconsin Magazine of History* 66 (Summer 1983): 274–91; John Quist, "Polygamy among James Strang and His Followers," *John Whitmer Historical Association Journal* 9 (1989): 34, 38; *Frontier Guardian*, Feb. 7, 1849, 2; D. Michael Quinn, *The Mormon Hierarchy: Origins of Power* (Salt Lake City: Signature Books/Smith Research Associates, 1994), 224; revelation to William Smith, Mar. 20, 1850, in *Melchisedek & Aaronic*

The Cutlerites were no exception. Alpheus Cutler, an intimate of Joseph Smith before his murder in 1844 and a member of the secretive Council of Fifty, as well as a leader at Winter Quarters, Iowa, led the Church of Jesus Christ (Cutlerite) from 1853 until his death in 1864. Cutler and his followers, first in Mills County and then Fremont County, Iowa, lived their own form of Mormonism without a temple, although this sect, as with other branches of the Mormons, included a form of sacred rites. According to Cutlerite expert Danny L. Jorgensen, Cutler's sacred ritualism "involved a secretive initiation, assignment of a sacred personal identity, passwords to the celestial world, endowments (or blessings), ritual cleansing by water and anointings with oil, the receipt of a sacred undergarment, and ritual reenactment of sacred myths."[6] Other ordinances included baptism by proxy for the salvation of the dead as well as monogamous celestial marriage. The endowment of the first generation, coupled with the quickly decreasing numbers of followers after the death of Cutler in 1864, eventually limited ordinances to the ritual baptism for the dead.[7]

Thus, among the members of the Mormon diaspora, the environs of a temple were not necessary for the rites associated with it. The Cutlerites practiced them in Iowa, and the Wightites, discussed more fully below, did the same in Texas before building the Pedernales temple. Brigham Young, at the request of many of his Latter-day Saints in Winter Quarters, years before the Endowment House was built in Salt Lake City, approved the performance of eternal sealings, marriages, and adoptions.[8] The Strangites, the Wightites, and the Utah LDS Church attempted to build, built, or use other buildings for rites associated with Mormon temple ritual.

The social and material landscape of Zodiac Mormonism included

---

Herald, Apr. 1850, 4 pp., photocopy; Joseph Smith III and Heman C. Smith, *The History of the Reorganized Church of Jesus Christ of Latter Day Saints*, 6 vols. (Independence, Missouri: Herald House, 1951–70), 3:35. George Miller's newspaper articles may be compared with *The Life of George Miller, Written by Himself*, ed. H. W. Mills, as "De Tal Palo Astilla," in *Annual Publications of the Southern Historical Society* (1917), 88–156.

6. Danny L. Jorgensen, "The Fiery Darts of the Adversary: An Interpretation of Early Cutlerism," *John Whitmer Historical Association Journal* 10 (1990): 75.

7. Jorgensen, 67–70, 74, 75–76, 83.

8. Richard E. Bennett, *Mormons at the Missouri, 1846–1852: "And Should We Die ..."* (Norman: University of Oklahoma Press, 1987), 189–91.

an infrastructure of temple ritualism, economic exclusiveness, and plural marriage, which fused the sacred and the secular in this frontier community of faith. From their early beginnings in Wisconsin, the Wightites had defined social, familial, and individual needs in religious terms. The role of Apostle Lyman Wight as the community prophet and leader provided direct, authoritarian guidance. The Zodiac temple with its rituals defined the focus of family and individual goals. Temple ritualism bound the community together: husbands and wives, parents and children, leaders and followers. It gifted (or endowed) families with continuity, transcending mortality, sublimating death to eternal life, unraveling the bindings of secular time and space. Those in Zodiac believed their temple work endowed them beyond the grave with everlasting exaltation: for themselves, their families, and their familial dead. The environment of Zodiac, Lamoni Wight wrote many years later, had presented his family and friends with the opportunity to worship "according to our desires, unity, peace, and harmony prevailing."[9]

John Hawley remembered that "Lyman [Wight] told us we must build a house for to attend to the baptism for the dead and also the ordinance of washing of feet and a general endowment in the wilderness. So we … built a good little Temple to worship in." It was completed on February 17, 1849, the first Mormon temple west of the Mississippi. The large, two-story log building functioned as a multi-purpose center for Zodiac, a company storehouse as well as an upstairs room for temple ritual. Of the two Mormon schools enumerated in the census of 1850, one met in the building. The Zodiac High Council gave permission for William Leyland to hold his classes in the large room on the second floor. Heman Hale Smith, RLDS Church historian and descendent of a Zodiac family, incorrectly believed that the building was "only in name" a temple.[10] It was, in fact, a functioning Mormon temple on the Texas frontier.

---

9. Levi Lamoni Wight, "Autobiography of L. L. Wight," *Journal of History* 9 (July 1916): 265.

10. John Hawley, "Autobiography of John Hawley," unpublished manuscript, 1889, 7, Community of Christ Library–Archives, Independence, Missouri; hereafter CCLA; "The Mormon Colony (Zodiac) Near Fredericksburg, Texas," 1969, in the Cotter Collection, unpublished manuscripts compiled by John Cotter and Dorothea (Weinhiemer) Cotter, in the Pioneer Heritage Memorial Library, Fredericksburg, Texas; William Leyland Journal, in Heman Hale Smith, "The Lyman Wight Colony in Texas," manuscript prepared for the

Various ordinances performed in the Zodiac temple involved married and unmarried individuals. These activities included the distinctive rites of baptism for the dead; washings of feet, head, and body; a general endowment; various anointings; adoptions; the sealing (marriage) of men and women for time and eternity; and the setting apart of kings, queens, and priests for eternity. Zodiac ritualism, on at least one occasion, reorganized families as well as united them. In the spring of 1849, the Leyland siblings, who hated George Miller, their stepfather, encouraged Lyman Wight to use the ceremonies to separate them from Miller's rule. William Leyland noted in his journal that on April 8, 1849, he received the endowment portion of "the washing of feet under the hands of the Twelve High Counsellors and their presidents along with sixteen elders and their presidents and on the 9th received the washings of the body and anointing." The following month, William Leyland and his sisters Sophia, Sarah, and Eliza were ritually adopted into the Lyman Wight family. Although the girls were only "adopted until they were of age," William wrote that he was "adopted under the oath and covenant of the priesthood unto my salvation or damnation until I could save my father and raise him to be a king and priest."[11]

John Hawley is the only individual to experience and compare the endowment ritual of both the Wightite and Utah LDS branches of Mormonism. He celebrated the ceremony at Zodiac (1849) and later in Utah (1857, 1868). Under sworn oath in the Temple Lot Case

---

Reorganized Church of Jesus Christ of Latter Day Saints (Lamoni, Iowa, 1920), 21, 25, CCLA. Heman H. Smith (son of Heman C. Smith and grandson of Spencer Smith, both members of Zodiac), great-grandson of Lyman Wight, and a church leader and historian for the RLDS Church, prepared the manuscript from the Lyman Wight Journal, the Spencer Smith Journal, and the William Leyland Journal, all later destroyed by fire.

11. William Leyland Journal, in Smith, "Lyman Wight Colony," 21–22. Hawley either considered the type of ceremony in which Leyland participated as not an endowment or was unaware that Leyland had received anointings and washings without the sealing ceremony to a woman for time and eternity. Hawley carefully distinguished, in the Temple Lot Case, at page 455, the difference between the first ordinances and marriage sealing, noting that while in Salt Lake City young men could receive the first part of the endowment without the sealing ceremony for time and eternity—such was not the case in Zodiac. Hawley's temple experiences are recorded in three different documents: John Hawley to Bro. Joseph, the *Saints' Herald*, June 28, 1884, 412; Hawley, "Autobiography of John Hawley," 7; and *The Reorganized Church of Jesus Christ of Latter Day Saints, Complainant, vs. The Church of Christ at Independence*, et al. (Lamoni, Iowa: Herald House, 1893), 451–62.

(1893),[12] he compared in federal court the various ordinances and clothing associated with these rituals. It should be noted that Hawley was testifying in the Temple Lot Case on behalf of the RLDS Church, which defended Joseph Smith well into the twentieth century against the accusation that he was the foundation of Mormon polygamy. Hawley was a devout member of the RLDS Church during the last four decades of his life. His "Autobiography" describes his sealing for time and eternity to his first wife, Harriet Hobart, near Austin, Texas, in 1846 and also to his subsequent, non-plural spouse Sylvia Johnson in 1849 (at which time both were endowed).[13] In the Temple Lot testimony, Hawley was referring to the Wightite endowment with Sylvia in 1849, as well as its comparison to the LDS ceremonies of their sealing in Salt Lake City (in 1857) and later his second anointing (in 1868).

Hawley's writings during the 1880s and 1890s clearly indicate a bias against Brigham Young and the LDS Church, while understating the complexity of Wightite attitudes toward polygamy. For instance, family lore mentions that Hawley nearly became a polygamist, but in his autobiography, he discusses that fact yet skips his own brother's role as a polygamous husband.[14] He does not note that his sister Mary was Lyman Wight's fourth wife. His brother George was a plural husband for nearly ten years in Texas and the Utah territory.[15] Nor do the later writings and sworn testimony of John Hawley note that he served as the presiding elder of the LDS Church in Pine Valley, Washington

---

12. [Temple Lot Case] The Reorganized Church of Jesus Christ of Latter Day Saints, Complainant, Vs. the Church of Christ at Independence, Missouri: Richard Hill, Trustee; Richard Hill, Mrs. E. Hill, C.A. Hall [and Others] … as embers of and Doing Business Under the Name of The Church of Christ, at Independence … United States. Contributor, Circuit Court (8th Circuit) (Herald Publishing House, 1893). An excellent examination of the case is found in Richard Donald Oullette, "The Mormon Temple Lot Case: Space, Memory, and Identity in a Divided New Religion," PhD diss. (University of Texas–Austin, 2012).

13. Hawley, "Autobiography of John Hawley," 6–7, 10. John and Sylvia were sealed for time and eternity a second time by Brigham Young in Salt Lake City in 1857.

14. Hawley, "Experiences," in "Autobiography of John Hawley," 234.

15. Brigham Young to Bishop Zadok K. Judd, Feb. 24, 1860, and Brigham Young to Bishop Z. K. Judd, Fort Clara, May 22, 1860, Church History Library, Church of Jesus Christ of Latter-day Saints, Salt Lake City, Utah; hereafter CHL; Freddijo Passey Burk, Joseph Hadfield Story: An Incredible Odyssey (Scottsdale, Arizona: Concept Management Corporation, 2008), 188, 362; Johnson, Polygamy on the Pedernales, 57. Hawley married George's third wife, Jenet, to the Hawley ward, Joseph Hadfield, in 1860.

County, Utah territory, during the 1860s.[16] Thus his writings concerning his temple experiences, compared to his reticence about Wightite and family polygamy, become more compelling with their forthright and lucid descriptions of them.

Hawley's testimony stated that, to the best of his personal understanding, Young and Wight both believed they had the priesthood authority to seal men and women together for time and eternity in an endowment ceremony. Participants in each sect's rite used holy clothing known as "garments." Unlike the Utah Mormons, the Wightites of Zodiac wore their religious garments only for special occasions, including for sealing ceremonies and for burial. They believed the garment robes were patterned on a design worn by the ancient Book of Mormon prophet Moroni, an angelic messenger whom Joseph Smith said had visited him and shown him the golden plates. This outer garment was a loose frock without markings, described as an "entire covering of linen," leaving bare only the extremities of the hands, feet, and head. The garment and an apron, a facsimile of those supposedly worn by Adam and Eve to cover their nakedness after their expulsion from the Garden of Eden, were bare of markings. In contrast, so Hawley testified, the Utah garment was always worn by the initiated, who were counseled never to take it off, even to leaving one leg in the garment while bathing. The Utah apron and the tight-fitting garment, joined together at the waist and legs to make one piece of clothing, had special markings. The temple clothing also included a robe with a "bandage" that came down from the shoulders, moccasins, and a cap.

---

16. John Hawley to Bro. Joseph, 412; Hawley, "Autobiography of John Hawley," 6–7; T. R. Turk, "Mormons in Texas: The Lyman Wight Colony," typescript manuscript, 1987, photocopy, CHL. Turk, "Mormons in Texas," 44–45, 46–47, incorrectly dates George Hawley's marriage to Ann Hadfield in either 1848 or 1849; Hawley, *Temple Lot Case,* 452, 453, 457; Journal History of the Church of Jesus Christ of Latter-day Saints (a chronological scrapbook of typed entries and newspaper clippings, 1830–present), Mar. 22, 1863; May 8, 1864, 3; and Dec. 31, 1866, 2, CHL. The marriages of the Hawley siblings on July 4, 1846, took place at or near Sycamore Springs, four miles north of Austin, revealing once again the continuing Mormon pattern during the second half of the nineteenth century that eternal marriage sealings could take place outside of a temple. For examples, see Quinn, *Mormon Hierarchy,* 54, 191, 494–95, and 657, of such sealings being performed from 1842 to 1845 before the Nauvoo, Illinois, temple was dedicated and at p. 657 for examples in 1846 after the Latter-day Saints had abandoned the Nauvoo temple.

Hawley testified he first encountered endowment practices in Zodiac, that "Lyman Wight was the first person that taught [to Hawley] anything about endowments according to my best recollection." The Zodiac endowment, he alleged, involved only matrimonial concerns, the sealing of a man and women "together in order to enjoy each other's society in eternity." He described the doctrine as "spiritual wife marriage," a negative term used by the RLDS Church (and others) during that era to attack the plural marriage practices of Utah Mormonism, the language of which was guaranteed to offend LDS sensibilities. Hawley testified further that sealings for time and eternity were performed for monogamous as well as polygamous couples in Zodiac.

Nonetheless, having more than one concurrent wife, according to Hawley, led to the accrual of extra spiritual advantages: "Those that were in spiritual marriage were said to be in polygamy, as well as those that were not. The understanding was that they would enjoy the same glory as others, but the ones that had more than one wife would enjoy a greater portion of it." He further offered that it "was not a necessary and logical sequence" that those who had been married for time and eternity would have to practice the doctrine of plural marriage. If a man took more than one wife, however, then his "glory which was in eternity would be greater" than the husband who had only one wife.[17]

Wight was always concerned that the rite of eternal marriage, or patriarchal marriage, be correctly performed, and that couples were married for eternity as well as for time. He earlier had ordained Pierce Hawley, John's father, as a patriarch because, in Mormon theology, he would have the authority, through the power of his office, to determine an individual's family, or tribal, line. Pierce Hawley discerned that his son was from the tribe of Ephraim and of the royal blood and lineage of Joseph of Egypt. Antebellum eternal marriage under the Wightite system, like other Mormon factions, did not need to be performed in a temple.[18]

An example follows. In 1846, Lyman Wight and Pierce Hawley had made marriage selections for John Hawley (Harriet Hobart), Priscilla Hawley (John Young), and George Hawley (Ann Hadfield). On July 4, presumably at Sycamore Springs to the north of Austin, Texas,

17. Hawley, *Temple Lot Case*, 453–56.
18. Hawley, "Autobiography of John Hawley," 6, 7.

with Pierce Hawley and Otis Hobart officiating, John Hawley was ordained a king and priest and anointed with oil after first having his feet washed. John then washed Harriet's feet, anointed her head with oil, and ordained her a queen. Lyman Wight sealed John and Harriet for time and eternity. Hawley testified later that the use of "the power of the priesthood" differentiated religious sealings from civil rites. The Mormons used them "instead of the legal form of marriage and at that time we looked upon it as being more binding for eternity than the other form of marriage."[19]

Hawley compared the Utah and Zodiac ceremonies. He asserted that the rites he underwent at in Salt Lake City were "not the same endowments that I took under Lyman Wight's administration." The Zodiac endowment consisted of only the one ceremony of sealing for time and eternity, but also the following ordinances: the washing of feet, an anointing with oil, and the ordaining of the initiates as "kings, queens, and priests," which Hawley averred consisted "the sum and substance" of the Zodiac endowment. The Utah endowments, however, distinguished between marriage and resurrection ordinances. His testimony cited that "Wilford Woodruff [an LDS apostle] did the anointing and washing and Brigham Young [LDS Church president] did the sealing" for Hawley and his wife. Unlike the Zodiac endowment, the couples in Hawley's ceremony in Salt Lake City were separated by gender in different rooms. The Utah endowment involved the washing and anointing with oil of the entire body and feet of the initiate.

Hawley stated that the Utah endowment did not include ordinations of the celebrants as kings, queens, and priests. The Utah rituals included two other major additions that differed from the Texas rite. They required the participants to swear oaths "to avenge the blood of the prophets" in addition to resurrection and marriage ordinances. The Utah penalty for revealing the "grip and oath" associated with the avenging of Joseph and Hyrum Smith "was disembowelment." Brigham Young had added a second endowment, wrote Hawley, that included "an anointing and setting apart for the resurrection, and" a power to be

---

19. Turk, "Mormons in Texas," 43, 52, 83; Hawley, *Temple Lot Case,* 452; Hawley, "Autobiography of John Hawley," 6, 7, 10–11.

called "to rise from the dead, and to raise others." The candidate then received "a name we would be called for from the grave by."[20]

The issue of privacy also differentiated the endowment ceremonies of Zodiac and Utah. Hawley testified that in Zodiac anyone could attend. In Salt Lake City, "it was done secretly and no one was permitted to see them only the officers and the ones taking the endowments. No one else was present or permitted to be present simply because no one else had any business there and they were not permitted to be there." The availability of facilities was probably one reason for the difference in practice. Zodiac was a frontier community with a two-story log building, its only community building other than the mill, and it served as the temple, the storehouse, the high council meeting place, and one of the schools. The Endowment House in Salt Lake City, on the other hand, had, according to Hawley, "a good many departments" with "a reception room, a small stairway to the veil, and it was pretty much all on the ground floor. Had dressing rooms, washing rooms, a prayer circle, and an altar."[21] The Mormons of Utah had the time, the opportunity, and the security to build a private structure in which to house a much more intricate ceremony than that in Zodiac.

Temple ordinances continued at Zodiac from 1849 to 1851, including baptism for the dead. On February 10, 1851, Lyman Wight signed an attestation of purpose concerning the principle of such baptism. He was convinced by scripture, the words of Joseph Smith, and "twenty years in the cause of God," the Zodiac leader wrote, "that baptism for the dead is one of the most essential ordinances given to us by Christ our redeemer." Only a covenanted people, he declared further, dedicated "even unto the principle of all they have and being placed under the controll of the Almighty God" could build an appropriate house and font for the sanctification of God's followers. Wight averred that never, in his opinion, had a site before been worthy of such an edifice and for the rites held within it. According to Wight, "the Lord Almighty [had] accepted" the Zodiac temple.[22] That same day, Stephen

---

20. Hawley to Bro. Joseph, 412; Hawley, *Temple Lot Case,* 453, 454, 457, 458.

21. Hawley, *Temple Lot Case,* 454, 456.

22. Lyman Wight, "Revelation on Baptism for the Dead," Feb. 10, 1851, Archives of the State Historical Society of Iowa, Des Moines, Iowa.

Curtis administered the rite to Lyman Wight as a proxy candidate for his grandfather Levi Wight and to Harriet Benton Wight, proxy for Levi Wight's wife, Susanna Wight. Official witnesses were Pierce Hawley, Sarah Schroeder, Joseph D. Goodale, and George Hawley.

More than half a dozen sessions were held from February 11 to March 11, 1851. The women normally used their maiden names rather than those of their husbands. Recorders included John Young and Stephen Curtis, with Andrew Ballantyne, Stephen Curtis, and J. D. Goodale as administrators of the ritual. Proxy candidates included Pierce and Sarah Schrader (Schroeder) Hawley; George Montague Sr., and his plural wife Eliza Segar; Stephen Z. Curtis; John F. Miller and Margaret Frances Andrews; Ralph Jenkins and Verona Brace; Irvin Carter and Mary Ann Six; Jennet Turnbull and Andrew Ballantyne. Witnesses included George Hawley, John Hawley, Priscilla Hawley, I. F. Carter, Spencer Smith, Rodney Bray (Brace), Andrew Ballantyne, George W. Bird, Pierce Hawley, E. W. Curtis, Eber Johnson, William Ballantyne, Alaxe St. Mary, (Marion) Frances Andrews, J. S. Goodale, and Margaret Ballantyne.[23]

Lyman Wight's attestation of and participation in baptism for the dead in Zodiac clearly reveal his rejection of the post-Joseph Smith churches of Nauvoo and Salt Lake City. It was his rebuff to the authority of Brigham Young and the rites performed in the Nauvoo temple. Wight obviously believed the Nauvoo temple was not worthy of religious rituals, thus underlining the futility of its ordinances before the Lord and the world. The implications of the Texas directive are clear: the worthiness of such rites could only be performed by a covenanted people who had dedicated all they owned and who had been accepted and directed by the Lord God Almighty. The conclusion of that train of logic was equally clear: Lyman Wight, not Brigham Young, was the Lord's appointed messenger. Obviously, Wight believed some form of common-stock association was the religious and economic foundation necessary for a covenanted people, rather than the stewardship and tithing programs of Utah Mormonism. Dated February 10, 1851, the document logically

---

23. Baptism for the Dead Record, Lyman Wight Records in Zodiac, Feb. and Mar. 1851, CCLA. I have included parenthetical corrections and annotations to clarify the identification of certain individuals.

infers that Wight believed not only could he officiate in such a position but that the Mormons of Zodiac, with Wight at their head, could build an acceptable temple and worthily perform its rites.

The writings of John Hawley and William Leyland and records of baptism for the dead reveal the extent of Zodiac temple activities. They involved the wearing of garments, the receiving of endowments, and the performance of other religious rituals. It is obvious that the statements of Wight, Hawley, and Leyland, as well as the records for baptism of the dead, reveal an active and functioning Mormon temple on the banks of the Pedernales River in frontier Texas before the Civil War. The Zodiac temple, the first Mormon temple west of the Mississippi River, no longer exists, but its record does.

TEN

"TO COVER YOUR NAKEDNESS"
THE BODY, SACRED SECRECY, AND
INSTITUTIONAL POWER IN THE INITIATORY

JOHN-CHARLES DUFFY

In February 1846, the *Warsaw Signal*, an Illinois paper, ran an exposé of a secretive ceremony, called "the endowment," that Mormons were allegedly performing in their not-quite-finished temple in nearby Nauvoo.[1] A shrill voice against Mormonism since the early 1840s, the *Signal* reveled in the outrage of this latest shocking disclosure: "There must always be two candidates, a male and female presented for the endowment, at once. ... The candidates are first taken into a room together, where they are stripped of all their clothing and are made to wash each other from head to foot. ... [Afterward] the candidates are brought together, still in a state of nudity, into a room where they are allowed to remain together, alone, as long as they see proper."[2]

Two months later, the *Signal* published a letter by a disaffected Mormon signing herself Emeline. Though she had come to regard the Mormon leadership as "vile, corrupt, licentious libertines" and the endowment as "a laughable farce," Emeline wished to set the record straight about alleged sexual improprieties during the ceremony, perhaps out of fear for her own reputation. It was true, she wrote, that in the temple she had been "divested of all [her] apparel, and in a state of perfect nudity ... washed from head to foot." But, she continued, "all this was done by sisters in the church—none others were present—it is false to say that men and women are admitted together in an indecent

---

1. I owe thanks to several individuals who commented on earlier versions of this essay: Kathleen Flake, Pamela J. Stewart, Andrew Strathern, Thomas A. Tweed, and two anonymous reviewers for the *Journal of Ritual Studies*.

2. "Ceremony of the Endowment," *Warsaw Signal*, Feb. 18, 1846.

manner."[3] Elaborating on her experience, Emeline provided history's first published eyewitness account of Mormon temple ceremonies.

As the exchange between Emeline and the *Signal* illustrates, rumors of nudity in temples have been a source of scandal since Mormons first started administering the washing rite that Emeline described—a rite still practiced today, albeit in altered form, in temples of the Church of Jesus Christ of Latter-day Saints (hereafter LDS), the largest denomination to arise from early Mormonism. Unlike the LDS Church's much more numerous meetinghouses, where Sunday services are held, temples are closed to the public following dedication; at the beginning of 2019, there were 150 operating LDS temples worldwide,[4] whereas meetinghouses probably numbered between 10,000 and 20,000.[5] In temples, LDS members perform rites—"ordinances," in LDS parlance—which prepare the faithful to receive the fullness of God's blessings in the world to come. The washing rite is part of an ordinance that LDS today usually refer to as the initiatory.[6] During this ordinance, adult initiates are washed and anointed in preparation for becoming kings and priests, or queens and priestesses, in God's kingdom. They are also clothed for the first time in the temple garment, which they will thereafter wear throughout their lives as underclothing.[7]

Until the beginning of the twentieth-first century, the initiatory was administered while initiates were in a state of nudity—entire during the nineteenth century, partial during the twentieth. Only in early 2005 did

---

3. Emeline, "Mormon Endowments," *Warsaw Signal*, Apr. 15, 1846.

4. "Temple List," at www.lds.org/temples.

5. Although the LDS Church publicizes various statistics that illustrate its worldwide growth, including numbers of temples, missions, missionaries, family history centers, congregations, and members, it does not publicize numbers of meetinghouses. See "Facts and Statistics," at www.mormonnewsroom.org/facts-and-statistics. In the late 1990s, a pair of journalists calculated that the church had over 12,000 meetinghouses. Richard Ostling and Joan K. Ostling, *Mormon America*, rev. ed. (San Francisco: HarperOne, 2007), 408. If construction of new meetinghouses has continued at the same rate, as of 2018 the number of meetinghouses would approach 20,000.

6. In the sequence of temple ordinances, the initiatory is followed by a Masonic-style drama. It is this drama that contemporary LDS usually have in mind when they speak of the "endowment," the term used by the *Warsaw Signal*. However, "endowment" can also refer, as in the *Signal's* usage, to the initiatory and the allegorical drama together, treated as a unit.

7. Allen Claire Rozsa, "Temple Ordinances," in *Encyclopedia of Mormonism*, ed. Daniel H. Ludlow, 4 vols. (New York: Macmillan, 1992), 4:1444–45.

church leaders revise the initiatory so as to abolish nudity. This essay traces the history of the decline of nudity in the initiatory and interprets that decline by setting it against intersecting LDS discourses about the body and the sacred. During the twentieth century, it became common for LDS to invoke a metaphor of the body as temple to proscribe exposure of the body outside marriage: like the rites of the temple, the body is to be concealed on the grounds that it is sacred. The decline of nudity in the initiatory extended the imperative to conceal the body into a realm where that imperative was formerly, anomalously, suspended. Attention to the power dynamics involved in this shift yields a complicated picture. The covering up of initiates' bodies works to protect their privacy, a change that many temple-goers have no doubt welcomed. But the change also works to conceal the potentially unwelcome power that the church, as an institution, holds over members' bodies—the power to require members to expose their bodies, if church leaders see fit, in ways that historically some members have experienced as a personal violation.

STUDYING RELIGIOUS SECRETS

Before beginning my historical analysis, I must address the ethics of studying temple ritual. LDS members frequently insist that temple ordinances are too sacred to be discussed outside temples. Kathleen Flake cites as typical one LDS individual's assertion that "discussing the temple ceremonies openly is as insensitive as burning the Torah, stomping on the Eucharist and desecrating a mosque."[8] Given this attitude, is it ethical for scholars to publish studies of these ordinances? Discussions of the ethics of studying religious secrets have typically envisioned scenarios where an outsider seeks access to secrets of a group to which he or she does not belong. The trend of such discussions, not unexpectedly, is to advocate respect for others' privacy. That advocacy is most emphatic when the groups in question have been objects of Western colonialism, upon whom scholars fear to perpetrate further cultural violence.[9] Calls to respect religious privacy may be more

---

8. Kathleen Flake, "'Not to be Riten': The Mormon Temple Rite as Oral Canon," *Journal of Ritual Studies* 9, no. 2 (1995): 6; reprinted in the present compilation.

9. On respecting religious secrets to avoid cultural violence, see Nancy Scheper-Hughes, "The Best of Two Worlds, the Worst of Two Worlds: Reflections on Culture and Field Work

qualified in cases of secretive new religious movements, which outsiders may suspect of having something shady to hide.[10] Scholars doing work on LDS temple worship have sought to respect religious privacy by repeating only what is found in official descriptions of the rites published by the church or, in the case of qualitative research, by taking pains not to cross boundaries signaled by LDS informants. Examples of these approaches include LDS scholar Kathleen Flake's historical study of temple ritual as an oral tradition (included in this compilation); non-LDS scholar Colleen McDannell's interview-based study of the meanings that temple garments have in the lives of LDS individuals; and a master's thesis by then-LDS graduate student Janet Kincaid that used interviews to examine how LDS young adults responded to temple ritual.[11] By contrast, non-LDS scholar Douglas Davies has been rather freer about describing elements of temple ritual that are explicitly covered by covenants of nondisclosure, something that LDS would generally find extremely offensive (although Davies is nevertheless regarded by many LDS scholars as friendly toward their religion).[12]

The ethical question becomes more complicated when we move from scenarios in which scholars are *probing* for information about religious secrets to scenarios in which religious insiders are *volunteering*

---

among the Rural Irish and Pueblo Indians,"*Comparative Studies in Society and History* 29, no. 1 (1987): 56–75; Jill D. Sweet, "'Let 'Em Loose': Pueblo Indian Management of Tourism," *American Indian Culture and Research Journal* 15, no. 4 (1991): 59–74; Kenneth M. George, "Dark Trembling: Ethnographic Notes on Secrecy and Concealment in Highland Sulawesi," *Anthropological Quarterly* 66, no. 4 (1993): 230–46; and Hugh B. Urban, "The Torment of Secrecy: Ethical and Epistemological Problems in the Study of Esoteric Traditions," *History of Religions* 37 (1998): 209–48. Though he does not refer to secrecy, Ronald L. Grimes's call for scholars to avoid desecration of native burial sites likewise moves in the vein of promoting respect for colonized peoples' sacred boundaries; see Ronald L. Grimes, *Ritual Criticism* (Columbia: University of South Carolina Press, 1990), 75–79.

10. See, for example, Benjamin Zablocki and Thomas Robbins, eds., *Misunderstanding Cults: Searching for Objectivity in a Controversial Field* (Toronto: University of Toronto Press, 2001), 12–14; and Janja Lalich, "Pitfalls in the Sociological Study of Cults," in *Misunderstanding Cults*, 144–47.

11. Flake, "'Not to be Riten,'" 1–21; Colleen McDannell, *Material Christianity: Religion and Popular Culture in America* (New Haven: Yale University Press, 1995); Janet M. Kincaid, "'Tell Eve about Serpent!': A Qualitative Study of the Effects of Temple Participation in the Lives of Young Adult Mormons," master's thesis (Graduate Theological Union, 2000).

12. Douglas J. Davies, *The Mormon Culture of Salvation* (Aldershot, England: Ashgate, 2000), 123, 131, 139n34.

information. The most detailed information publicly available about LDS temple ordinances comes from exposés by former members. It is difficult to dispute that a scholar ought to respect an informant's reticence to disclose religious secrets. But what should be the scholar's attitude toward an informant who desires disclosure, as in the case of a disaffected initiate who publicizes her knowledge of temple ritual to strike against an institution she has come to regard as immoral or oppressive? Once such a figure appears on the scene, it is no longer adequate to resolve the question of how a researcher should treat religious secrets by invoking a general imperative of respect for others. Rather, the question becomes unmistakably one of how scholars should position themselves in relation to conflicts internal to the group being studied. It becomes, in other words, a question of taking sides—in this case, with the LDS Church or with its detractors—or, alternatively, of exerting oneself diplomatically to avoid the appearance of taking sides.

In such a case, the considerations governing a well-informed decision about self-positioning will be localized, pragmatic, and overtly political. Such decisions will be shaped by the relationships and loyalties that researchers have developed in the course of their work; concern for their reputation or the reputability of their discipline; their perceptions about which course of action will protect future research opportunities, for themselves or for others; and their sense of the likely consequences of concealing or publicizing religious secrets for those whom the researchers see as having the most to gain or lose.[13] Scholars who have taken sides with an interest group may be inclined to make absolutist claims on its behalf couched in the language of ethical or legal imperatives. Sociologist of religion Jeffrey Hadden provides an example of such an absolutist claim when he asserts that "to deny a religious group the right to protect its esoteric knowledge ... constitutes a denial to that group [of] the protection of the Free Exercise clause of the First Amendment of the constitution of the United States."[14]

---

13. Considerations such as these are laid out in the 1998 Code of Ethics of the American Anthropological Association.

14. Quoted in Douglas E. Cowan, "Contested Spaces: Movement, Countermovement, and E-space Propaganda," in *Religion Online: Finding Faith on the Internet*, ed. Lorne L. Dawson & Douglas E. Cowan (New York: Routledge, 2004), 255.

But claims such as this need to be understood as arguments in defense of particular interests, not as categorical imperatives handed down from a position of impartiality. Hadden's assertion was literally made in the context of taking sides with an interest group, that is, as part of an *amicus curiae* brief Hadden filed in support of the Church of Scientology, which was suing a critic for publishing Scientologist texts on the internet. A position such as Hadden's advances the interests of parties who wish to conceal certain kinds of information, but it does not acknowledge the complexity that conflicting interests produce for scholars' ethical decision-making.

Matters are complicated further in my study by the fact that I am an initiate, having received the initiatory and accompanying temple ordinances in 1991, at age eighteen, as part of my LDS upbringing. As an initiate, I am committed to maintaining the obligations of non-disclosure I took when I received the ordinances. But I am also in a position of seeing something that may be opaque to non-initiates: that LDS claims about the privacy of temple rites are contestable on the rites' own terms. The oaths of nondisclosure administered to initiates explicitly apply only to selected features of the ordinances, specifically the Masonic-style grips, signs, and passwords that initiates learned.[15] LDS sociologist Armand Mauss has therefore argued that "there is no real reason that even devout Church members could not talk more about the temple ceremonies than they do," which Mauss believes would "facilitate understanding among both Mormons and non-Mormons in certain historical and scholarly respects."[16] Adopting

---

15. By the time I received the endowment, one category of information covered by covenants of nondisclosure had been removed from the rite: a set of symbolic gestures known as "penalties," which were excised in a 1990 revision. The penalties are not pertinent to my discussion of the initiatory, but I mention them here because they raise additional complications for navigating the ethics of religious secrecy. Since I never covenanted not to disclose the penalties, do I have a religious obligation, as an endowed initiate, not to discuss them? Since the penalties are no longer part of the endowment, would it still be as offensive (allegedly) for outsiders to discuss the penalties as it would be to burn the Torah, stomp on the Eucharist, etc.? If something once considered secret by a religious group continues to demand inviolability even after it is no longer in use, are modern-day scholars, such as archaeologists or historians of ancient Gnosticism, obliged not to probe the religious secrets of cultures past?

16. Armand L. Mauss, "Culture, Charisma, and Change: Reflections on Mormon Temple Worship," *Dialogue: A Journal of Mormon Thought* 20, no. 4 (Winter 1987): 77. Because I am citing Mauss in support of a more transparent discussion of temple rites than

a position akin to that articulated by Mauss, I do not include in my discussion of the initiatory any information explicitly covered by covenants of nondisclosure. In addition, I do not reveal any information about the initiatory that has not already entered the public realm—that is, that could not already be obtained through some other written source, print or electronic. This represents my understanding of an ethical approach to discussing secret ritual as well as of my religious obligations as an initiate.

However, my position does not resolve the ethical problem as neatly as it might seem to outsiders. Even though I maintain that I do not violate explicit covenants of nondisclosure, many LDS might find my presentation unacceptably transparent. This is because LDS routinely apply, and LDS leaders have enforced through church discipline, a broader standard of sacred secrecy than that spelled out by the obligations administered during the rites. Gordon B. Hinckley, at the time a counselor in the First Presidency, preached in 1990, "I remind you of the absolute obligation to not discuss outside the temple that which occurs within the temple. Sacred matters deserve sacred consideration. We are under obligation, binding and serious, to not use temple language or speak of temple matters outside." [17] In fact there is no point in the temple ceremonies at which initiates consent, in such broad terms, to "not use temple language or speak of temple matters outside," but Hinckley's much wider interpretation of the obligation of silence is common among LDS church members. Just days after Hinckley's sermon, church leaders implemented revisions in the endowment which, among other things, enacted a more egalitarian relationship between husbands and wives and suppressed a satirical representation of a Christian minister. Church members who commented (positively) on the revisions to reporters were summoned for questioning by local church leaders, and some were disciplined, on the premise that they had violated their sacred obligations, even though those particular aspects of the ceremony were not covered by

---

LDS Church leaders would authorize, I should note, in fairness to Mauss, that I do not know whether he would approve of my discussion specifically.

17. Gordon B. Hinckley, "Keeping the Temple Holy," *Ensign*, Apr. 1990.

the covenants of nondisclosure that initiates make during the cere-mony.[18] Non-LDS scholar Colleen McDannell unintentionally ran afoul of LDS leaders' broad construal of the obligation of silence in her ethnographic work on the wearing of the temple garment. Even though McDannell had taken care to respect what her LDS interview-ees understood to be the boundaries of sacred secrecy, the church's highest governing bodies alluded to her work in an official statement deploring public discussions of temple worship as sacrilegious.[19]

Similarly, though I maintain, on the basis of my experience as an ini-tiate, that my presentation does not violate the boundaries of the sacred, other fellow initiates might dispute that claim, operating out of differ-ent ideas about where the boundaries lie. The fact that this essay makes no disclosures about the ceremony that have not already been made in other published sources would not prevent other LDS from viewing my study as an unwelcome exposure of private religious practices.[20]

In sum: a general mandate to respect LDS members' sacred bound-aries does not provide adequate direction for resolving the ethical problem, because the location of those boundaries is subject to dispute among LDS themselves. This problem exists in other cases of religious secrecy as well. A scholar's determination to respect, for example, the sacred boundaries of "the Pueblo" (rhetorically cast as if they were a unitary entity, all sharing the same sensibilities of the sacred) ob-scures conflicts among the Pueblo about where those boundaries lie and thus obscures the power relations that produce the boundaries.

---

18. Lavina Fielding Anderson, "The LDS Intellectual Community and Church Lead-ership: A Contemporary Chronology," *Dialogue: A Journal of Mormon Thought* 26, no. 1 (Spring 1993): 33–34. See, more recently, the official LDS statement that attended the pub-licity surrounding the church's revisions of the endowment to reflect greater gender equality: "Official Statement," Jan. 2, 2019, at www.mormonnewsroom.org/article/temple-worship; and, for context, Peggy Fletcher Stack and David Noyce, "LDS Church Changes Temple Ceremony," *Salt Lake Tribune,* Jan. 3, 2019.

19. Colleen McDannell, "Sacred, Secret, and the Non-Mormon," *Sunstone,* Apr. 1997, 41–45.

20. In a controversial but oft-cited address that aimed to delimit the boundaries within which LDS scholars ought to work, one high-ranking church leader denounced as fallacious the claim "that so long as something is already in print, so long as it is available from another source, there is nothing out of order in using it in writing or speaking or teaching." Boyd K. Packer, "The Mantle Is Far, Far Greater Than the Intellect," *BYU Stud-ies* 21, no. 3 (1981): 271.

Anthropologist Elizabeth Brandt has observed that religious secrecy among the Pueblo allows leaders to impose their will, without explanation, over objections from other factions in the community because the leaders can claim to be acting on the basis of religious knowledge to which only they have access. Brandt recounts how one faction who sought to challenge the leadership consulted studies published by anthropologists who had transgressed the boundaries of secrecy drawn by tribal leaders. The information disclosed by the anthropologists gave the faction "some understanding and access to the secrets so necessary for a secular political challenge to Pueblo leadership."[21] Scholarship on secret rites cannot help but become implicated in such internal conflicts—and shying away from such scholarship to avoid becoming implicated is itself a move with political consequences, serving some parties' interests over others'.

Finally, a note on sources: Because of the LDS Church's expectations about sacred secrecy, the most extensive descriptions of temple rites available to scholars have come from church members who became disaffected. Especially in the nineteenth century, such members may have experienced the rites once in their lives, years before the time they described the rites publicly. Obviously, scholars must approach such accounts with a healthy dose of skepticism. My having received the rites is helpful because it gives me a broader knowledge base from which to make judgments about the reliability of descriptions of the rites which otherwise cannot be corroborated. Confronted with a range of nineteenth-century claims about the initiatory (including, as we will see, allegations of sexual activity in temples), I give more credence to those exposés that more closely resemble the rite I witnessed in the late twentieth century.[22] In deciding which accounts of

---

21. Elizabeth A. Brandt, "On Secrecy and the Control of Knowledge: Taos Pueble," in *Secrecy: A Cross-Cultural Perspective*, ed. Stanton K. Tefft (New York: Human Sciences Press, 1980), 143. For more characteristic appeals from scholars to respect the Pueblo's right to preserve secrets, see Scheper-Hughes, "The Best of Two Worlds," 56–75; Sweet, "'Let 'Em Loose,'" 59–74.

22. I became acutely aware of the advantage of insider status when a polemical website, hostile to the LDS Church, first broke the news of the 2005 revision to the initiatory. Because I no longer held a temple recommend (required to participate in temple rituals), I could not corroborate the report by witnessing the new initiatory for myself. It took some

the initiatory deserve most credence, I have also been aided by existing work on the historical development of temple worship by David John Buerger, who employed documents from LDS Church archives that were available during the 1970s but were subsequently withdrawn from public access.[23] The uncertainties endemic to research on LDS temple rites require me to qualify many of my assertions about the initiatory's history; but as my notes indicate, those assertions rest on extensive reading in the available primary literature.

THE DECLINE OF NUDITY IN THE INITIATORY

The initiatory was inaugurated in Nauvoo, Illinois, in the early 1840s. Historical documents indicate that men and women received the initiatory in separate parts of the temple, at the hands of same-gender officiators: that is, men administered this ordinance to men, women to women, a practice that continues today.[24] After removing all their clothing, initiates reclined in a tub to be washed by officiators, then stood to be generously anointed with scented oil. While applying water and oil to different body parts, officiators reportedly pronounced appropriate blessings: "your eyes, that you may see the glory of God; your

time for me to obtain corroboration from non-hostile eyewitnesses who were willing to volunteer that information and whose reliability I trusted.

23. David John Buerger, *The Mysteries of Godliness: A History of Mormon Temple Worship* (San Francisco: Smith Research Associates, 1994). Since I first wrote this essay in 2005, many primary sources tracking the evolution of LDS temple ritual, including typescripts collected by Buerger, have been made available in Devery S. Anderson, ed., *The Development of LDS Temple Worship, 1846–2000: A Documentary History* (Salt Lake City: Signature Books, 2011).

24. The initiatory is currently the only LDS ordinance administered by women. During the nineteenth century, LDS women also anointed the sick in a rite patterned after the initiatory. Linda K. Newell, "A Gift Given, A Gift Taken: Washing, Anointing, and Blessing the Sick among Mormon Women," in *The New Mormon History: Revisionist Essays on the Past*, ed. D. Michael Quinn (Salt Lake City: Signature Books, 1992), 101–20. The use of female officiators for the initiatory is very difficult to explain within the framework of LDS doctrine because the valid performance of ordinances requires priesthood authority, which is held exclusively by men. I surmise that the use of female officiators was a doctrinally anomalous exigency to preserve a sense of propriety given that initiates received the rite in the nude. However, other commentators, notably D. Michael Quinn, have cited the initiatory and other temple ordinances to argue that LDS women have a claim on the priesthood. D. Michael Quinn, "Mormon Women Have Had the Priesthood Since 1843," in *Women and Authority: Re-emerging Mormon Feminism,* ed. Maxine Hanks (Salt Lake City: Signature Books, 1992), 365–409.

ears, that you may hear His voice," and so on through nose, mouth, back, breast, vitals, loins, arms, hands, legs, and feet.[25] Following the anointing, officiators dressed initiates in the temple garment, a specially marked undergarment, with the instruction that initiates should wear this throughout their lives. Initiates then donned additional clothing, over the garment, before moving to other parts of the temple for further ordinances.[26]

Nudity in the initiatory was not only a practical convenience facilitating the washing and anointing of the body. It also re-enacted the nakedness of Adam and Eve in the Garden of Eden: when it came time for initiates to be clothed in the garment, they were told that this represented the coats of skin that God gave to Adam and Eve to cover their nakedness (Gen. 3:21). Notwithstanding the symbolic significance of nudity in the initiatory, eyewitness accounts intimate that from very soon after the ordinance was inaugurated through the early twentieth century, various gestures were made, albeit inconsistently, toward preserving initiates' privacy: throwing a blanket around an initiate during

---

25. Increase M. Van Deusen, *Positively True: A Dialogue between Adam and Eve, the Lord, and the Devil, Called the Endowment* (Albany, New York: C. Killmer, 1847), 6. The formulae for blessing body parts have been fixed since at least the beginning of the twentieth century; nineteenth-century accounts present different formulae from those now in use, but it is unclear whether this reflects actual differences in how the initiatory was administered or imprecision of informants' memories.

26. A number of accounts, spanning nearly a century, are reasonably consistent in their descriptions of the initiatory as performed prior to the revisions of the 1920s, although some offer more detailed description than others. Emeline "Mormon Endowments"; Van Deusen, *Positively True*; T.B.H. Stenhouse, *"Tell It All": The Story of a Life's Experience in Mormonism* (Hartford, Connecticut: A. B. Worthington, 1874), 359–61; Ann E. Young, *Wife No. 19: Or, the Story of a Life in Bondage, Being a Complete Exposé of Mormonism* (Hartford, Connecticut: Dustin, Gilman & Co., 1876), 358–61; G.S.R., "Lifting the Vail: The Endowment House Mysteries Fully Exposed …," *Salt Lake Daily Tribune*, Sep. 28, 1879; F. E. Bostwick, *As I Found It: Life and Experience in Utah among the Mormons …* (St. Louis: n.p., 1893), 73–74; *Mysteries of the Endowment House and Oath of Vengeance of the Mormon Church* (Salt Lake City: Salt Lake Tribune, 1906); Daniel S. Tuttle, *Reminiscences of a Missionary Bishop* (New York: Thomas Whittaker, 1906), 315–17; Thomas P. Marshall, *Mormonism Exposed, by Thomas Philip Marshall, Ex-Elder of the Utah Mormon Church, with the Secret Workings, Washings, Anointings, and Ceremonies Performed in Their Temples …* (St. Louis: Ponath-Bruewer Printing Company, 1908); Stuart Martin, *The Mystery of Mormonism* (London: Odhams Press, 1920), 247–48; *Temple Mormonism: Its Evolution, Ritual, and Meaning* (New York: A. J. Montgomery, 1931).

the anointing;[27] using dim light in the washing room;[28] washing and anointing each initiate privately behind a curtain;[29] letting initiates clothe themselves in the garment (more on this momentarily);[30] bathing initiates while they wore a "chemise;"[31] and allowing initiates to anoint their own "secret parts" during the blessing on the loins.[32] It is noteworthy that the 1902 text which attests to initiates being allowed to clothe themselves in the garment is actually a record of the St. George, Utah, temple president instructing temple workers to *stop* allowing initiates to clothe themselves. One wonders: Had temple workers taken the initiative to adapt the ceremonial procedure because they, or the initiates, or both, were uncomfortable with the physical intimacy involved?

Nudity in the initiatory was more dramatically curtailed—with church approval—in the early twentieth century through the introduction of the "shield." This development probably occurred as part of a revision to temple ordinances enacted by church leaders during the 1920s.[33] I have no information to indicate whether the design of

---

27. Emeline "Mormon Endowments"; Catharine Lewis, *Narrative of Some of the Proceedings of the Mormons Giving an Account of Their Iniquities* ... (Lynn, Massachusetts: Catharine Lewis, 1848), 8.

28. Van Deusen, *Positively True*, 5; John H. Beadle, *Life in Utah* (Philadelphia: National Publishing Co., 1870), 487.

29. G.S.R., "Lifting the Vail."

30. Temple Minute Book, St. George, Dec. 19, 1902; reproduced in Anderson, *Development of LDS Temple Worship*, 129.

31. Tuttle, *Reminiscences of a Missionary Bishop*, 317.

32. Marshall, *Mormonism Exposed*, 49.

33. On the 1920s revisions, see Buerger, *Mysteries of Godliness*, 136–54; Anderson, *Development of LDS Temple Worship*, xxxii–xxxv. It is impossible to date precisely the introduction of the shield because of lack of access to historical materials. The earliest reference to the shield I have located appears in a set of instructions for first-time female temple-goers written by Salt Lake temple worker Zina Y. Card. I encountered Card's instructions, while researching the first version of this article in 2005, as a typescript in the H. Michael Marquardt Papers, Special Collections, J. Willard Marriott Library, University of Utah, Salt Lake City; Card's instructions have since been published in Anderson, *Development of LDS Temple Worship*, 205–207. The typescript version of Card's instructions bears no date. However, Card refers at one point to modifications to the temple garment that we know were made in 1923; the document must therefore date to sometime between 1923 and 1931, when Card died. Devery Anderson's published version of the text dates it to "ca. 1923." My theory that the shield was introduced as part of the 1920s revisions to temple ordinances is supported by the fact that the shield is not mentioned in the 1931 exposé *Temple Mormonism*, which, notwithstanding its publication date, describes the endowment as performed prior to the 1920s revisions.

the shield evolved; but at least by the late twentieth century, the shield was a broad, loose, shin-length robe, comparable to a poncho. It covered the initiate in front and back but was open at the sides to allow officiators to touch the various body parts to be blessed. With the introduction of the shield, the washing and anointing were reduced to a token dabbing of water and oil on the requisite body parts. Tubs fell into disuse, and initiates received the washing and anointing while seated on a stool. Officiators helped initiates step into the garment and pull it on underneath the shield.

In January 2005, a revision to initiatory procedures practically eliminated nudity. Initiates were now instructed to clothe themselves in the garment in the privacy of a changing-room cubicle, then to place the shield on top of that before being presented to the washing room. The shield was now closed at the sides, making it, essentially, a robe. The closing of the shield was possible because officiators no longer touched any part of the initiate's body other than the head. As the revised rite began, initiates were told that they would be washed and anointed "only symbolically"; this symbolic washing and anointing was restricted to dabbing water and oil on the initiate's forehead or crown. Officiators still pronounced the traditional blessings on individual body parts, but they did so while laying hands on the initiate's head, a gesture that would be familiar to LDS from church ordinances performed outside temples, such as confirmations, ordinations, and health blessings. At the point of the initiatory where officiators had formerly clothed initiates in the garment, officiators now made a declaration that the garment the initiate had donned in the changing room was "authorized"; the officiator then went on to provide the customary instructions about wearing the garment throughout one's life.[34]

I say that the 2005 revision "practically" eliminated nudity because the continued wearing of the shield, even though now closed at the sides, could be interpreted as a vestigial or symbolic nudity—a *reduced*

---

34. On the very day the 2005 revision was implemented, a detailed description was posted by a former member of the LDS Church to his polemic website, www.JosephLied.com. LDS temple-goers have confirmed to me the accuracy of this description. The description was later removed from the website. A description of the 2005 revision, derived from the information posted at JosephLied.com, appears at "The Initiatory (2005)," *The LDS Endowment*, at www.ldsendowment.org.

state of dress and a reminder of the earlier, more exposing procedure, at least for those who had experienced or knew of the pre-2005 initiatory. However, in 2016 even this vestige of nudity was eliminated. Henceforth initiates would receive the rite wearing not the shield but the same costume that constitutes basic dress for other temple rites: white shirt, trousers, and tie for men, a white dress for women.[35] For nearly 175 years, participants in the initiatory had experienced, in one form or another, sensations arising from having their bodies exposed and touched in unaccustomed ways; in theory, those sensations had invited initiates to imagine themselves as replicating experiences of Adam and Eve. As of 2016, after a long incremental decline, that sensory experience was no longer part of the initiatory.

REACTIONS TO NUDITY IN THE INITIATORY

From the beginning of the initiatory's history, rumors of nudity inspired salacious interest and contributed to allegations of sexual licentiousness in temples. The February 1846 *Warsaw Signal* exposé I quoted at the beginning of this essay, with its claims about nude male and female initiates washing one another and its hints at sexual coupling, appeared just two months after the initiatory began to be administered in the Nauvoo temple. Subsequent temple exposés, written during the furor over LDS polygamy in Utah, offered further allegations of sexual impropriety: that female initiates were washed by lecherous male elders; that initiates were naked not only during the initiatory but also during the ordinances that followed; that actors playing Adam and Eve appeared nude and performed sexual acts before the temple-going audience; and that the temple ceremonies culminated in an orgy.[36] Disaffected LDS member Fanny Stenhouse, in her own

---

35. The implementation of the 2016 change was discussed by LDS or former LDS members in online message boards: "Temple Initiatory Change," *StayLDS.com*, May 29, 2016, at www.forum.staylds.com; "Less Temple Laundry?" *Wheat & Tares*, June 25, 2016, at www.wheatandtares.org.

36. Nelson W. Green, *Fifteen Years among the Mormons: Being the Narrative of Mrs. Mary Ettie V. Smith, Late of Great Salt Lake City* (New York: Charles Scribner, 1858), 50–51; *The Gates of the Mormon Hell Opened, Exhibiting the Licentious Abominations and Revellings of the High Priest of the Latter-day Saints, Rev. Brigham Young and His 90 Wives ...* (London: Hewitt, Wych Street Strand, n.d.), 5.

1874 exposé, derided these sorts of claims as "absurd," "strange," and "revolting," and she insisted that nothing "indecent or immoral" occurred during the temple ordinances she experienced in Salt Lake City. On the other hand, she thought it possible that "the most disgraceful things" were done in the Nauvoo temple, before her time.[37] Government investigation of temple ordinances during the hearings to decide whether LDS apostle Reed Smoot should be allowed to retain his seat in the US Senate, 1904–06, did much to dispel nineteenth-century rumors. Still, subsequent exposés were reluctant to give up the suspicion that temple rites had sexual dimensions.[38] Allegations of a man and a woman being half-naked together were made in a temple exposé published as late as 1922.[39]

A few nineteenth-century exposés were titillating to a point that approached the pornographic. One male author reminded readers three times in two pages that the female initiate was naked during her washing and anointing, then invited readers to imagine "the great excitement produced" in the initiate by this "most excitable ceremony."[40] An exposé authored by Nelson Green, but written as a first-person narrative from a female informant, played an elaborate game of concealment and revelation—a textual striptease—that literally encouraged readers to let their imaginations run wild. Describing the allegorical drama set in the Garden of Eden that follows the initiatory, Green's female narrator apologized that she "felt compelled to omit" some information "most distasteful to the recollection of a pure woman." In "compensation" for that (as she put it), she offered the following: "I call the attention of the reader to the fact, that ... I have *not* mentioned the *dress* of '*Adam* and *Eve*,' nor the nature of the 'FRUIT' by which each was in turn tempted; I think he [the reader] will admit that while I have said *enough*, I have also left more unsaid

37. Stenhouse, *"Tell It All,"* 353, 356.

38. See John D. Nutting, ed., *The Secret Oaths and Ceremonies of Mormonism* (Cleveland, Ohio: Utah Gospel Mission, 1912); Stuart Martin, *The Mystery of Mormonism* (London: Odhams Press, 1920).

39. Craig L. Foster, "Victorian Pornographic Imagery in Anti-Mormon Literature," *Journal of Mormon History* 19, no. 1 (Spring 1993): 122–23.

40. Thomas White, *The Mormon Mysteries: Being an Exposition of the Ceremonies of "The Endowment"* (New York: Edmund K. Knowlton, 1851), 6–7.

than the imagination, held with the loosest possible rein, would be likely to picture ..." A footnote, presumably commentary from Green, added, "It is perhaps needless to say that 'Adam' and 'Eve' were both entirely nude: from which the nature of the '*fruit*' may well be imagined." Green went on to lament that "a false estimate of propriety" prevented a full exposure "of these Mormon debaucheries."[41] The exposé that most blatantly appealed to pornographic interests was by William Jarman. Introducing his subject, Jarman explained that "as this book will not be sold in a sealed envelope, or be given to the public as obscene literature, I am compelled to omit very much that I would like to have an opportunity to whisper in men's ears." He then dropped in an advertisement for his "private lectures to men only" which purportedly offered an unexpurgated account of what transpired in temples.[42]

Descriptions of the initiatory authorized by LDS Church leaders avoided mention of nudity, suggesting that church leaders found the practice so sensitive, they preferred not to explain it. *The House of the Lord* (1912), authored by Apostle James E. Talmage,[43] was surprisingly forthcoming in describing the interior of the Salt Lake temple, including the Holy of Holies, a room associated with the church's most esoteric ordinance and one that not even temple-goers are usually permitted to see. Yet when Talmage described the rooms where the initiatory was performed, he became elliptical, informing readers only that there are a number of "dressing rooms" used to perform "certain ordinances of anointing," with no mention of washing. Talmage assured readers that "in these ordinances only women administer to women and men to men," but he did not explain why such assurance would be necessary.[44]

41. Green, *Fifteen Years among the Mormons*, 50–51.

42. William Jarman, *U.S.A., Uncle Sam's Abscess: Or, Hell upon Earth for U.S., Uncle Sam* (Exeter: H. Leduc's Steam Printing Works, 1884), 67.

43. James E. Talmage, *The House of the Lord: A Study of Holy Sanctuaries Ancient and Modern* (Salt Lake City: Signature Books, 1998; rpt. ed.), 138–41.

44. An unauthorized photograph of a washing room, with tub, was taken in 1911 by Gisbert Bossard, an alienated church member who sneaked into the Salt Lake temple while it was closed for cleaning. Bossard took photographs throughout the temple, planning to either extort or embarrass church leaders. Talmage's book, with its much finer photographs of the temple interior, was published to preempt a sensationalistic exhibition of Bossard's photographs in New York. Bossard's photograph of the washing room can be seen in Kent

Apostle Boyd K. Packer was similarly elliptical in his book *The Holy Temple* (1980), assuring first-time temple-goers that "in the temple the ideal of modesty is carefully maintained" but saying nothing about the washings and anointings beyond the fact that ordinances with those names occur as required by scripture. This vagueness is consistent with Packer's instruction that local church leaders preparing first-time temple-goers should speak of the initiatory and other ordinances only "in the most general terms."[45]

Nineteenth-century allegations about mixed-gender nudity in temples were an occasion for much moral outrage, as well as titillation. By contrast, when informants described temple-goers of the *same* gender being naked in one another's presence or touching one another's bodies—the actual LDS practice—their tone was often matter-of-fact. This matter-of-fact quality becomes more readily apparent when contrasted to the embarrassment that some informants experienced in a mixed-gender setting immediately following the initiatory. It was customary during the nineteenth century that, after being clothed in the garment, male initiates further donned a nightshirt and female initiates a nightdress. So attired, initiates of both sexes were then brought into the same room for the allegorical drama that follows the initiatory. Appearing before initiates of the opposite sex in what they considered a state of partial dress occasioned moderate shame for informants Fanny Stenhouse and Ann Eliza Young.[46] By contrast, informants did not usually express shame about appearing in a state of nudity before members of their own sex during the washing and anointing. This fact suggests that same-gender nudity provoked little sense of scandal during the nineteenth century. Hence, former church members, such

Walgreen, "Inside the Salt Lake Temple: Gisbert Bossard's 1911 Photographs," *Dialogue: A Journal of Mormon Thought* 29, no. 3 (Fall 1996): 22. The same Bossard photo appears as Plate 11.1 in Signature Books's 1998 special reprint edition of *House of the Lord* (188). However, consistent with his silence about the washing rite in the text, Talmage's original book included no photograph of a washing room.

45. Boyd K. Packer, *The Holy Temple* (Salt Lake City: Bookcraft, 1980), 29, 71, 154–55.

46. Stenhouse, *"Tell It All,"* 361–62; Young, *Wife No. 19*, 363. Similarly, comments about how ashamed or ridiculous the men looked, standing in front of the women in their nightshirts, can be found in G.S.R., "Lifting the Vail"; and in a fictionalized account from Alvah M. Kerr, *Trean: Or, the Mormon's Daughter* (Chicago: Belford, Clarke, & Co., 1889), 134.

as Emeline, who were concerned to rebut allegations of impropriety could support their case by holding up the fact that nudity occurred only in same-gender settings.[47]

An exception to my claim that same-gender nudity provoked little sense of scandal during the nineteenth century is an 1879 exposé signed "Mrs. G.S.R." This author was scandalized by the blessings on her breast and loins, administered to her by a female officiator, and she expected readers to share that sentiment: "I must ask my readers not to think I want to tell this part of the story, but I do want people to know the truth, and how disgusting and indelicate this thing is. Mormon people deny many of these things, and civilized and decent people can scarcely realize that this institution is as infamous as it really is."[48] G.S.R.'s feeling that it was "disgusting and indelicate" to be intimately touched by someone of her sex became more commonly expressed in the early twentieth century. Probably due to growing awareness of homosexuality, Americans generally, and the LDS specifically, came to see same-gender nudity and touch as indecent or potentially erotic. As symptoms of this shift in LDS attitudes, historian D. Michael Quinn has cited the illegalizing of nude swimming during the early 1900s and the proscribing of affectionate touch in photographs of athletic teams

---

47. Emeline, "Mormon Endowments"; see also Stenhouse, *"Tell It All,"* 356, 359. Of course, a certain sense of scandal haunts all nineteenth-century discussions of nudity in the initiatory, which is why exposés lent themselves to pornographic interest. Perhaps to resist such scandal, some informants refrained from using the words "naked" or "undressed" in describing their experience: Lewis, *Narrative of Some of the Proceedings of the Mormons,* 8; Stenhouse, *"Tell It All,"* 359; Young, *Wife No. 19,* 358; Apostate, "The Endowments: The Story of One Who Took There Orders …," *Salt Lake Daily Tribune,* Dec. 8, 1878. Other accounts omit reference to the breast or loins when naming the body parts that are washed and anointed, or they state that the blessings given to body parts are unfit to print: John Hyde, *Mormonism: Its Leaders and Designs* (New York: W. P. Fetridge, 1857), 91–92; Stenhouse, *"Tell It All,"* 359–60; Emily Faithfull, *Three Visits to America* (Edinburgh: D. Douglas, 1884), 164; Hubert H. Bancroft, *History of Utah: 1540–1886* (San Francisco: The History Co., 1889), 357n17; Bostwick, *As I Found It,* 74. One exposé writer, Increase Van Dusen, apologizes that his subject is "rather … delicate" for a work "designed to be read by all classes of both sex." Van Deusen, *Positively True* 5. But these moves reflect a concern to avoid *public discourse* that is scandalous, which is not the same as finding nudity in same-sex settings scandalous *per se.*

48. G.S.R., "Lifting the Vail."

by the 1920s.[49] The introduction of the shield in the early twentieth century likewise betokens a growing discomfort with same-gender nudity. In the late 1930s, officiators at one temple were instructed to keep their eyes closed while administering initiatory ordinances; this may be another sign of discomfort with same-gender nudity.[50]

Even following the introduction of the shield, some initiates expressed discomfort about the exposure of their bodies. In some cases this discomfort appeared to arise from initiates not realizing in advance that they would be required to remove their clothing and allow their bodies to be touched. Because of the church's policy of withholding details about temple ordinances, even in temple preparation courses for church members, first-time temple-goers often know very little about what will occur, although local church leaders, family members, or friends may volunteer more concrete information, depending on their understanding of the boundaries of sacred secrecy. (Today the internet offers easier access than ever before to temple exposés, and it would be interesting to know to what extent some uninitiated LDS may consult those sources prior to their first-time temple experiences. But temple exposés are highly stigmatized in LDS culture, so it's hard to imagine that many LDS use them to educate themselves about temple ordinances.) One participant in a study of LDS young adults' reactions to temple worship, conducted between 1997 and 1999, told interviewer Janet Kincaid that he "would have flipped out during the washings and anointings if I hadn't known a bit of what to expect" from talking with his bishop. Another respondent told Kincaid that on the basis of her first-time temple experience, "If I were escorting someone, or teaching a temple prep course, I would ... actually say, 'at some point you're going to have to undress, at some point you're going to have to change your clothing ...'"[51]

For other pre-2005 initiates, the exposure of the body was disconcerting independent of any foreknowledge about the logistics of the

---

49. D. Michael Quinn, *Same-Sex Dynamics among Nineteenth-Century Americans: A Mormon Example* (Urbana: University of Illinois Press, 1996), 95–96, 323–24.

50. Manti Temple Historical Record, May 1, 1938; reproduced in Anderson, *Development of LDS Temple Worship*, 246.

51. Kincaid, "Tell Eve about Serpent!" 74, 76.

ordinance, because they perceived that the semi-nudity required of them ran counter to LDS teachings about modesty and chastity. A respondent in Kincaid's study said that she felt "nervous about the washing and anointing part of the temple, 'cause I had had several friends get married in the temple and they told me it [the initiatory] was very bizarre and not all like … the way the Mormon religion is practiced. So I was really worried."[52] Disaffected LDS have been the most emphatic in their antipathy to exposing their bodies, attributing to the initiatory unwelcome sexual overtones or potentialities. The ex-member who first publicized the 2005 revision to the initiatory online wrote that the change meant an end to that "icky naked feeling … because the old men (and old women for the ladies) no longer reach under the Shield and touch you all over your naked body." On the same website, another disaffected initiate wrote: "I can[']t speak for women, but as a man, I don't relish the thought of being touched on the loins by another man, and I'm pretty sure most other men don't …"[53] (Contrary to the impression that remark may give, the genitals were not touched during the blessing on the loins in late twentieth-century practice, although the touching was nevertheless intimate.)[54] Other disaffected initiates characterized the touching of body parts in the pre-2005 initiatory as "violation of personal boundaries," "sexual harassment," or "borderline traumatic." Some even claimed to have repressed their memories of the rite, by analogy to repressing memories of sexual abuse.[55] In these circles, there was speculation that the church implemented the 2005 revision in response to a lawsuit. The speculation is most likely groundless; but the fact that some disaffected initiates found this speculation plausible is a measure of the extent to which they regarded the semi-nudity and touch practiced in the initiatory prior to 2005 as a personal violation—i.e., they imagined it could be prosecuted in court.

52. Kincaid, 73.

53. "Newsflash," *The LDS Temple Endowment Site*, 2005, at www.lds-temple.org.

54. Former LDS who dissected the matter in an online bulletin board recalled that during the blessing on the loins they were touched on the base of the back, on the belly, or between the groin and hip. "Naked Touching in the Mormon Temple. Is It for Real?" *Recovery from Mormonism*, n.d., at www.exmormon.org/mormon/mormon366.htm.

55. "Naked Touching in the Mormon Temple."

Not all initiates reacted negatively to the intimacy of the pre-2005 initiatory. Essayist Ruth Knight wrote in 1990 that the washing and anointing of her body left her "awash in the sensible purposes of mortality. ... I knew then that the physical and the spiritual were sides of the same precious coin."[56] The author of a 2004 ex-LDS memoir characterized her first temple experience as distressing: among other things, she had "felt ashamed of [her] nakedness under the shield." But she appreciated the "anonymous gentleness" of the officiators who washed and anointed her during a subsequent temple visit. "I liked their touch, the sound of female voices in my hair, the way they spoke blessings on the head, the spine, the loins."[57] Even Deborah Laake, author of the high-profile 1993 exposé *Secret Ceremonies*, described the intimate, relational aspects of the initiatory in positive terms: the grandmotherly officiator's "chanting and ... cool fingers were both song and dance."[58] On the other hand, Laake thought the shield and garment were ugly and was scandalized by the obligations of secrecy imposed in the course of temple ordinances.

Appreciative literary reactions to the initiatory are paralleled by conclusions that Janet Kincaid drew from her qualitative research in the late 1990s. For Kincaid's female respondents, "without fail the initiatory ranked at the very top of their list of favorite ordinances," while male respondents commented consistently (and positively) on the "level of intimacy" experienced in the initiatory. At the same time, Kincaid noted that "very few" of her respondents had ever repeated the initiatory after their first experience.[59] This might be read as a suggestion that her respondents were ambivalent about the initiatory: they assigned positive meaning to the rite but were not keen to experience it again. That reading would be consistent with speculation that church leaders implemented the 2005 revision in the hope that temple-goers would volunteer more frequently to perform the initiatory vicariously

---

56. Ruth Knight, "Carrying On," *Dialogue: A Journal of Mormon Thought* 23, no. 3 (Fall 1990): 153.

57. Heidi Hart, *Grace Notes: The Waking of a Woman's Voice* (Salt Lake City: University of Utah Press, 2004), 23–25.

58. Deborah Laake, *Secret Ceremonies: A Mormon Woman's Intimate Diary of Marriage and Beyond* (New York: William Morrow & Co, 1993), 78.

59. Kincaid, "Tell Eve about Serpent!" 79, 92–93.

for the dead, after having received it for themselves, if they were not required to expose their bodies.[60] Again, whether that speculation is correct or not, the fact that some LDS or ex-LDS found the speculation plausible is a window into their own attitudes—their own disinclination to volunteer to perform this rite for the dead out of aversion to the semi-nudity required.

SACRED SECRECY AND THE BODY

LDS Church leaders are not in the custom of explaining revisions to temple ordinances, either to the public or to church members, so the motives for the elimination of nudity from the initiatory remain a matter for speculation. Concerns about public image and expressions of discomfort by church members are plausible motivating factors. It is also plausible that the 2005 and 2016 revisions reflect a widespread anxiety about touch in contemporary American society, an anxiety which elsewhere has led to no-touch policies in schools, day-care centers, psychiatric units, and so on, fearful of litigation.[61] Alternatively, considering the church's international growth, accompanied by a boom of temple-building around the globe, the revisions might have less to do with American attitudes toward the exposure of bodies than with sensitivity to how nudity and touch in the initiatory would be perceived in different cultural contexts.[62] In any case, I am less interested in the intentions behind the decline of nudity than I am in its effects. That is, what does this change in ritual procedure *do*—more specifically, what does it do when articulated in terms of LDS discourse about the body? My answer is that the decline of nudity extends into the ritual space of the initiatory an imperative, already in force outside

---

60. "Newsflash," *The LDS Temple Endowment Site*; Michael Norton, "Major Changes Made to Initiatory Ordinances Starting on Tues. Jan. 18, 2005," at www.josephlied.com.

61. Tiffany Field, *Touch* (Cambridge, Massachusetts: MIT Press, 2001), 2–5. The stigmatization of touch in American society has prompted researchers to worry that Americans are being deprived of healthy physical contact with others. Ashley Montagu, *Touching: The Human Significance of the Skin*, 3rd ed. (New York: Perennial Library, 1986); Stanley E. Jones, *The Right Touch: Understanding and Using the Language of Physical Contact* (Cresskill, New Jersey/Annandale, Virginia: Hampton Press & Speech Communication Association, 1994).

62. Thanks to an anonymous reviewer of this essay for reminding me to place LDS Church governance in an international, not only a US, context.

temples, to conceal the body in the name of concealing the sacred. At this point in my study, I seek to analyze the power relations enacted on initiates' bodies during the initiatory.

Since the beginning of the twentieth century, LDS have been accustomed to speak of the body as sacred.[63] More specifically, the body is figured as a temple, following 1 Corinthians 3:16–17: "Know ye not that ye are the temple of God?" The trope of body-as-sacred or body-as-temple has been frequently invoked, especially since the mid-twentieth century, in exhorting youth to keep the Word of Wisdom (the church's health code), to be modest and sexually chaste, and, more recently, to refrain from body piercing and tattooing.[64]

At the same time, LDS are accustomed to speaking of an obligation to preserve as private—in effect, to conceal—things that are sacred. The most obvious example of this is the silence surrounding temple ordinances, but the principle of concealing the sacred is extended to other practices or experiences as well. A patriarchal blessing (given to members, usually in their teenage years), for example, is supposed to be kept private on the grounds that it is sacred: "It might be appropriate to share a patriarchal blessing with close family members, but it is sacred and should not be discussed lightly."[65] Similarly, church leaders have discouraged members from speaking publicly about dramatic experiences such as visions or miracles, and leaders have refrained from describing their own revelatory experiences, again on the grounds that

---

63. The following discussion about LDS attitudes toward the body focuses on teachings about the sanctity of the body in the specific contexts of modesty and chastity. For a broader (though necessarily less "thick") discussion of LDS embodiment, see Davies, *Mormon Culture of Salvation,* 107–39.

64. My claims about historical trends in LDS discourse are based on keyword searches that I performed in 2005 using (1) the LDS Church's *Gospel Library,* an electronic archive of church magazines and selected publications from the 1970s to the present, available at www.lds.org, and (2) the CD-ROM *GospeLink 2001,* a commercially produced database of about 2,000 LDS publications, including major periodicals of the nineteenth and twentieth centuries (prior to the 1970s). Searching *GospeLink* for the keyword combinations "body AND sacred" and "body AND temple" within ten words of each other produced virtually no relevant hits in publications prior to 1900.

65. "Gaining Strength through Patriarchal Blessings," *Ensign,* June 1994, at www.lds.org. See also "Teaching Children about Patriarchal Blessings," *Ensign,* Oct. 1987, at www.lds.org; Boyd K. Packer, "The Stake Patriarch," *Ensign,* Nov. 2002.

"there are some things just too sacred to discuss."[66] The principle of concealing the sacred has also been invoked to explain why couples should not discuss their sexual life with others.[67]

The intersection of these discourses—the body as temple, the body as sacred, the sacred as private—produce an imperative for concealing the body, for veiling it in what observer Douglas Davies calls "sacred secrecy."[68] Davies uses the term to refer to the privacy surrounding temple rites, but it could be applied as well to the less conspicuous privacy surrounding patriarchal blessings, dramatic spiritual experiences—and bodies. The temple garment that initiates receive during the initiatory to "cover [their] nakedness" sets a standard of modesty that requires concealment of the body in everyday life: initiates must henceforth wear clothing that covers their bodies from shoulder to knee.[69] The obligation to observe this standard of modesty is most emphatic for initiates, but the standard is normative for all LDS, whether they have received the initiatory or not. LDS discourse exhorting modesty is closely related to discourse exhorting chastity. In both discourses, the sanctity of the body-as-temple is explicitly cited as the grounds for holding the body in reserve from being viewed or handled by others.[70]

---

66. Boyd K. Packer, "The Spirit Beareth Record," *Ensign*, July 1971. Packer made this statement while rebuking church members for asking him whether, in connection with his calling as an apostle, he had been privileged to see Jesus Christ in vision. For other cases of church leaders typing their revelatory experiences as too sacred to discuss, see Alexander B. Morrison, *The Dawning of a Brighter Day: The Church in Black Africa* (Salt Lake City: Deseret Book Co., 1990), 59–60; Russell M. Nelson, *The Gateway We Call Death* (Salt Lake City: Deseret Book Co., 1995), 94; M. Russell Ballard, "Special Witnesses of Christ," *Ensign*, Apr. 2001. For exhortations to lay members not to discuss sacred experiences such as miracles, see Dallin H. Oaks, *The Lord's Way* (Salt Lake City: Deseret Book Co., 1991), 96; John L. Hart, "Teaching, Learning 'by the Spirit,'" *LDS Church News*, Jan. 2, 1993, 11.

67. Boyd K. Packer, *That All May Be Edified* (Salt Lake City: Bookcraft, 1982), 28; Brent A. Barlow, "They Twain Shall Be One: Thoughts on Intimacy in Marriage," *Ensign*, Sep. 1986.

68. Davies, *Mormon Culture of Salvation*, 81. I use the term, as Davies does, to sidestep the frequent LDS objection that temple ceremonies are "sacred, not secret."

69. Prior to 1923, the everyday temple undergarment covered the initiate's body from wrist to ankle.

70. My search of *GospeLink* produced over 100 references to the body as temple in LDS publications across the twentieth century, becoming progressively more numerous from the 1940s on (partly, no doubt, as a function of increased LDS publishing). A search of the church publications archived at the church website, www.lds.org, yielded around 200 additional references to the body as temple from the 1970s to 2005, when I conducted the search for the first version of this essay.

The following passage from a devotional work by LDS apostle Mark E. Petersen is an especially well-elaborated example of a commonly deployed metaphor.

That which is sacred has long been protected from the eyes of the curious public. ... Did the masses of the people obtain admission to the sacred tabernacle of ancient Israel? Could they view or handle the [A]rk of the [C]ovenant? Were they admitted into the sacred precincts of the Holy Temple built anciently to the name of the Lord? Are they permitted into the Holy of Holies of any age?

The human body is as sacred as any building ever erected, whether temple or tabernacle itself. It provides a mortal home for our own spirits, which are divine, the very offspring of God, and it may be a resting place for the Holy Spirit to which all followers of God are entitled. ... Is it not as much an act of desecration to expose the sacred human temple to the public gaze, as it would have been for ancient Israel to expose the Ark of Covenant to the eyes of the jeering mobs?[71]

An instance of the body-as-temple figure more recent than Petersen's exhorts LDS to keep their bodies, like temples, "closed to the eyes of the world."[72]

At times, rhetoric about the sacred secrecy of the body has been joined to warnings about the danger of unleashing the body's sexual powers, as when Apostle Bruce R. McConkie wrote that temple garments "cover that nakedness which when exposed leads to lewd and lascivious conduct."[73] Until recent decades, LDS discourse on the dangers of exposing the body focused especially on the female body and its ability to tempt young men into unchaste behavior.[74] In the early

---

71. Mark E. Petersen, *Toward a Better Life* (Salt Lake City: Deseret Book Co., 1960), 311–12.

72. John S. Tanner, "To Clothe a Temple," *Ensign*, Aug. 1992.

73. Bruce R. McConkie, *The Mortal Messiah: From Bethlehem to Calvary* (Salt Lake City: Deseret Book Co., 1980), 2:295–96.

74. Mark E. Petersen, for example, speaking in the 1950s, related "the sanctity of the body" to the "sanctity of sex," then went on to remark: "I wish you girls could sit behind the curtain sometimes when we have private interviews with boys, and these boys really express themselves, man to man, about how they feel concerning modesty of dress. They were tempted, right on the dance floor, just by what they could see, just by what was not properly covered up." Petersen, *Toward a Better Life*, 125. More recent church publications avoid blaming young women for male immorality and make a point of exhorting young men to dress modestly, too. There remains, though, some tendency to focus more specifically

twenty-first century, Relief Society president Ellen W. Smoot warned of the spiritual harm that immodesty does to young women and men alike, but she repeated the familiar move of equating exposure of the sacred body with exposure to destructive power: "When we wear clothing that is unseemly or too tight, that exposes or otherwise belittles the sacredness of our bodies, we play with fire. And sometimes the scars of even a small burn mar our souls for a long, long time. Back away from the fire and head in the right direction."[75]

As the sanctity of the body is invoked in prohibitions against displaying the body, so also it is invoked in prohibitions against touch. LDS parents have been instructed to teach their young children "that our bodies are too personal and sacred to be handled inappropriately by ourselves or by others."[76] Discourse forbidding touch of the body outside marriage can be stern, especially when directed to youth. A typical example is Apostle Richard G. Scott's preaching that "any intentional contact with the sacred, private parts of another's body, with or without clothing[,] is a sin and is forbidden by God."[77] A more emphatic variation on this injunction comes from Boyd K. Packer, whom I cited earlier on the obligation to conceal details about the initiatory from first-time temple-goers. "Do not let anyone at all touch or handle your body," Packer stated in an article for youth, "not anyone!"[78]

By piling up quotations about the obligation to conceal the body, I hope that I have conveyed its force in LDS discourse. By extension, I hope that I have clarified why some LDS would perceive that the semi-nudity and intimate touch they experienced during the initiatory prior to 2005 were "not at all like ... the way the Mormon religion is practiced" (as expressed by one of the young adults interviewed by

---

on female dress, as in this passage from a widely disseminated official church brochure for youth: "Young women should wear clothing that covers the shoulder and avoid clothing that is low-cut in the front or the back or revealing in any other manner. Young men should also maintain modesty in appearance." *For the Strength of Youth: Fulfilling Our Duty to God* (Salt Lake City: Intellectual Reserve, 2001), 16.

75. Mary Ellen W. Smoot, "Seeking Solutions," *Ensign,* Feb. 2002.

76. "Lesson 9: Chastity and Modesty," *The Latter-day Saint Woman: Basic Manual for Women, Part A* (Salt Lake City: Church of Jesus Christ of Latter-day Saints, 2000), 60–65.

77. Richard G. Scott, "Making the Right Choices," *Ensign,* Nov. 1994.

78. Boyd K. Packer, "Why Stay Morally Clean," *Ensign,* July 1972.

Janet Kincaid).[79] Nudity in temples predated frequent deployment of the body-as-temple metaphor in LDS Church discourse; but following the emergence of that discourse in the twentieth century, the continuing practice of temple nudity (or semi-nudity after the introduction of the shield) meant that the initiatory was a space where otherwise emphatic prohibitions against immodesty and touch were suspended. This suspension of prohibitions created a disparity between the way LDS were taught to treat bodies outside the temple and the way their bodies were treated during the initiatory. Young adults attending the temple for the first time would be especially likely to perceive that disparity, having been the target of frequent injunctions to conceal the body during adolescence.

The disparity between nudity in temples and injunctions to conceal the body is not the only instance of a tension between the LDS Church's *exo*teric (public) discourse and *eso*teric (private) practice. Throughout the twentieth century, LDS sought to dispel sinister interpretations of the silence around temple ordinances by repeating that the ordinances were "sacred, not secret." Nevertheless, temple-goers took upon themselves what were called "obligations of secrecy" until a sweeping revision of temple ordinances in 1990, when the word "secrecy" was eliminated, leaving only references to the ceremonies being "sacred." Thus public claims and private realities were belatedly harmonized. The elimination of nudity in 2005 could likewise be interpreted as a case where esoteric practice was belatedly brought into line with exoteric discourse: post-2005, the sacred secrecy of the body enjoined outside temples would be enforced inside them as well.

PRIVACY AND POWER

To speak of the revised initiatory as *extending* or *enforcing* an imperative to conceal the body may be counterintuitive. One might have expected me to speak, rather, of the revised initiatory as *protecting* or *shielding* the body from exposure. By opting instead for a rhetoric of extension and enforcement, I emphasize the ways that sacred secrecy, in the initiatory and other settings, enacts lopsided power relations between individual LDS

---

79. Kincaid, "Tell Eve about Serpent!" 73.

and their church (the latter represented by church leaders and function-aries). Catherine Bell, a scholar of religious studies, has urged students of ritual to examine "how ritual strategies construct distinct forms of domination and resistance." This means examining not only how par-ticipants are dominated by those who "more or less control the rite" but also how the rite enacts limits on the power of those in control such that "domination involves a negotiated participation and resistance that also empowers" those who are dominated.[80] Applying Bell's approach to analyzing the decline of nudity in the initiatory reveals a complicated relationship between individual privacy and institutional power.

Outside the initiatory, injunctions to sacred secrecy establish cer-tain zones of privacy for LDS members. Teaching that a couple's sex life is sacred, and therefore not to be discussed outside the marriage, potentially shields couples from prying by local ecclesiastical leaders who might desire to police their sexual practices.[81] The sacred secrecy with which LDS usually surround temple rites means that there is a dearth of official commentary on the rites; that, in turn, frees initi-ates to invest the rites with private meaning. Inasmuch as it establishes boundaries or privacy, sacred secrecy can be represented as protecting or empowering individuals.

But sacred secrecy can also function as an instrument of institu-tional power seeking to control individuals. When church leaders enjoin members not to speak of "sacred" (that is, private) personal revelations, they prevent the development of prophetic charismas that might compete with the more bureaucratic style of leadership that has come to typify the LDS hierarchy.[82] LDS anthropologist David

---

80. Catherine Bell, *Ritual Theory, Ritual Practice* (New York: Oxford University Press, 1992), 211.

81. The First Presidency has instructed local leaders that during temple recommend interviews, they are not to ask about "personal, intimate matters about marital relations." It appears that the First Presidency found this instruction necessary because local leaders had been asking interviewees if they engaged in, for example, oral sex, a practice of which the First Presidency had previously expressed disapproval even within marriage. Romel W. Mackelprang, "'They Shall Be One Flesh': Sexuality and Contemporary Mormonism," in *Multiply and Replenish: Mormon Essays on Sex and Family*, ed. Brent Corcoran (Salt Lake City: Signature Books, 1994), 59–60.

82. In the nineteenth century, the charisma of LDS apostles was bound up in an ex-pectation of their having visionary experiences. In the twentieth century, as church leaders

Knowlton has connected church leaders' insistence on the privacy of temple ordinances to a wider-reaching "politics of the unspeakable" that legitimizes strategies to silence writers whose views leaders regard as deviant—that is, who are speaking what should not be spoken.[83] The official silence the church maintains around the temple rites, in addition to empowering initiates to make their own interpretations of the rites, also aims to limit public knowledge of features of the rites that could create problems for the church's public image.[84]

Following Bell, we can say that the elimination of nudity from the initiatory produces a particular complex of domination and resistance. Within that complex, individual privacy and institutional power intertwine in such a way as to weight the power relation toward the

---

increasingly came from professional backgrounds, apostles and others became suspicious of visionary charisma, downplayed the importance of visions in speaking of their role as witnesses of Christ, and invoked the principle of sacred secrecy to justify silence about their spiritual manifestations. D. Michael Quinn, *The Mormon Hierarchy: Extensions of Power* (Salt Lake City: Signature Books/Smith Research Associates, 1997), 1–6. By contrast, leaders of new, rival movements within Mormonism often invoke the visionary charisma of Joseph Smith Jr. by claiming visions of heavenly beings, delivering oracular revelations in the style of "Thus saith the Lord" or producing translations of lost scriptural texts. John-Charles Duffy, "The Making of Immanuel: Brian David Mitchell and the Mormon Fringe," *Sunstone*, Oct. 2003, 34–35.

83. David C. Knowlton, "Intellectual Politics and the Unspeakable in Mormonism," *Sunstone*, Apr. 1997, 46–51.

84. Such features include an oath to pray for vengeance on the United States for the assassination of Joseph Smith, which formed part of the endowment until the 1920s and came under scrutiny during the attempt to unseat LDS senator Reed Smoot; the violent penalties that accompanied covenants of nondisclosure until 1990; in general, the Masonic-like nature of the ceremony, which pulls against recent efforts to minimize LDS difference from the Christian mainstream; and, of course, the practice of nudity. Recently, church officials have even used the principle of sacred secrecy to circumvent potentially awkward questions about baptism for the dead, a rite to which obligations of silence have not, historically, applied. On April 12, 2005, while I was working on this essay, I heard an episode of *Radio West* (a public radio program produced at the University of Utah) in which David Rencher, a public relations official for the LDS Church, addressed the latest instance of a recurring controversy over vicarious baptisms performed for Jews killed during the Holocaust. Rencher claimed that individuals for whom vicarious baptisms have been performed are not considered to be, nor are counted as, members of the LDS Church. Another guest challenged Rencher on this point by observing that during the rite of confirmation for the dead, individuals *are* declared to be members of the church. Rencher side-stepped this challenge by refusing to discuss the wording of sacred temple ordinances, and he hinted that the critic's knowledge of the content of these ordinances was illicit: "I'm not sure how you're privy to that information." While I am accustomed to hearing sacred secrecy invoked in connection with the initiatory and the endowment, this was the first time I had heard sacred secrecy extended to baptism and confirmation for the dead.

institution. When the revised initiatory extended the injunction to conceal the body into a realm where formerly that injunction had been suspended, it established a zone of individual privacy around initiates' bodies—but it did so as a function of the church's power over initiates' bodies. That is to say, the privacy of initiates' bodies was *granted* by church leaders who had the power to mandate how the rite should be administered and thus the power to dictate whether initiates would receive this rite naked or clothed. Notwithstanding the frequency of injunctions to conceal the body, and notwithstanding the sensitivities about modesty that church leaders and temple officiators have demonstrated in different ways across the initiatory's history, privacy of the body was not a given in the universe of LDS discourse. It was not a right that initiates could demand or that temple officiators had to request permission to transgress.

Temple-goers uncomfortable with the exposure of their bodies had limited options for resisting the institution's requirement of nudity or semi-nudity, especially if they did not know in advance—as a consequence of sacred secrecy—what would occur during the initiatory. The author of one nineteenth-century exposé reports that when she was required to undress and step into the tub to be washed, she "objected strongly to this part of the business, but was told to show a more humble spirit"—whereupon she complied.[85] It is not hard to empathize with her predicament: short of turning around and walking out, what else was she to do? We have seen how, after the fact, some initiates have complained—either privately to one another or, in the case of disaffected initiates, more publicly—about the exposure of their bodies. We have also encountered the suspicion that temple-goers may have refrained from repeating the initiatory during subsequent temple visits as a way of evading further exposure. It is even conceivable that some members expressed objections to church leaders, although the hierarchical nature of authority in the church tends to inhibit critiques of church policy, and injunctions not to discuss temple ordinances outside the temple would further inhibit communication on this subject. All of these are ways in which LDS individuals have, or conceivably

---

85. G.S.R., "Lifting the Vail."

could have, resisted the institution's power to denude their bodies. But the key point to note here is how limited was their ability to resist.

The end of nudity, after 2005, ended as well the tensions caused by initiates' discomfort about the exposure of their bodies. One way to state this is that *in concealing the body, the revised initiatory also conceals the extent of the church's power over its members' bodies.* When initiates were nude or semi-nude, the institution's power was, one might say, naked. It was palpable. The discomfort that some initiates have expressed about the exposure of their bodies is a consequence and therefore a sign of the institution's power to require that exposure. Allowing initiates to preserve the privacy of their bodies diminishes the discomfort or vulnerability produced by the church's power over bodies—but, crucially, it does not eliminate the church's power over members' bodies. If, tomorrow, church leaders decided to return to the earlier practice of semi-nudity, or even full nudity, in the initiatory, the way that authority is structured in the LDS Church would give leaders the power to implement this decision, and church members would have no more leverage to resist the requirement of nudity than they ever did. The end of nudity can be validly interpreted in positive terms as an act of sensitivity on the part of church leaders, a demonstration that they listen to members' concerns. But the change can also be interpreted, just as validly, in more negative terms: by refraining to exercise their power to require church members, like it or not, to receive the initiatory nude, church leaders make the fact that *they still possess that potentially unwelcome power* more difficult to detect. I hasten to clarify that I am not proposing this as an account of church leaders' motivations for the post-2005 revisions. I am offering, rather, a reading of the revision's effects—its psychological implications for initiates and the cultural work it accomplishes.

I am sensitive to the fact that my reading's focus on power—specifically, the LDS Church's power over bodies—bears resemblance to a long-standing tradition of polemicizing against ostensibly dictatorial LDS leadership, a tradition that dates back to nineteenth-century anxieties about polygamy and theocracy and that endures in new permutations today.[86] It is not hard to imagine how my reading of the

---

86. Terryl L. Givens, *The Viper on the Hearth: Mormons, Myths, and the Construction of Heresy* (New York: Oxford University Press, 1997).

initiatory might be co-opted by disaffected initiates who characterize the pre-2005 initiatory as sexual harassment. As I noted at the beginning of this essay, scholarship on religious secrecy cannot help but become implicated in such controversies. For what it may be worth by way of resisting the co-option of my reading by interest groups I disfavor, let me state that my own associations with the intimate nature of the pre-2005 initiatory are positive. I regret, in fact, the elimination of semi-nudity and the touching of body parts, given what those symbolized. On the other hand, I do not know how I would have responded to receiving the rite before the advent of the shield, and I have no doubt that my positive reaction to the rite was influenced by my having known in advance that semi-nudity would be required.

Additionally, I must steer away from a facile reading of the opposition my reading invokes between "institution" and "individual." I am convinced that the opposition does useful work in this case: the fact that initiates are taken one by one behind a curtain to be washed and anointed by church functionaries who act according to centrally mandated protocols makes it appropriate to speak of the initiatory in terms of a relationship between individuals and an institution. But it is also true that individuals constitute institutions, which makes an opposition between the two unstable. The form of institutional power that was at work when temple-goers allowed their bodies to be exposed and touched despite finding this uncomfortable has to be understood not simply as imposed from above but as arising out of initiates' relationships with other LDS family members and friends, with teachers and local leaders, and with the church, its hierarchy, and its teachings as abstractions. To put it simply: I do not wish to be read as alleging that nudity in LDS temples has been coerced. As Catherine Bell observes, following French philosopher Michel Foucault, "power must be grasped as quite different from the forces of violence or coercion."[87] One must speak, rather, of complicity—in the case of the initiatory, of the trust that LDS members place in their church and in the leaders they sustain as living prophets.

At the same time, we must not lose sight of the power imbalance

---

87. Bell, *Ritual Theory*, 201.

involved in the relationship between an individual initiate and the church as an institution—a power imbalance that is quite literally *covered up* in the post-2005 initiatory by the covering up of initiates' formerly denuded bodies. Bell's caution against speaking of "coercion" underscores the agency of individual initiates: their complicity in the power relationship that exists between them and the church, as well as their abilities, however limited, to resist what the church requires of them. Bell's caution in this regard has its uses. But too emphatic an insistence on initiates' agency and consent would risk eclipsing the power differential that is at work in a rite whose participants occupy a basically passive role (initiates *are washed, are anointed, are blessed*); who submit to these ritual acts, in many cases, without having known in advance what the acts would consist of; and who are naked, semi-naked, or clothed as a result of decisions made, without consultation or explanation, by upper-level church leaders.

Nevertheless, the following must also be said: If it is true that the concealment of initiates' bodies conceals the extent of the church's power over bodies, it is also true that the concealment of initiates' bodies simultaneously reveals and conceals *limits* on the church's power over bodies. I have said that in the universe of LDS discourse, the privacy of the body is not a right that initiates can demand. But neither initiates nor church leaders operate only in that discursive universe. Earlier I noted that some disaffected members have speculated that the 2005 revision was a response to the threat of litigation. While I do not give credence to those speculations, the fact that they exist—the fact that someone could imagine a litigation scenario—underscores the constraints to which the church is subject by virtue of its position in a larger social landscape. The church's power over its members' bodies is limited by the church's relation to other social agencies and forces, including civil law, the current widespread American anxiety about touch, and prevailing norms about the privacy of bodies as exemplified by the legal and ethical protocols that regulate exposure of bodies in institutions such as law enforcement and medicine.

The imperative to conceal the body, in the name of concealing the sacred, provided a ready-made means to negotiate such constraints on the church's power. Covering up initiates' bodies allowed the church to avoid legal or ethical liability but without having to relax the broadly interpreted obligation of sacred secrecy for temple ritual preferred by church leaders—that is, without having to provide first-time temple-go-ers with enough foreknowledge about semi-nudity and touch in the initiatory to stand as informed consent for ethical purposes (which might have been an alternative solution). By shrouding initiates' bodies in the name of sacred secrecy, church leaders avoided compromising the secrecy with which they prefer to shroud temple ritual. Again, we see a complicated connection between privacy and power: establishing a zone of privacy around initiates' bodies protects—indeed, strengthens—the principle of sacred secrecy, a principle that, in turn, serves, in various ways, to promote the church's institutional power. I reiterate that this is an observation about the effects of the revision, not an attempt to reconstruct motivations. Whether or not church leaders *intended* the post-2005 revisions to produce the effect I just described—preserving sacred secrecy, while avoiding potential legal and ethical liability—is not a question I seek to answer for the purposes of this analysis.

CONCLUSION

In tracking and interpreting the decline of nudity in the initiatory, I have grappled with ethical and methodological issues that have broader rele-vance for ritual studies. I have argued that the study of religious secrets cannot be governed by generalized mandates about respecting others but rather must be approached in localized, pragmatic terms, as a question of where scholars will choose to stand vis-à-vis conflicts and power rela-tions internal to the group being studied. Deciding whether to respect or transgress a particular case of religious secrecy becomes a question of deciding whose interests to serve. In the case of the initiatory, some LDS members profess to be pained by what they see as exposure of their sacred ritual practices; at the same time, there are other LDS who profess to have been pained by the exposure of their bodies during temple rites. My goal has been to steer responsibly across a terrain where ethical con-cerns flow in multiple directions and where parties vie for my allegiance with competing claims that their private selves are threatened.

From the time of the Nauvoo temple, the practice of nudity in the initiatory scandalized some LDS members and helped fuel sometimes wild rumors among outsiders about sex in temples. Nineteenth-century sources offer glimpses of possibly unofficial efforts by temple workers to preserve initiates' privacy. Although the introduction of the shield in the twentieth century officially reduced nudity to semi-nudity, sources indicate that the experience remained uncomfortable for some initiates. The exposure and intimate touch that initiates experienced inside the temple clashed with injunctions outside the temple not to allow one's body to be viewed or handled. Different injunctions to practice sacred secrecy worked together to create (unintentionally, one presumes) the potential for LDS to experience the initiatory as intrusive. Injunctions to treat one's body as sacred, therefore not to be seen or touched, created taboos that were unexpectedly suspended during the initiatory; while injunctions not to discuss temple ordinances outside the temple could make the initiatory an entirely unforeseen, and thus even more jarring and unsettling, experience for participants.

The 2005 and 2016 revisions to the initiatory ended even the semi-nudity of the twentieth century. I have identified various effects of this change. It reconciled exoteric church discourse about concealing the body, in the name of modesty and chastity, and the esoteric ritual of the temple. It eliminated sensory experiences that had held positive meaning for some initiates: identifying with Adam and Eve, feeling a union of the physical and the spiritual, being comforted or strengthened by others' touch. Most significantly, in my view, the end of nudity concealed the institutional church's power over its members' bodies by eliminating an experience that had formerly made that power palpable in a way that some members found uncomfortable, even distressing. By extending the mandate of sacred secrecy that applies to LDS bodies outside the temple into the temple's washing rooms, church leaders reasserted their use of sacred secrecy as an instrument of institutional power. The history of nudity in the initiatory reveals—one could say, uncovers—a persistent power differential between the LDS Church as an institution and its individual members. If members find that differential harder to detect now than they did before 2005, that is because the church now refrains from applying its power to the sensitive terrain of naked flesh.

CONTRIBUTORS

R. Jean Addams has published articles dealing with the Church of Christ (Temple Lot, Independence, Missouri), including the monograph *Upon the Temple Lot: The Church of Christ's Quest to Build the House of the Lord* (2011). His is also the author of the essay "The Bullion, Beck, and Champion Mining Company and the Redemption of Zion" (2014). He was president of the John Whitmer Historical Association from 2012 to 2013. "A Contest for 'Sacred Space'" first appeared in the *John Whitmer Historical Association Journal* 31, no. 1 (Spring/Summer 2011): 44–68.

Devery S. Anderson is co-editor of *Joseph Smith's Anointed Quorum, 1842–45: A Documentary History* and *The Nauvoo Endowment Companies, 1845–46: A Documentary History;* editor of *The Development of LDS Temple Worship, 1846–2000: A Documentary History* and *Salt Lake School of the Prophets, 1867–1883;* and the author of *Emmett Till: The Murder That Shocked the World and Propelled the Civil Rights Movement.* "The Anointed Quorum in Nauvoo, 1842–45," first appeared in the *Journal of Mormon History* 29, no. 2 (Fall 2003): 137–57.

Richard E. Bennett is former chair of the Department of Church History and Doctrine and Associate Dean of Religious Education at Brigham Young University. He has published extensively in Latter-day Saint nineteenth-century history. He has recently edited and published *The Journey West: The Mormon Pioneer Journals of Horace K. Whitney with Insights by Helen Mar Kimball Whitney* (Brigham Young University, 2018). His book-length study entitled *Temples Rising,* a history of LDS temple worship, is forthcoming from Deseret Book. He served as president of the Mormon History Association, 2013–14. He thanks the staff at the Church History Library, Church of Jesus Christ of Latter-day Saints, Salt Lake City, for their advice, input, and support. He also thanks his assistant, Wendy Top, for her invaluable research assistance, keen insights, and commitment; his colleagues at BYU for their input; his department secretary, Linda Godfrey, for typing the manuscript; and his wife, Pat, for her never-ending faith, encouragement, and support. "'The Upper Room': The Nature and Development of Latter-day Saint Temple Work, 1846–55," first appeared in the *Journal of Mormon History* 41, no. 2 (April 2015): 1–34.

John-Charles Duffy is visiting assistant professor at Miami University and past William N. Reynolds Fellow at the University of North Carolina at Chapel Hill. He has published essays in *Victorian Literature and Culture*, *Dialogue: A Journal of Mormon Thought*, *Journal of Mormon History*, and *Sunstone*; has contributed to *Peculiar Portrayals: Mormons on the Page, Stage, and Screen* and *Mormons and Popular Culture*; and written entries on Mormonism for *Homosexuality and Religion* and *Hispanic American Religious Culture*. An earlier verison of "'To Cover Your Nakedness': The Body, Sacred Secrecy, and Institutional Power in the Initiatory" was first published in, and appears here in its present form with appreciation to, the *Journal of Ritual Studies* 21, no. 2 (2007): 1–21.

Kathleen Flake is the Richard Lyman Bushman Professor of Mormon Studies at the University of Virginia and the author of *The Politics of American Religious Identity: The Seating of Senator Reed Smoot, Mormon Apostle* (2004). Her current research project is "Mormon Matriarchy, a Study of Gendered Power in Antebellum America." "'Not to Be Ritten': The Mormon Temple Rite as Oral Canon" was first published in, and appears here with appreciation to, the *Journal of Ritual Studies* 9, no. 2 (Summer 1995): 1–21.

Melvin C. Johnson is a writer, speaker, columnist, historian, and has taught at several colleges and universities. He retired from Angelina College as a tenured professor of English and history. He has published numerous articles and book review articles in the *East Texas Historical Association Journal*, *WTHA Yearbook* (now *West Texas Historical Review*), *John Whitmer Historical Association Journal*, *Environmental History*, *The Jeffersonian*, *Cross-Cut*, *Journal of Civil War Regiments*, and *Journal of Mormon History*. He is the author of the Smith–Pettit Foundation award winner for Best Book at the annual John Whitmer

Historical Association Conference (2006), *Polygamy on the Pedernales: Lyman Wight's Mormon Village in Antebellum Texas, 1845–58*. The article "'So We Built a Good Little Temple to Worship In': Mormonism on the Pedernales–Texas, 1847–51," first appeared in the *John Whitmer Historical Association Journal* 22 (2002): 89–98.

Christin Craft Mackay and **Lachlan Mackay** reside in Nauvoo, Illinois. Christin is director of the Joseph Smith Historic Site and book review editor for the *John Whitmer Historical Association Journal*. Lachlan, a member of the Council of Twelve Apostles of the Community of Christ, heads the church's Northeast USA Mission Field and leads its Historic Sites and Church History teams. "A Time of Transition: The Kirtland Temple, 1838–80," first appeared in the *John Whitmer Historical Association Journal* 18 (1998): 133–48.

Tonya Reiter is an independent historian residing in Salt Lake City. "Black Saviors on Mount Zion: Proxy Baptisms and Latter-day Saints of African Descent," which received the Editors Best Article Award from the Mormon History Association in 2018, first appeared in the *Journal of Mormon History* 43, no. 4 (October 2017): 100–23.

Brian H. Stuy is compiler and publisher of the five-volume set *Collected Discourses Delivered by President Wilford Woodruff, His Two Counselors, the Twelve Apostles, and Others, 1886–1898,* and is founder and owner Research-China. "'Come, Let Us Go Up to the Mountain of the Lord': The Salt Lake Temple Dedication, 1893," first appeared in *Dialogue: A Journal of Mormon Thought* 31, no. 3 (Fall 1998): 101–24.

Ryan G. Tobler is a PhD candidate in Religions of the Americas at Harvard University, where he studies the intellectual, cultural, and religious history of colonial North America and the early American Republic. His dissertation, "American Worship: Religion and the Politics of Ritual in the Early United States," explores religious practices and their controversies in the nineteenth century. "'Saviors on Mount Zion': Mormon Sacramentalism, Mortality, and Baptism for the Dead" first appeared in the *Journal of Mormon History* 39, no. 2 (Fall 2013): 182–238.

ABOUT THE EDITOR

Christian Larsen is an independent writer and historian, practicing Episcopalian, and fourth-generation Mormon. Professionally he works in digital publishing and content marketing. He received his master's degree in publishing from George Washington University in 2018, and two bachelor's degrees—history and Latin American studies—from the University of Utah in 2014. He and his husband, Jacob, reside in Salt Lake City, Utah.